THE DIVINE RIGHT
OF KINGS

by

JOHN NEVILLE FIGGIS

INTRODUCTION BY
G. R. ELTON

GLOUCESTER, MASS.

PETER SMITH

1970

TO

THE MEMORY

OF

EDWARD HENRY MOULE

THE DIVINE RIGHT OF KINGS

Introduction to the Torchbook edition copyright © 1965 by G. R. Elton

Printed in the United States of America

First published in 1896; second edition, 1914. It is here reprinted by permission of Cambridge University Press. The Torchbook Edition omits two sections of the appendix: "Aaron's Rod Blossoming or Jus Divinum in 1646" and "Bartolus and the Development of European Political Ideas," and the short Prefaces to the first and second editions.

First HARPER TORCHBOOK *edition published 1965 by Harper & Row, Publishers, Incorporated 49 East 33rd Street New York, N.Y. 10016.*

Reprinted, 1970, by Peter Smith Publisher, Inc. With the Permission of Cambridge University Press

THE DIVINE RIGHT
OF KINGS

TABLE OF CONTENTS

THE MAJOR WRITINGS OF
J. N. FIGGIS

The Divine Right of Kings (Cambridge, 1896; revised edition, 1914)

Studies of Political Thought from Gerson to Grotius (Cambridge, 1907)

"Political Thought in the Sixteenth Century," *Cambridge Modern History,* vol. iii (Cambridge, 1907), 736–769

The Gospel and Human Needs: Hulsean Lectures at Cambridge (London, 1909)

Churches in the Modern State (London, 1913)

Fellowship of the Mystery: Bishop Paddock Lectures, General Theological Seminary, New York (London, 1914)

The Political Aspects of S. Augustine's City of God (London, 1921)

INTRODUCTION TO THE
TORCHBOOK EDITION

BY G. R. ELTON

JOHN NEVILLE FIGGIS was born on February 2nd, 1866, at Brighton in Sussex, even then something of a place of resort and retirement for the upper middle classes. His father, the Reverend John Benjamin Figgis, was a minister in the sect known as the Countess of Huntingdon's Connexion, a narrowly Calvinist by-product of the eighteenth-century Methodist movement. In 1886 he went to St. Catharine's College, Cambridge, to read mathematics; moderate success in that Tripos (1888) was followed next year by a brilliant performance in the Historical Tripos. In reaction against his upbringing, he turned agnostic, in the undergraduate fashion of his day, but his father's powerful personality never let him be himself, and he looked for father-substitutes for the rest of his life. In his early twenties he attached himself to Mandell Creighton, Regius professor of history at Cambridge and later bishop of London; there followed a move into the Anglican Church, ordination in 1894, and an unsatisfactory year as curate in the market town of Kettering (Northamptonshire). From 1896 to 1902 he was very busy indeed, combining a teaching post in history at St. Catharine's with the chaplaincy of Pembroke College and a curacy at the University church. Singlehanded he gave to his old College, notorious even in the Cambridge of its day for its low standards and philistinism, a respectable position in the University. But in 1902 preferment called him to the rectory of Marnhull (Dorset) where he spent five rather frustrating years, an intellectual parson in a backward village which respected but hardly understood or used him. Then, in 1907, he took the decisive and in many ways disastrous step of moving to the wing of his Church right opposite that with which by upbringing he should have had most sympathy. Strongly influenced by the relentless and magisterial figure of W. H. Frere, he joined the Anglican monastic community at Mirfield in Yorkshire. A busy but, to him, barely tolerable life of austerity was spent in the religious duties of the house, in preaching and writing, and in American lecture tours. On his third trip, he was torpedoed in January 1918; and though he survived, his health suffered permanent damage. Early in 1919 his mind gave way, and he died in a mental home on April 13th, 1919[1].

Figgis was fundamentally an unhappy man with a sad history. By nature large, greedy, desperately untidy, kind, lively, gregarious, spontaneous, he suffered through life from a heavy sense of sin and inadequacy. He was manifestly an unconscious homosexual, surrounded by young friends and

---

[1] For Figgis's life and person I have relied on W. H. Frere's curiously unsympathetic account in *Dictionary of National Biography;* Maurice G. Tucker's *John Neville Figgis* (London, 1950), a simple piece of hero-worship; and on memories still current at Cambridge. Tucker's book makes reading between the lines both easy and necessary.

pupils, uneasy with women unless they were much older and could be met on the intellectual level only. He entered the communal life in a search for the discipline which he believed he needed and could not find within himself. Like many a good College man before and since, he was shamelessly overworked and exploited by colleagues who were only too willing to leave the hard work to the willing horse. The stringent régime of Mirfield helped to undermine his health and—possibly worse—forced him to devote his intellect to the ephemera of ecclesiastical and theological argument at the low level suitable to the aspirant cleric. Though in his circle he had a high reputation as a preacher, he displayed in his sermons and correspondence much of that distance from the world of men characteristic of his age, class and calling. In particular, he bore the two unmistakable hallmarks of this remoteness: he (as he himself might have put it) commonly larded his discourse with misapplied slang and excruciatingly bad jokes, so that the luminous and lucid style usually at his command suffered lapses into mental stuttering which are painful to read. The collapse of his mind did not come out of nowhere. Though no doubt assisted by the severe strains within himself, it was in the main brought on by the labours of his acquaintances, well-wishers as well as indifferents, who would not let him be himself. From his father to his superior, he was always attaching himself to simpler, stronger men who knew what was good for him; uncoordinated and diffuse in himself, he humbly accepted their guidance, and between them they destroyed him.

All this must be said in order to bring out more clearly Figgis's positive and very remarkable achievement. Contrary to what he himself was led to believe, this lay in the work of a university teacher and a student of history. As a historian, too, he over-eagerly sought guides and heroes, and here too he displayed less than perfect judgment. After Creighton, the two men he most admired were F. W. Maitland, the great legal historian, and Lord Acton, Creighton's successor as Regius professor. But while he always acknowledged the superb quality of Maitland, he followed more readily the inspiration of Acton, away from institutions and laws to the history of ideas. When Maitland discussed ideas (as he often did) he never forgot that they are only meaningful with reference to the people who hold or denounce them. He never fell victim to the fallacy which sees the past solely through the books written in the past, for he had the discipline of the record to steady his passionate interest in the world of thought and speculation. This Acton lacked, despite all his notable gifts and his wide involvement with men of affairs. Acton may have been a wise man, but he was an indifferent historian, often surprised by the discovery of intrigue or double-dealing behind an official façade into a somewhat amateurish reaction: astonishment at the commonplace, overemphasis on the insignificant, heavily moral attitudes. But his powerful presence and public figure, together with the influence, just beginning to be felt, of Ranke's school, set an imprint on the incipient Cambridge school of history. International relations and the history of ideas, both unusually selfcontained forms of historical enquiry and both capable of being studied in printed books, were to form its staple for a long time. Maitland left a glowing memory, much admiration, and no disciples.

In one respect Figgis did better than his mentor: he wrote

books, serious and good works of history in his chosen field. If today he is himself worthy of memory, as he is, he owes this entirely to his two studies in the history of political thought, *The Divine Right of Kings* (1st edition, 1896), and *From Gerson to Grotius* (1907; Torchbook edition, 1960). The second book in many ways follows up the suggestions of the first, fills in some gaps and corrects some errors of interpretation. Most competent critics would probably agree that it represents not only wider knowledge but also more adequate views. Nevertheless, it is with his first book, a prize essay written before he was thirty, that Figgis's name is commonly linked; and this is just. *From Gerson to Grotius* was based on lectures; *The Divine Right of Kings* is much more of a book. It rests on astonishingly wide reading, carried out, before the days of modern editions, in clumsy sixteenth and seventeenth century versions[2]. Unlike his later work, it is unaffected by his conversion and the religious preoccupations which increasingly interfered with a clear view of the past. And it is more truly original in that it discusses not this writer or that but one particular idea. Most of the vast work done in English in what one may call pure political theory—before sociology, psychology and social anthropology complicated the situation by introducing important but indigestible dimensions—follows in some measure from the great impression made by Figgis's youthful work. He established the method: to study the writers from the point of view of a particular problem, collect and collate their views, establish lines of influence and descent. He stressed

---

[2] For this reason, no attempt has here been made to clear up Figgis's footnotes which, as a rule, make it very difficult to know what particular editions he was using.

the importance of the historical setting, a sufficiently new notion then, now the merest tired commonplace. He directed attention to the leaders of thought and the purer intellectuals, where (unfortunately) it has in the main stayed since. If Figgis's book does not today read like a work seventy years old, this is because in method and approach writers on the history of political thought have added remarkably little to his, though they have thickened the texture, enlarged the catchment area, and rendered the argument more sophisticated. In the process, it may be added, too many of them have also lost his skill in conveying complex problems in simple and attractive language. There is no jargon in Figgis, and he would be worth re-reading for that fact alone.

Since his book has retained its life for such a long time— long in the academic context—he has naturally exerted even more influence in his chosen field than in the whole genre. When Figgis started work on the divine right of kings, no one took that theory seriously. John Locke had effectively destroyed it in the seventeenth century; all men with ambitions to be thought well-informed knew that it was laughable—a huge joke. Figgis soon discovered its logical coherence and its ancient ancestry; he realised that, given a point of view which saw in politics the hand of God, the doctrine was both more obvious and more convincing than the utilitarian liberalism which dominated English thinking in his own time. He therefore spent much labour in defending his choice of subject and explaining the link which, in the seventeenth century and earlier, had connected theology and political thought. All this is now so familiar that the reader may be bored by Figgis's insistence; but there is historical value in these constant affirmations. If at times Figgis seems excessively aware of his potential readers' preconceptions, it is worth remembering, once again, that he was a pioneer, addressing an audience particularly ill-qualified to grasp the religion-dominated and king-oriented thought of a lost past, a past before Enlightenment and Bentham and John Stuart Mill and Darwin and Mr. Gladstone had been. Since Figgis's day, on the other hand, it has been difficult to free the sixteenth and seventeenth centuries from an air of being exclusively peopled by divinely entitled and therefore absolutist kings. Theories of kingship which stressed the rights of subjects and the dominance of law have tended to be overlooked in the dazzling light of God-granted authority. Figgis himself redressed the balance a little in *From Gerson to Grotius,* and constitutional historians have long been pointing to the institutional and practical limitations upon divine-right kingship; but the serious analysis of doctrines opposed to the absolute assertion of divine right—doctrines inevitably less straightforward or logically conclusive within their own terms—has only recently been making progress and has not yet achieved the coherence of statement which Figgis gave to the other side[3]. Figgis's book was almost too successful in displacing the contempt and neglect which he disputed.

Naturally enough, a book so many decades old—decades filled with an ever-widening stream of historical research, analysis and description—can be corrected in a good many details. Figgis saw the English middle ages through the eyes

[3] See esp. William F. Church, *Constitutional Thought in Sixteenth-Century France* (Cambridge, Mass., 1941); John G. A. Pocock, *The Ancient Constitution and the Feudal Law* (Cambridge, 1957); J. W. Gough, *Fundamental Law in English Constitutional History* (Oxford, 1955); Franklin L. Baumer, *The Early Tudor Theory of Kingship* (Cambridge, Mass., 1938).

of Stubbs, and few today would interpret the fourteenth and fifteenth centuries so simply as times of constitutional conflict between prerogative and feudal or popular rights of consent[4]. Widely read as he was, he could not anticipate future labours: the important medieval canonists and civilians, especially, were less well known to him than they have since become[5]. He did not grasp how traditional and even commonplace—how unrevolutionary—the political thinking of leading reformers like Luther and Calvin really was. But what strikes the mind forcibly is the degree to which some of his suggestions proved seminal, to be traced further by others, even if some of these developments do not now command general acceptance. He introduced writers in English to the notion that the middle ages, holding to a Platonic and Thomist concept of human law as reflecting the eternal law of God (the order of the universe), could not strictly conceive of the possibility that man might *make* law: this view was to underlie all C. H. McIlwain's massive work, though we have come to realise that it both underestimates medieval realism in such matters and overestimates the exclusive hold of

[4] E.g. below, 28, 73ff., 81. For more recent interpretations, see May McKisack, *The Fourteenth Century* (Oxford, 1959) and E. F. Jacob, *The Fifteenth Century* (Oxford, 1961), with good bibliographies; and particularly, Stanley B. Chrimes, *English Constitutional Ideas in the Fifteenth Century* (Cambridge, 1936), and his edition of Sir John Fortescue's *De Laudibus Legum Anglie* (Cambridge, 1942).

[5] E.g. Cecil N. S. Woolf, *Bartolus of Sassoferrato* (Cambridge, 1913), Walter Ullmann, *The Medieval Idea of Law as represented by Lucas da Penna* (London, 1946), and *Medieval Papalism* (London, 1949); Brian Tierney, *Foundations of Conciliar Theory* (Cambridge, 1955); and the works mentioned in notes 10 and 16 below. There are useful bibliographies in Kantorowicz (see note 10) and Lewis (see note 6).

Thomist thought on the fourteenth and fifteenth centuries[6]. Earlier than anyone else, Figgis realized how much the political thought of sixteenth-century France influenced the arguments of seventeenth-century England; this has been followed up only to a limited extent[7]. Figgis treated the political thought of Elizabethan puritanism with more respect than was usual in his day, and his view that Thomas Cartwright, for instance, believed in the existence of "two kingdoms" (a clear separation of Church and State) formed the basis of A. F. Scott Pearson's work on that writer[8]. The insight and rapid association of ideas which mark Figgis's mind are characteristic of the best work done in the history of political theories; are indeed required for it. They are

[6] Charles H. McIlwain, *The High Court of Parliament* (New Haven, 1910); *The Growth of Political Thought in the West* (New York, 1932), esp. 323ff.; *Constitutionalism Ancient and Modern* (Ithaca, N.Y., 1947). Attacks on his views are widely scattered, e.g. through the works of Gaines Post and Brian Tierney cited in notes 15 and 16; for a useful summary of the problem see Ewart Lewis, *Medieval Political Ideas* (London, 1954), ch. I, esp. 18ff.

[7] G. P. Gooch, *English Democratic Ideas in the Seventeenth Century* (Cambridge, 2nd ed. 1927; Harper Torchbook edition 1959), Ch. I; J. H. M. Salmon, *The French Religious Wars in English Political Thought* (Oxford, 1959).

[8] *Thomas Cartwright and Elizabethan Puritanism* (Cambridge, 1925); *Church and State: Political aspects of sixteenth-century Puritanism* (Cambridge, 1928). I cannot agree with this view which ignores the essential Puritan belief in theocracy—government on earth by God's ministers—and forgets the degree to which pamphleteers adapted their tenets to the pressures of political circumstance. Figgis himself says (below, 190) that in Cartwright's teaching the Church was to dictate the use of the sword held by the State; where, then, are the two independent kingdoms? The vast literature of puritanism is outside our present concern; see, e.g., M. M. Knappen, *Tudor Puritanism* (Chicago, 1939), and C. H. and K. George, *The Protestant Mind of the English Reformation* (Princeton, 1961), for useful bibliographies.

certainly more noteworthy than the inevitable errors and insufficiencies of the pioneer. Figgis's is a mind worth meeting, and his book must still be read by anyone interested in the subject. After seventy years, that is a considerable achievement[9].

*   *   *

A good many threads run through this book, but some may be isolated as particularly important to Figgis himself. He believed that the seventeenth-century doctrine of the divine right of kings, as he found it in the teaching of Stuart apologists and French absolutists, was peculiar and in essence distinguishable from earlier views which linked monarchy with delegation of power from God. He held that the doctrine grew out of the necessity to find a positive theoretical support for the rejection of papal claims to spiritual, and sometimes temporal, overlordship, that the political thought of the Reformation (in particular, Luther's) formed one major pillar for it, and that the concept of sovereignty (resulting in the separation of Church and State, the emancipation of the State from clerical control) could never have been developed except by way of the divine right of kings. That is to say, he regarded medieval thought on society and political authority as essentially different from modern: the first stage of the modern situation was embodied in the emergence of national states ruled by absolutist princes claiming God-granted authority. Both in general and in par-

9 This present edition reprints the second edition of 1914, overseen and a little corrected by Figgis himself. Of the essays which he added to that edition, only that on Erastus, the last word on the subject, is here retained. The one on Bartolus was immediately superseded by Woolf's book (above, note 5); and the discussion of one particular civil-war pamphlet is outdated.

ticular, these points have been much debated, further developed, and often attacked.

Since 1896 a great deal has been written on medieval kingship[10]. Study has in the main concentrated on theories in justification of royal power and on the symbolism with which monarchy surrounded itself; the result—perhaps predictably—has been to bring out the mystic, semi-priestly, and potentially autocratic elements, to the relative neglect of such limitations, theoretical and practical, as undoubtedly existed. Through most of the middle ages, those who wrote on such topics were necessarily clerics, which helped to direct attention to this more religious side of kingship. Royal coronations partook of the character of episcopal ordinations; the anointing replaced the old Germanic "election" or acclamation as the chief element in the making of a king; some kings even used a holier oil than the bishop's chrism, while the papacy would permit only an inferior grade to the emperor. (The king of France was *rex Christianissimus,* the Most Christian king, because the oil used in his coronation had come direct from heaven, the unlikely recipient being that barbarian of genius, the Merovingian Clovis.) Comparisons with Christ, claims to Christ's vicariate on earth, were freely made. All this royal semi-divinity was

[10] A small selection: Frederick W. Maitland, "The Crown as Corporation," *Select Essays,* ed. Hazeltine, Lapsley and Winfield (Cambridge, 1936), 104ff.; Marc Bloch, *Les Rois Thaumaturges* (Strasbourg, 1924); Percy E. Schramm, *A History of the English Coronation* (Eng. trans., Oxford, 1937); *Der König von Frankreich* (Weimar, 1939); *Herrschaftszeichen und Staatssymbolik* (Stuttgart, 1952—4); F. Schulz, "Bracton on Kingship," *The English Historical Review,* 1945, 136ff.; Jean de Page, *Le Roi Très Chrétien* (Paris, 1949); E. Kantorowicz, *The King's Two Bodies* (Princeton, 1957); Walter Ullmann, *Principles of Government and Politics in the Middle Ages* (London, 1961), Part II.

worked out and stressed at the very beginning of medieval kingship, from the eighth to the tenth centuries. It was then that divine-right (theocratic) kingship was at its height, summed up in the phrase which, from Charlemagne onwards, kings came generally to use: the phrase *dei gratia*. They were kings by the grace of God, by God's gift and permission; and this was elaborated to mean that they could be held responsible only to God, that the governed people were by God committed to their charge (*populus mihi commissus*), even that the body of subjects were in the position of a minor, in tutelage to the guardian instituted by God. There is very little in seventeenth-century views of divine right that may not be traced in the claims put forward by the Carolingian, Saxon or Salian kings of Germany, in the practice of Anglo-Saxon kings calling themselves emperors, in the writings of an extreme defender of the rights of kings like the eleventh-century Norman Anonymous. The systematic study of Roman law renewed in the twelfth century, added to the armoury of royal pretensions with such famous texts as that "what has pleased the prince has the force of law" or that the prince is "free of the laws" (*legibus solutus*), and the fourteenth-century definition, *rex est imperator in regno suo,* ascribed to kings the attributes to be found in the Roman emperor. But none of this could raise royal claims above those of a Charlemagne, a William the Conqueror, or of a man like the emperor Henry III who appointed popes at his pleasure.

In fact, so far from the divine right of kings being developed against the papacy, it would to some extent be truer to turn the notion round. The divinity of early-medieval kingship arose not only from the *dei gratia* concept and the example of Constantine; it owed a great deal also to the practical facts which left kings alone capable of acting as God's agents on earth in the protection of men's bodies and souls. Before the eleventh century at least, the Church could not help but look to kings for the preservation of order, the safeguarding of its property, and the advance of God's cause. "Proprietary churches," whether the individual benefice controlled by a local lord or the body of a regional (national) Church controlled by a king, were the necessary order of the day. Where else should authority lie? True, the papacy had from an early date put forward claims which could extend to a universal monarchy. The superiority of the spiritual to the temporal was generally acknowledged, but kings were granted possession of spiritual authority, too. Melchisedek, king and priest, was to the monarchists of the middle ages the prototype of kingship. The collapse of the papacy in the tenth century left the field to kings. Thereafter the great papal revival, culminating in the world monarchy of Innocent III and the unrealistic assertions of Boniface VIII, altered the position: in theory, at least, kings were deprived of their spiritual authority, quarrels developed over rival jurisdictions and powers, popes asserted a superiority which might include a claim to make and unmake kings. The outward attributes of divine right remained (kings were the Lord's anointed, *divi* and *sacri*), but no late-medieval king was so manifestly God's deputy in matters both spiritual and temporal as had been his tenth-century ancestor. In truth, as a developed doctrine, the king's divine right to rule preceded the pope's divine right to oversee all rule. When one remembers that the papacy had a long struggle before it was accepted as leader even of the estate of the clergy, whereas kings could look to Constantine and Charlemagne as models, this may seem less surprising.

It was indeed the peculiar strength of medieval kingship
that it never abandoned the notion of a God-given authority
not mediated by the pope; the supposedly grander medieval
emperor always suffered from being linked in a notional
world monarchy with a partner who, by crowning him, sym-
bolised his own primacy.

Of course, once the reformed papacy got down to business,
its spiritual eminence, its universal reach and claim, its exceptional organisation, and its mass of agents and propagan-
dists enabled it to proclaim the full logic of its position in a
way that neither kings nor emperors could ever emulate.
The divine right of a priest like the pope was more probable and manifest than the divine right of kings. Figgis was
therefore quite right to interpret the doctrines of the sixteenth and seventeenth centuries against the background of
the break with the papacy. When Henry VIII of England
adopted the title of supreme head of the Church, his position owed a great deal to the supremacy, resting on right
divine, which papal doctrine had erected upon the *successio
Petri*. While divine right is a term which one would readily
apply to tenth-century kingship, *plenitudo potestatis*, the
pope's special preserve, is not. The divine right of Henry
VIII and Elizabeth inherited at least elements of this papal
fullness of power which had not been present in the "thau-
maturgical" kingship of the Anglo-Saxons or the practical
divine right of that protector of the Church, William the
Conqueror. But when Henry claimed, as he did, that he was
merely restoring the true preeminence of kings, long dis-
turbed by papal interference and usurpation, he was neither
so wrong nor so hypocritical as is usually alleged. There
were real links between the divine-right monarchy of the
Tudors and the *dei gratia* monarchy of the Carolingians;

and both quite properly looked back to Constantine the
Great.

Certainly they were not the same in every essential. Tudor divine right, and even up to a point the Bourbon monarchy of the seventeenth century, contained far less of that
magic or mystic element that distinguished the newly Chris-
tianised barbarian kings. Mysticism there was, but attenuated; religion formed the ceremonial dress rather than the
passionate essence of post-medieval kings by right divine.
On the other hand, their actual power over both State and
Church was as a rule markedly greater; the machinery, the
economy of their realms saw to that. More significantly, a
different aspect of the complex doctrine came to receive chief
attention, and it did so (as Figgis divined) because the doctrine was reconsidered under the stress of the attack on Rome
and of the Reformation of which this attack formed a part.
The aspect now stressed was not so much the will of God in
making the king, or the king's duty to govern his people on
God's behalf (though no one doubted these points), as the
subject's duty towards his king. The theory of the divine
right of kings resolved itself into a discussion of obedience
and resistance. And it did so, to be brief, because the Reformation everywhere introduced revolutionary situations in
which men's loyalties could easily divide.

Luther himself has often enough been credited with an
excessive worship for princes; it is even supposed that he
really transformed political thought by demanding obedience
at all costs. This is going far too far, though there is some
truth in it. The Reformation in a sense revived the situation
of the tenth century when order and the struggle against
anarchy depended exclusively on the power of secular
princes; the end of the papal monarchy, however purely

theoretical it had already become, left kings again as the necessary residuary legatees, and the theory of divine right stood ready to exalt them into sole occupation of the saddle. Luther, a true conservative, was extremely sensitive to the danger that what he regarded as a necessary return to an uncorrupted condition in the Church could lead to the dissolution of all secular ties and therefore to disastrous anarchy in God's natural creation. The government of this creation, he believed to be the consequence of the Fall; God's order for the fallen universe involved obedience to constituted authority. St. Paul's few words in Romans, 13, run right through all post-Reformation writing on authority and obedience. To Luther, the only liberty worth thinking about was Christian liberty, by which he meant salvation—nothing to do with men's temporal state. It did, however, lead him to make an important reservation to his general injunction of obedience: if the ruler ordains anything contrary to the truth of God, as revealed in Scripture, obedience is unlawful. So, however, is resistance: the Christian must confine himself to non-obedience, taking the consequences in this life and bliss in the next.

Calvin's teaching was in essentials the same, though he hinted at the possibility that there might exist inferior magistrates (like the Spartan ephors or modern Parliaments) who, having their power also from God, might in given circumstances be entitled to preserve God's good order against a tyrant. Here lay the germ of a useful idea, to be tended and developed by later generations of Calvinists when they came into conflict with their princes. In general, however, all the leading reformers preached non-resistance because kings were kings by right divine, responsible to God and punishable by Him alone, and because resistance meant the dissolution of God's decree for the fallen creation. Just because they saw the kingdoms of this world in so much worse a light, by comparison with the kingdom of God, than had the theorists of the later middle ages, they would not consider the questions of political liberty or limitations upon the powers of the magistrate. But that is only to say that they were good Augustinians, not Thomists, stressing the logical implications of ancient tradition.

Naturally this suited princes. The *Homily of Obedience* of 1547 expressed the whole doctrine of obedience and non-resistance in terms which no devotee of divine right in Louis XIV's France or Charles II's England could have bettered. "We may not resist, nor in any wise hurt, an anointed king, which is God's lieutenant, viceregent and highest minister in the country where he is king." The whole history of the divine right of kings, both its ancient belief in the sole source of royal power and its more recent preoccupation with obedience, is here neatly summed up. What, then, could the Stuarts add to it—to a doctrine not only, as Figgis thought, as old as the Reformation but in fact as old as Christian kingship? Yet there was an element missing, or at least not firmly stated, and here James I put in his pennyworth[11]. He added indefeasibility—or rather, since the notion of royal power as inalienable and, once created, irremovable also had a long history, the identification of indefeasibility with hereditary succession by primogeniture in the legitimate line. The one question left open in Tudor

---

[11] For James I see *The Political Works of James I*, ed. with a valuable introduction by C. H. McIlwain (Cambridge, Mass., 1918). A remarkable variant of the doctrine, deriving royal power from biblical and sociological patriarchalism, was put forward by Sir Robert Filmer in his *Patriarcha:* see the edition by T. P. R. Laslett (Oxford, 1949).

divine right teaching was this: who is the king appointed by God? The Tudor answer was pragmatic: whoever happens to be recognised as king. Anything more philosophical would have been awkward for a dynasty whose original claim was very weak and which encountered a series of succession problems. But the Stuarts, safer in their descent and happier in their production of progeny, felt able to claim that God's choice was announced by birth: at any given moment, there was always only one true king, whether or not he in fact ever managed to sit on a throne, and he was his predecessor's legitimate heir. Thus the doctrine received its final logical elaboration, and also (characteristically) the one touch of true absurdity to be found in it.

Figgis thus underestimated the antiquity and foundations of the doctrine and overestimated the contribution made by the Reformation. Yet he was right to see the particular form it took in the seventeenth century as the product of the situation, political as well as doctrinal, which grew from the rejection of the papacy and the breakup of Christendom. Next, he argued that this development led to the formulation of a true theory of sovereignty, and that nothing else could have done. When he talked of sovereignty he was thinking of the definition given by John Austin in lectures published in 1832: that sovereignty resides in the individual or aggregate body to whom a given society is in the habit of rendering obedience or submission, but who himself is not in the habit of obeying any determinate human superior. Austin's sovereign is principally a law-maker whose edicts command habitual obedience (or punishment for disobedience) and are the emanation of his sole will. It is generally agreed, with Figgis, that in this special sense sovereignty cannot be said to exist in a society which acknowledges a variety of intermediate or sectional superiors, or one whose laws are treated as the reflection of transcendental law, to be judged good or bad, valid or invalid, according to their consonance with it. However, many would now doubt whether "Austinian" sovereignty is to be found even in the seventeenth century: some argue that it had never really existed anywhere, while others hold that even if it ever had reality it is too narrow to be treated as universally valid. There is therefore now a tendency to trace such sovereignty as is supposed to have existed in the seventeenth century further and further back into the middle ages[12].

The conventional notion, propounded by Figgis, was that sovereignty could not exist before the political developments of the sixteenth century (the growth of selfcontained nation states) which were first clearly summed in Jean Bodin's definition of the "modern" notion of sovereignty (*Six Books of the Republic*, 1567). As against this, we are now commonly told two things: one, that late medieval states were quite as selfcontained and "sovereign" as their post-Reformation successors, and two, that the limitations upon sovereignty which operated in the seventeenth century (respect for natural law, respect for customary rights and restraints) made the sovereignty of Stuart kings and Bourbon monarchs more like that of their Yorkist and Valois predecessors than that of the nineteenth century. Both points have force; neither is entirely true. The political situation in the later middle ages is not really relevant if it remains

[12] For Austin see H. L. A. Hart's edition of his *The Province of Jurisprudence Determined* (London, 1954), esp. 193ff.; for an attack on his views, see Hans Kelsen, *General Theory of Law and State* (Eng. trans., Cambridge, Mass., 1949).

true that those societies regarded themselves as seriously
constrained by abstract laws (which to some extent they
did) or as sharing power among a variety of authorities
(which they certainly did). And the second point is less
important than it might seem, because the real question is
whether at any given moment a single authority exists on
the earthly plane, rather than whether respect remains for
superhuman authority. However attenuated, some such respect nearly always remains, which means that the discussion
would have to turn upon degrees of approximation to an
ideal definition rather than upon the realities of political
thinking. In some very important respects the State of the
sixteenth and seventeenth centuries could entertain an opinion of itself which gave it selfsufficiency and selfcontrol; its
predecessor could sometimes demonstrate these qualities but
did not consciously believe in their existence. In practice
this meant that sovereign activity increased quite as much as
doctrines of sovereignty, which makes the distinction important.

Nevertheless, Figgis's outright denial of the possibility of
sovereignty in the middle ages will not do. Some scholars
have found in the claims of the papacy the full equivalent
even of Austinian sovereignty: not only did the *plenitudo
potestatis* include all power to govern, not only was the pope
thought free of all earthly superiors, but when in the later
middle ages it came to be more widely held that law depended for its validity solely on the ruler's will papal legislation, claimed to be universally applicable, achieved true
sovereignty[13]. Papalism could assuredly lead to this view.

---

[13] Michael J. Wilks, *The Problem of Sovereignty in the Later Mid-
dle Ages* (Cambridge, 1963), esp. 151—83. For papal doctrine see also
Walter Ullmann, *The Growth of Papal Government in the Middle
Ages* (2nd ed., London, 1962), and *Principles etc.*, Part I.

Some writers came to eliminate the division between secular and ecclesiastical power, drew the logical conclusion from the God-given and monopolistic power of the Church's ruler, and subordinated all other authority, ecclesiastical or lay, to the papal monarchy which was thus invested with all the attributes of a genuine sovereignty—that is, with total irresponsibility. It may be objected that this was only one strand, and that the constitutionalist doctrines of those who in the fifteenth century advocated conciliar rule in the Church prove the existence of quite different views among the defenders of ecclesiastical preeminence[14]: but the brief importance of such teaching resulted simply from the accident of the papal schism, and the rapid restoration of papal despotism proved where the mainstream ran.

A more weighty objection to this identification of papalist doctrine with true sovereignty lies in the reminder that in practice late-medieval popes exercised no such powers. Secular states, at least closely resembling those found in modern Europe, are easily found in the fourteenth and fifteenth centuries, and their rulers, asserting a form of divine-right monarchy, may be credited with an equal claim to the possession of sovereignty. After all, they were usually called sovereigns. But this is where the term has proved too protean. By redefining it, scholars have found sovereignty in the thirteenth-century lawyer Accursius, allegedly nearer to present-day teaching on the subject than to Austin[15]; both canonists

[14] E.g. Brian Tierney, "Some recent works on the political theories of the medieval canonists," *Traditio*, 1954, 594ff.

[15] Brian Tierney, " 'The Prince is not bound by the laws:' Accursius and the origins of the modern state," *Comparative Studies in Society and History*, 1963, 378ff. His argument does not convince me: he creates modernity in Accursius by smudging all proper distinctions and never comes to grips with the problem of the *making* of law as distinct from living with that which exists.

and civilians from that time on have been interpreted as ex-
pounding doctrines according to which "the state itself,
being superior to all private rights, was by the mid-thirteenth
century becoming sovereign," such sovereignty being in
practice vested in its head, the prince, with his power "of
legislating, judging and administering, of doing all that was
necessary for the common and public welfare[16]." That such
unequivocal assertions are immediately followed by very
large exceptions and reservations, from the law of God to
the rights of subjects, sounds a warning to those who would
like to wipe out the distinction between medieval and modern. However, late-medieval kings could do most of these
things most of the time, and could do them with only in-
termittent interference from elsewhere, or from inferiors:
Figgis's "radical discontinuity" between these ages does not
convince either. We no longer believe in a "new monarchy"
in the sixteenth century. In both England and France clear-
cut concepts of sovereignty remained difficult to develop as
long as theorists acknowledged the presence of such limitations as *leges imperii* (fundamental laws which no human
agency could alter) or the supposed ability of the existing
law to control the validity of new law[17]: McIlwain refused
to see any recognition of real sovereignty as late as the

[16] See the writings of Gaines Post in *Traditio*, 1943, 355ff., and
1953, 281ff.; *Speculum*, 1954, 417ff.; *Welt als Geschichte*, 1961, 8ff.,
71ff. The above quotations come from Mr. Post's summary of his own
views in his review of Wilks's book (see note 13), in *Speculum*, 1964,
365ff.

[17] Bodin believed in fundamental laws; it has even been possible
to treat him simply as a constitutionalist (which he was not): Beatrice
Reynolds, *Proponents of Limited Monarchy in Sixteenth-Century
France* (New York, 1931). For common law and statute law in England see the summary in G. R. Elton, *The Tudor Constitution* (Cambridge, 1960), 233f.

age of Louis XIV[18]. Figgis's clear distinction has become blurred by medievalists looking to the practical effects of kingship and by modernists paying heed to conventional limitations on freedom of action. The fact that, with reservations, Figgis was probably nearer the truth is worth restating.

For one thing, the attack on Austin has gone too far. His definition fits best the sort of unitary, centrally controlled and all-powerful state which he had before him in nineteenth-century England; and the excesses practised by such states in conditions of twentieth-century totalitarianism have done much to discredit his somewhat rigorous opinion. A country like the United States, with its fundamental constitution and its devolution of powers upon constituent states, may be said to practise a system in which there is no room for Austin's sovereign. The British Commonwealth on Nations, resting (in law) upon the Statute of Westminster (1931) in which the sovereign law-maker renounced the power of sovereign law-making, forms an even more striking argument against it[19]. But these are superficial views. The excesses of Hitler or Stalin do not prove that the essence of the state is not found in its right to demand obedience to its laws. The United States has several times shown itself possessed of the power to amend its constitution or coerce its component parts: there is an ultimate, if rarely used, sovereign authority there somewhere. And the Commonwealth is only in the process of proving that it has ceased to be relevant to the discussion: it no longer is, in Austin's phrase, "a society political and independent" but a loose collection of

[18] But see George L. Mosse, *The Struggle for Sovereignty in England* (East Lansing, 1950), for a strong dissenting view.

[19] These are the instances used by Tierney (note 15).

sovereign states. Austin did seize on the crucial point, whereas his critics drift around the edges. Kelsen's definition of law as "norm," as a rule of conduct generally accepted by a given society, may be wider and jurisprudentially more useful than Austin's law as command. But we are concerned with sovereignty, which is a dynamic quality: the power and right to make new law, the ability to order the doing or abstaining from something not hitherto enjoined or forbidden. And every non-Austinian definition of law sooner or later grounds upon this rock: whence does new law derive its authority and effect?

If legislation, then, is the criterion which must define the nature of the power structure within a state, the late-medieval concept of sovereignty will be seen to differ significantly from the modern. The pope was then the only possible medieval sovereign (in the modern sense) because he claimed superiority to all other laws for his edicts. So far Mr. Wilks's theorists are right. But because the pope's "sovereignty" was so universal—because his "state" embraced all Christendom—his sovereignty had no reality. Everywhere, the law of the secular community, the prince's law, rivalled the pope's, either co-existing with it or occasionally superseding it. But the prince's law was no more sovereign because everywhere the validity of the papal law in certain defined spheres of life was fully admitted. All this is quite apart from the view still firmly current that law, to be good, must please God, that there existed a superior standard of validity in the non-human law of nature. In practice, medieval legislators may not have been more notably bound by purely moral or religious scruple, though in fact it seems clear to me that the force of these beliefs declined in the course of the sixteenth century. The point is not important, any more than is the real meaning of natural law in the seventeenth century. As has already been said, men at all times make reservations to their total freedom to act as they please. What really limited medieval sovereignty was the existence of the papacy and its at least theoretically overwhelming claims. In the later middle ages, sovereignty meant no more than supremacy, chief magistracy, the right to govern within the agreed and limiting confusion of laws and legislative authorities. The Reformation was required to release sovereignty from its limitations and turn it into the power to make law superior to any other within a given society. This was most easily seen in such countries as England or Sweden where the medieval sovereign (the prince regnant) absorbed his rival's powers and so became sovereign in quite a different sense[20]. But in due course it became manifest also in states in which the papacy continued to exercise a theoretical influence. Figgis was right when he pointed to the separation of Church and State as the hallmark of sovereignty, though the story and the problems were much more complicated than he realised and the last word has certainly not yet been said. The middle ages did have a concept and practice of sovereignty, but these differed from what, quite slowly in most places and more slowly in most minds, developed from it after the Reformation. As for divine right, Figgis correctly supposed that it was closely involved in the emergence of clearer thinking about sovereignty and the state, but he mistook an accident for a causal relationship. Though quite often sovereignty and divine right went hand in hand, they did not have to do so; other concepts of monarchy and society

[20] For England and its mixed sovereignty, see G. R. Elton, *England under the Tudors* (London, 1955), 160f.; *The Tudor Constitution*, 230ff.

existed which were equally capable of reconciling themselves to the notion of sovereignty.

*　　*　　*

This raises the whole question of the dilemma of medieval and early modern kingship. Figgis, concerned with the divine right of kings, ignored other strands in the history of monarchy. If I now briefly go outside the confines he set himself, that is because a wider view will throw light on the divine right itself and help to explain the collapse of a doctrine which had so much logic and so much age to recommend it. The truth is that the medieval king combined within himself several dualities. There were the "two bodies" studied by Kantorowicz, the mystical entity which never died and the physical being which underwent the normal human vicissitudes. *Rex et sacerdos:* at least until the eleventh century, kings commonly claimed to be both. Reservoir of justice, reservoir of mercy: he was both. But these dualisms presented no difficulty to the single human being. It was otherwise with the double source of his power. To the fundamental questions—what made a man king, and by what right could he claim obedience—there were two discordant, even irreconcilable, answers. He was king by right divine, *dei gratia,* enjoying (to borrow Ullmann's graphic distinction) a power descending upon him from above. But he was also a king chosen by his people, bound in a relationship of mutual duty, enjoying a power ascending to him from below. From the ninth century onwards, the practical facts of a fragmented authority (feudalism) reinvigorated this second character of kingship by giving a political reality to his obligation to the governed. The people were subjects, committed to him and in his care. They were also vassals and counsellors whom he was bound to consult in what touched all: *quod omnes tangit ab omnibus approbetur* was no less serious a concept for being a tag. In the one capacity he is solely responsible to God, free of both control and punishment by any human agency, incapable of being sued for breaches of the law—strictly even incapable of being charged with any. In the other, he must observe the order acceptable to his subjects; he cannot touch their lives or property outside the established processes of the law, he must seek their advice, he cannot revoke grants and concessions once made, he can even be resisted and deposed. The dualism crops up in unexpected places. The very legists who read virtual absolutism into theocratic kingship and the dicta that the prince's pleasure is law and he is *legibus solutus,* also came to treat the supposed *lex regia,* by which the people had allegedly bestowed upon their ruler a power originally theirs, as grounds for the ruler's responsibility to the ruled.

This dualism is well exemplified, in English terms, by the meaning given to the royal prerogative. At heart this is nothing but those special rights, over and above those available to everybody, which the king enjoys by virtue of his office: they enable him to carry out his unique task in the State. Commonly they were divided into the two categories familiar from Chief Baron Fleming's famous judgment in Bate's Case in 1606: the ordinary and absolute prerogative. When one traces the terms back one finds the ordinary on occasion described as ordained (*potestas ordinata* instead of *ordinaria*)[21], and here lies the necessary clue. The ordinary power of kings is that which is laid down in the law—entitlement to certain revenues, powers of patronage, and so forth. His

---

[21] See J. Holub, "Ordinaria potentia—absoluta potentia," *Revue Historique de Droit Français et Étranger,* 1950, 92ff.

absolute power (*legibus soluta*) is that to which the law does not apply because it cannot: these are the rights of free action, unknowable until the occasion arises, which any ruler must possess if he is to deal with the crises of the body politic. His ordinary power he enjoys by agreement, by contract, with his people, a contract embodied in the binding details of the law accepted by both parties; his absolute because he is God's chosen instrument for the goverance of His people. The problems which arise in defining the borderline between the two, or in discovering whether the king is exercising a proper or improper "absolute" power, are a special case of the general dilemma which arises from the dual basis of royal authority[22].

For in the last resort there could be no theoretical resolution of this particular dualism. The king either held a descending power, in which case he looked only upwards for control over his actions and judgment on his misdeeds; or he held an ascending power, in which case he was at least in considerable measure responsible to his people. One medieval attempt to dispose of the problem has already been hinted at in what was said of the prerogative. There was always the law, the *tertium quid* between king and people, possibly even between king and God but at least the expression of God's order equally binding upon king and people. Bracton's famous assertion that the king, though under no man, is under God and the law tackled the dilemma in a way which proved satisfactory to many, though his inference that a king who

---

[22] The Tudors regarded the two kinds of prerogative as co-ordinate, each competent within its own sphere; the Stuarts held the absolute to be in control of the ordinary. A fine case study of the difficulties raised by divine right and the absolute prerogative in practice is provided by the Angevin monarchy of the twelfth century: J. E. A. Joliffe, *Angevin Kingship* (London, 1955).

fails to do justice thereby ceases to be king cannot be reconciled with any form of divine-right doctrine. But Bracton's answer really evades the problem by the characteristic device of supposing that the law somehow exists apart from men. Once again we are up against the question of legislation: the king may be under the law as it stands and is known, but what happens when the law requires addition, subtraction or modification?

It therefore remains true that the double authority of kings could not be brought into theoretical accord as long as sovereignty or supreme power was seen as vested in one being. This did not, needless to say, prevent kingship from working: graver problems of logic have not affected practical efficacy in institutions. But it did mean that there was a flaw in the system which only political competence—ability to operate an essentially double-ended position—could overcome, and this meant that crisis was built into medieval kingship. After a series of lesser crises, both French and English kingship met the conflict head on, as a consequence of the Reformation and the strains on loyalty which it introduced. In France the crisis came in the second half of the sixteenth century, in England in the first half of the seventeenth, as political and social stresses amalgamated with bewildered men's passionate doubts whether their God in heaven or His human deputy should receive their obedience.

Political theory really comes into its own only in a crisis, when the conventional beliefs and unargued assumptions of men are suddenly called in question. This accounts for the enormous output of relevant literature, running round and round the same issues, in both countries at those times. In both we find newly sharpened statements of divine right, clearer approaches to notions of sovereignty, fully worked out constitutionalist doctrines and even expressions of populist and democratic views. Medieval kingship was dissected into its component parts; if some of the tools were old (which accounts for the discovery of "predecessors" among medieval writers), some were newly provided by Protestantism and reformed Catholicism. This is particularly true of explicit doctrines of tyrannicide. The opening up of the question naturally revealed the flaw at the heart of kingship and worried away at it to the point where neither repair nor disguise was any longer possible. The results differed in the two countries. In France, divine right triumphed and the contractual side of the old kingship in effect vanished. In England, by 1688, the king was forced to abandon all claims *dei gratia* and to become his people's first official. The fact that both types of monarchy preserved some ceremonial vestiges of the attributes which they had lost is neither here nor there. This divergent outcome owed a good deal to the way in which the actual battle went, with the king emerging as saviour from a civil war in France, while the English monarchy experienced execution and abolition. It is, however, easy to see that past development had much to do with it— so easy that in England, at least, profound differences between French absolutism and English constitutionalism have commonly been backdated far beyond the truth.

The French triumph of divine-right kingship may have been unavoidable; the English crisis was much more unnecessary because a workable and intellectually possible solution to the dilemma had been provided by the Tudor monarchy. A better understanding of it might at least have saved the changes necessitated by time from involving civil war and revolution. The Tudor system rested on the concept of a unitary body politic, both State and Church, governed

respectively by a king and supreme head, one person executing two distinct functions definable as the rule of men's
bodies and the protection of their souls. So far it was pure
divine-right monarchy. But it had managed to accommodate
the contractual aspect of monarchy by recognising in Parliament (the assembly of king, lords and commons) a replica of
the body politic. It was a Tudor commonplace that the edicts
of Parliament were binding on all because all were there
present, in person or by deputy. The law there made was
valid because it carried both common consent and executive
sanction—was both "norm" and "command." By any-
body's standard, the Tudor king-in-Parliament was a true
sovereign. Unfortunately it was also a mixed sovereign, a
difficult thing to conceive of in theory and even more difficult
to operate in practice. The whole weight of past and present
opinion, and especially the hitherto clearest claim to true
supremacy (the pope's), all seemed to demand a single person
for sovereign. Bodin, summing up the tradition in a new situation, specifically denied the possibility of a collective sovereign power. When the crisis came it naturally took the form
of a struggle within the political machine, within what was
really the sovereign body, and those who by stages realised
that sovereignty was in issue were thus induced to locate it
in a single person, which meant that they asserted an unqualified doctrine of divine right. However ancient its basis,
Stuart divine right was revolutionary because it dispensed
with the contract and attacked an existing mixed sovereignty.
In due course, its opponents produced equally revolutionary
ideas of popular sovereignty, or even of the sovereignty of
the abstract State (Hobbes). The truer tradition was not
forgotten, but the few writers who in the midst of civil war

defended a mixed sovereign body met nothing but abuse[23].
On its return in 1660 the tradition was a little modified; at
the end of the struggle, in 1689, it overbalanced against
divine right. Divine right died in England because the kings
of the house of Stuart failed to accept the dual nature of
their authority and to use the political weapons of persuasion
and management upon which the Tudor reconciliation of the
irreconcilable had so successfully rested.

Figgis understandably studied the divine right of kings
when he could see it clearly defined in the floodlight thrown
by crisis. He therefore studied it on its deathbed, and though
he realised something if its ancient history he did not fully
grasp how permanent an attribute of European kingship
it had been. It was the contribution made by Christianity
to a form of government which also derived from Roman
imperialism (incorporating at least a trace of Hellenistic
kingship) and tribal barbarism. All things considered, it had
a long history, and it may well be doubted whether it was in
any way less defensible than the divine right of peoples.

Clare College
Cambridge, England
January, 1965

---

[23] See Charles H. McIlwain, "A Forgotten Worthy, Philip Hunton,"
Constitutionalism and the Modern World (Cambridge, 1939), 196ff.;
Margaret A. Judson, *The Crisis of the Constitution* (New Brunswick,
N.J., 1949), index entries under "Hunton, Philip" and "Parker,
Henry".

CHAPTER I

INTRODUCTORY

A MODERN essayist has said with truth, that "never has there been a doctrine better written against than the Divine Right of Kings[1]." But those, who have exhausted their powers of satire in pouring scorn upon the theory, have commonly been at little pains to understand it. That the doctrine is absurd, when judged from the stand-point of modern political thought, is a statement that requires neither proof nor exposition. But the modern standpoint is not the only one, and the absurdity of the doctrine in our eyes is the least interesting or important fact about it, except as driving us to seek further for its real meaning and value. Nor is "The Divine Right of Kings" differentiated by reason of its absurdity from other political theories of the seventeenth century. The rival doctrine of an original compact was no whit less ridiculous in theory, and (if we consider its

The Theory of the Divine Right of Kings commonly condemned as absurd.

But other theories of the time also absurd.

---

[1] Gairdner and Spedding, *Studies in English History*, 245. Cf. also Mr Gairdner's remarks in the preface to *Letters and Papers Illustrative of the Reigns of Richard III. and Henry VII.* XI—XIII.

influence upon Rousseau) infinitely more explosive in practice than the notions of Indefeasible Right and Passive Obedience. It is noteworthy, that, while Macaulay has nothing but contempt for the supporters of Divine Right, he does not find it needful to mention that its opponents would make no better figure among political thinkers of to-day. Instead of stating a fact, which is common to all obsolete doctrines, it were surely better to enquire into the notions of those, to whom the doctrine seemed natural, and to set it in relation to the conditions which produced it. Large numbers of men may embrace a belief without good reason, but assuredly they will not do so without adequate cause. And it is commonly of far greater importance towards the right understanding of a doctrine to know the causes, which lead to its prevalence or decay, than it is to be able to criticize the reasoning, by which men think to support it, while it is popular or to demolish it, as it grows obsolete[1].

The causes of the prevalence of the doctrine more important than the reasons against its validity.

Its import probably different from what it appears.

Further, although the theory may seem absurd, when framed into a set of bald propositions, it is not wise therefore to infer that it had no other meaning to its supporters, than that which it bears to us. It may prove to have been in the main a counter-theory to some other notion of Divine Right, more ridiculous and less useful. Judged in relation to the circumstances which produced it, and to the rival

---

[1] Mr Balfour takes these two theories as offering the most salient illustration of the fact that the causes of belief are widely different from the reasons for it, *Foundations of Belief*, 216—17.

doctrines it was formed to extirpate, the theory of
the Divine Right of Kings may prove to be necessary and even sensible. The import of the battle-
cries of "Passive Obedience" and "Ius Divinum" to
those, who were fighting the battle, must have been
very different from what it seems to those, who can
see no meaning in the cries, because they have forgotten that there was a battle. The method of
Whig historians is apparently to isolate the phenomenon, and to observe it *in vacuo*. Considered in
this way any theory of government must appear
ridiculous, so soon as it has ceased to influence
practice. It is not so that the true import and
value of 'forsaken beliefs' is to be gauged. It
has been shewn that the earlier free-traders were
at fault in treating the believers in the Mercantile
theory as conscious knaves or incurable fools. They
erred in supposing, that since a theory has become
obsolete, it therefore had never anything to recommend it, save the self-interest of the few and the
stupidity of the many[1]. May not the same thing
be true of some of those, who have poured out upon
the believers in the Divine Right of Kings ridicule,
that certainly has the merit of being obvious?

Nor again can the doctrine be dismissed as the *The
doctrine
not
academic
but
popular.* work of an isolated thinker with a turn for paradox.
It was essentially a popular theory, proclaimed in
the pulpit, published in the market-place, witnessed
on the battle-field. The names, which have come
down to us, as especially connected with it stand out

[1] Cunningham, *History of English Industry and Commerce*,
Part II. §§ 307, 357.

rather by lapse of time, than through any eminence of their own. Filmer is not to be regarded as a prophet or thinker, followed as a master by a crowd of inferior men. He was only slightly more able and far more notorious, than a host of other writers, whose names and works have faded from the general recollection. A belief so widespread was surely the product far more of practical necessity than of intellectual activity. No enthusiasm for a scheme of ideal politics, no quasi-scientific delight in discussions upon the nature of government could generate so passionate a faith. The pressure of circumstances could alone produce it. Nor as a matter of fact is the doctrine much regarded by the makers of Ideal Commonwealths in the sixteenth and seventeenth centuries. It might seem that no scheme of politics could be more purely ideal than one which asserts Divine authority for its basis. Yet there is no trace of propagandism in the works of royalist writers, whether in France or England. Some indeed are at pains to assert that they have no quarrel with other forms of government, when once established, whether elective monarchies or republics[1]. There is no desire to establish universal Kingship, akin to the passionate enthusiasm of French Revolutionaries for abolishing it. For the most part, the horizon of the politico-theological writers of the sixteenth and seventeenth centuries is bounded by a particular country in a definite stage of development. A Frenchman will indeed find in the Davidic kingdom the model of a state governed by

The outcome of actual needs.

---

[1] E.g. Hickes in *Jovian*.

the Salic law.   An Englishman will see in it the
Divine justification for the English law of succession.   But, except for the purpose of finding God's
authority for a given polity, neither really looks
beyond his own country.   The theory is the outcome of facts far more than it is of thinking.   From
the consideration of the popular acceptance and
practical object of the doctrine, some obvious conclusions may be drawn.   First, it seems clear that *The*
so general and enthusiastic a faith must have been *doctrine must have*
the expression of deep-seated instincts; secondly, *satisfied*
that a doctrine so fully elaborated and yet so *deep in- stincts*
eminently the product of a definite epoch must *and fulfilled a*
have been the result of a long chain of historical *function.*
causes, and that it must have been formed to meet
real needs.   If so, it had a definite function to fulfil
in the development of society.   It is the purpose
of this essay to enquire how far this was the case.

The theory of the Divine Right of Kings in its *Statement*
completest form involves the following propositions:— *of the theory.*

(1) *Monarchy is a divinely ordained institution.*

(2) *Hereditary right is indefeasible.*   The succession to monarchy is regulated by the law of
primogeniture.   The right acquired by birth cannot be forfeited through any acts of usurpation, of
however long continuance, by any incapacity in the
heir, or by any act of deposition.   So long as the
heir lives, he is king by hereditary right, even
though the usurping dynasty has reigned for a
thousand years.

(3) *Kings are accountable to God alone.*   Monarchy is pure, the sovereignty being entirely vested

in the king, whose power is incapable of legal limitation. All law is a mere concession of his will, and all constitutional forms and assemblies exist entirely at his pleasure. He cannot limit or divide or alienate the sovereignty, so as in any way to prejudice the right of his successor to its complete exercise. A mixed or limited monarchy is a contradiction in terms.

(4) *Non-resistance and passive obedience are enjoined by God.* Under any circumstances resistance to a king is a sin, and ensures damnation. Whenever the king issues a command directly contrary to God's law, God is to be obeyed rather than man, but the example of the primitive Christians is to be followed and all penalties attached to the breach of the law are to be patiently endured.

Illustrative quotations.

The following passages set the doctrine forth in the language of the time:—

"We will still believe and maintain that our Kings derive not their title from the people but from God; that to Him only they are accountable; that it belongs not to subjects, either to create or censure, but to honour and obey their sovereign, who comes to be so by a fundamental hereditary right of succession, which no religion, no law, no fault or forfeiture can alter or diminish[1]." "Obedience we must pay, either Active or Passive; the Active in the case of all lawful commands; that is whenever the Magistrate commands something which is not

---

[1] From an address of the University of Cambridge to King Charles II. in 1681, printed in the *History of Passive Obedience*, p. 108.

contrary to some command of God, we are then
bound to act according to that command of the
Magistrate, to do the thing he requires. But when
he enjoins anything contrary to what God hath
commanded, we are not then to pay him this Active
Obedience; we may, nay we must refuse thus to
act (yet here we must be very well assured that
the thing is so contrary, and not pretend conscience
for a cloak of stubbornness), we are in that case *to
obey God rather than man*. But even this is a
season for the passive obedience; we must patiently
suffer what he inflicts on us for such refusal, and
not, to secure ourselves, rise up against him[1]."

"If Adam himself were still living and now
ready to die it is certain there is one man, and but
one in the world who is next heir, although the knowledge who should be that one man be quite lost[2]."

The theory is commonly supported by a number
of Biblical illustrations and texts, of which some of
the most important may be mentioned :—Samuel's
description of a king, on the Jewish nation demanding one[3]; David's refusal to touch "the Lord's
anointed"; the text "By me kings reign and
princes decree justice[4]"; the passage describing
the vision of Nebuchadnezzar, asserting that "the

Common arguments in favour of the theory.

---

[1] *Whole Duty of Man*, Sunday xiv. § 5. The passage is quoted
by Hobbes as giving the best expression of "the doctrine of the
King's party." (*Behemoth*, Part i. p. 80.)

[2] Filmer's *Patriarcha*. Chap. i. § 9.

[3] 1 Sam. vii. 10—18. There is much controversy as to
whether Samuel intended to describe a good king exercising his
sovereign rights, or a tyrant.

[4] Prov. viii. 15.

Most High ruleth in the kingdom of men, and giveth it to whomsoever he will, and setteth up over it the basest of men[1]"; the command to·"render unto Cæsar the things that are Cæsar's[2]"; Christ's words to Pilate "thou couldest have no power at all against me except it were given thee from above[3]"; the behaviour of the primitive Christians; and above all the direct enjoining by both S. Peter and S. Paul of obedience to constituted authority, "The powers that be are ordained of God. Whosoever therefore resisteth the power, resisteth the ordinance of God. And they that resist shall receive to themselves damnation." "Ye must needs be subject, not only for wrath, but for conscience' sake[4]." "Submit yourselves to every ordinance of man for the Lord's sake—whether it be to the king as supreme, &c.[5]"

The Patriarchal form of the theory not essential to it. The Patriarchal theory, the most unqualified form of which Filmer and others profess to find in Genesis, forms the basis of the most symmetrical form of the doctrine of Divine Right, but it is far from universal and there is no reason for regarding it as of the essence of the theory.

No importance Nor, again, does the sacramental character of unction play much part in the exposition of the

[1] Daniel iv.   [2] S. Luke xx. 25.   [3] S. John xix. 11.

[4] Rom. xiii. 1—7. It was held of great importance to maintain that κρίσις meant damnation in the strict sense. There is a lengthy dissertation of Hammond to prove this single point.

[5] 1 Pet. ii. 13—17. A favourite argument to prove that kings are accountable to God alone is the text "Against thee only have I sinned" (Ps. li. 4). It is quoted by a French writer as having the authority of Otto of Freising, and is used by Leslie among others.

divine authority of kings. Richard II. undoubtedly *attached to unction.* believed that unction conferred an indelible mark, and the motion of the sacredness of royal power, as compared with all other constituted authority, was certainly strengthened by this ancient ceremony[1]. But it plays, in the controversies of the sixteenth and seventeenth centuries, a quite different part. In France the supporters of the League are found arguing, that unction is necessary to make a king, and that Henry IV., who as a heretic cannot be anointed by the Archbishop of Rheims, can therefore never be truly king. In England, the writers on the popular side are continually pointing to the coronation oath as evidence of the theory of compact, and as limiting the royal authority. Hence both in France and England, the counter-assertion is common that unction is of no importance, and confers no special grace; that the king is king before his coronation as fully as he is after; and that resistance to an 'uncrowned' king is verily damnable. The phrase, "the Lord's Anointed," is merely common form for the sacred person of the

---

[1] Shakespeare expresses the sentiment rather of Richard II. himself than of the believers in the Divine Right of Kings, in the famous lines :—

"Not all the water in the rude rough sea
Can wash the balm from an anointed king."

There can be no doubt that the notion of the sacred character conferred by unction was held by Richard, and that it long remained an element in popular feeling. But the exigencies of their position drove the supporters of the theory of Indefeasible Right to minimize the effect of unction. Any stress laid upon it tended to make the king a mere official, and to support the doctrine of the originally elective character of kingship.

King and is used by writers who are far from attri-
buting any sacramental character to the ceremony.
Undoubtedly the ordinary view is that of a royalist
divine, who declares in set terms that "Royal
Unction confers no grace, but declares a just title
only." Indeed no other view was really compatible
with the notion of indefeasible hereditary right[1].

[1] *The Royal Charter granted unto Kings*, Chap. III. *What is
meant by the anointing of Kings.* "*Unxit in regem* includes
nothing but a due title, excludes nothing but usurpations ; gives
him the administration to govern, not the gift to govern well ; the
right of ruling, not of ruling right." "Anointing is a sacred
signature betokening sovereignty, obedience to the throne, allegiance
to the Crown." Usher after quoting David's sentence on the Ama-
lekite for slaying the Lord's anointed goes on : "And this indeed
must be the main foundation not only of the observance but also
of all the other branches of that allegiance, which we do owe unto
our Prince ; that with the right which he hath obtained by Election
or Succession here below *we be careful to conjoin that unction
which he hath received from above.*" (*Power of the Prince*, p. 125.)
Clearly unction is regarded as equivalent to God's institution
of kings, not as a grace conferred by the sacrament of anointing.
Cf. Coke on Calvin's Case. "Coronation is but a *royal ornament*
and solemnization of the royal descent, but no part of the title."
He goes on to quote the case of two seminary priests, who claimed
that before his coronation it was not high treason to seize and
imprison King James. This doctrine was of course condemned by
the judges, who declared him to be as full king before coronation as after (7 *Reports*, 10 b). It is significant, that neither
The Maid's Tragedy nor *The Royal King and Loyal Subject*,
although each asserts most emphatically the sacred character
of Kingship, contains the slightest hint that this character is
acquired through unction. In France again, Servin writing on
behalf of Henry IV. distinctly denies that unction has any
significance, or is more than a pious ceremony. Blackwood
indeed appears to take a different view : "An non quemadmodum
sacerdotes sic et reges cum inaugurantur oleo id est divina quadam
virtute inunguntur ? Nam oleum, illud quo reges olim sacerdotes

Now a theory, such as that described, has plainly *The theory belongs to an age, when politics and theology were closely connected.* as much relation to theology as to politics, and cannot be judged from the standpoint of an age, when the two are sharply divided. Although something is heard at times of the importance of religious considerations in regulating international politics or state-inter-ference, yet no one now claims that politics is a branch of theology. Men may appeal with more or less of sincerity to Christian sentiment as a factor in political controversy, but they have ceased to regard political theory as a part of Christian doctrine. The theory of the Divine Right of Kings belongs to an age in which not only religion but theology and politics were inextricably mingled, when even for utilitarian sentiments a religious basis must be found if they were to obtain acceptance. All men demanded *The same methods are em-ployed by opponents of the theory.* some form of Divine authority for any theory of government. There is hardly a hint that those who disbelieved in the Divine Right of Kings had any quarrel with the methods of their opponents. Until towards the close of the seventeenth century, the atmosphere of the supporters of popular rights is as theological as that of the upholders of the Divine Right of Kings.

John Hall[1] indeed brushes aside the Biblical illustrations and authorities of the royalists; but most are content to argue on just the same lines as their

et prophetae perfundebantur, divinitatis symbolum erat ac *veluti sacramentum*" (*Apologia pro Regibus*, p. 15, cf. also *De Vinculo Religionis et Imperii*, pp. 232, 314). But this view is far less common than that given in the text.

[1] *The Grounds and Reasons of Monarchy* prefixed to *Harring-ton's Works*, p. 8.

opponents. They point out that Scripture has been misunderstood, that texts have been ignored which inculcate the right and duty of resistance, that the early Christians exhibited the virtue of Passive obedience merely because they could not help themselves. Even the original compact finds its biblical model in the 'law of the kingdom' laid down by Samuel. Towards the end of the seventeenth century, with Locke and Sidney and even the more able of the royalists, politics began to pass into a more modern stage. But most writers, of whom Johnson the author of *Julian the Apostate* is a fair specimen, have hardly a notion, that political theory can be framed except on a theological basis, or proved save by the authority of the Bible. Writers on behalf either of unlimited obedience or popular rights, though they are undoubtedly impelled by a pressing sense of the utility of resistance or *vice versâ*, yet seek by appealing to Scripture to establish their theory upon an immutable basis, and to base it upon transcendental grounds, of which no fresh view of what was merely expedient should ever destroy the force. To judge aright the political theories of the sixteenth and seventeenth centuries, we must not consider them from the standpoint of an age in which all political theory is confessedly utilitarian[1]; their true relations are to a time when theology and politics were closely united both in theory and practice. It is useless to demonstrate, what nobody doubts, that the theory of the Divine Right of Kings has

[1] Professor Sidgwick (*Elements of Politics* 34) bears witness to the exclusively utilitarian character of modern politics.

no affinity with the creed of any modern political party. Rather we must seek to find what political theories of ecclesiastical power met their countervailing influence in this theological theory of politics.

Again, the theory assumes the fact of "sovereignty." When it is borne in mind, that the idea of sovereignty in the Austinian sense was unknown in any single nation in the middle ages, it will at once become a matter for enquiry how far the uncompromising absolutism of the royalist writers may have been merely the expression of a thought, which came to them with all the force of a discovery. While the fact that the notion appears in the claims to universal supremacy of both Popes and Emperors, may point to the possibility of similar causes operating in the struggles on the part of the national states for independence of Papal control, it was not, perhaps, easy for a writer like Austin to see, how a theory of the state can ever be formed without the recognition, that there must be in it some ultimate authority, which because it can make laws is above law. Yet it is certain that this notion is modern, and that the idea of the complete supremacy of one body or person in the state did not enter the heads of those who wrote of the English polity in the middle ages. Bracton knows of no sovereign in the Austinian sense, and distinctly denies to the royal authority the attribute of being 'incapable of legal limitation[1].' How indeed could it have been

The theory involves the notion of sovereignty.

[1] Cf. Pollock and Maitland, *History of English Law*, I. 160. " That the king is below the law is a doctrine which even a royal

otherwise under the conditions of feudalism, however modified, and in the face of the admitted claims of the Papacy and the canon law[1]? In addition, then, to setting the theory of the Divine Right of Kings in relation to contemporary conflicts of politics and theology, it will be needful to enquire how far the doctrine is the expression of a dawning idea of sovereignty, whether or no this idea was realised by the opponents of Divine Right, and what are the true relations of the latter doctrine to the more systematic theory of sovereignty, expounded by Hobbes.

Origin of the theory to be sought in the conflicts of the Papacy and Empire.

The fact, that Imperialist writers in the middle ages, endeavouring to refute the claims of the Papacy, develope for themselves the essential notion of sovereignty, points, as was said, to the conflict with Rome as the true source of the theory of Divine Right. Again, the necessarily theological character of politics, so long as the Pope's claims to supreme political authority were a main factor in the situation, makes it yet more plain, that the history of the theory must be largely concerned with the political side of the Reformation struggle. But in order to learn how the weapons were forged, which were to be used in the seventeenth century, it will be needful to study the earlier conflicts of Pope and Emperor.

justice may fearlessly proclaim. The theory that in every state there must be some man or definite body of men above the law, some 'sovereign' without duties and without rights would have been rejected." See also p. 208, and Bk. II. Ch. II. § 13, The King and the Crown.

[1] Cf. Maine, *Early History of Institutions*, Lectures XII. and XIII. in which is shewn the practical inapplicability of Austin's theory to primitive societies and half developed states.

In these the Papalist writers first will be found
developing a theory of sovereignty for their Lord the
Pope, while this is met by the counter-contention
of the Imperialists that not the Pope but the
Emperor is truly sovereign, and that he is so by
God's direct appointment. Here clearly are the
main elements of the later doctrine.

That to the Reformation was in some sort due *If the*
the prevalence of the notion of the Divine Right of *doctrine was need-*
Kings is generally admitted[1]. If then it should *ful to*
prove that the doctrine was an essential element of *effect the Reforma-*
success in the struggle against the political claims *tion, it*
of the Papacy, it will be vain to condemn its *did good service.*
supporters for trying to set back the clock of time.
If the theory was needful, it did good work, and the
fact that the work is done is no reason for pouring
ridicule on those who took part in it. The value of
a doctrine is to be gauged, not from its having given
place to a better, but from its having superseded
one which was either pernicious or had become
obsolete.

The interest of the subject is great. It marks *History of*
the transition from mediæval to modern modes *the theory of interest,*
of thought. In studying it we see the links of *as mark-*
connection between thinkers like Dante and Ockham *ing the change*
on the one hand, and Locke and Rousseau on the *from*
other, while, despite the notion of natural rights, *mediæval to modern*
Locke and Sidney with their strong vein of utili- *thought,*
tarian sentiment are plainly the forerunners of *as proving the de-*
Bentham and Mill. But not only does the history *pendence of theory*

[1] See especially Mr Gairdner's valuable essay on the subject.
Gairdner and Spedding, *Studies in English History*, 245 sqq.

upon practice. of the doctrine serve to bridge the gulf between mediæval and modern thought. It also illustrates the inevitable dependence of theory upon circumstances. That facts are the parents of theories far more than theories of facts, that political thought is inevitably relative to political development, men are all too prone to forget. But no one who studies the origin and history of the theory of the Divine Right of Kings is likely to do so. On the other hand it is unquestionably true, that a doctrine produced by the pressure of circumstances may have a great practical work to perform. It gives expression to real needs, and strengthens men in their determination to make a stand, for what they instinctively feel to be of vital importance. No belief could be more the child of circumstance than that in the Divine Right of Kings; while it played no despicable part in giving the nation some sort of intellectual and doctrinal basis for its claim to independence of ecclesiastical control. These points it will be the aim of the following essay to elucidate.

CHAPTER II

EARLY IDEAS OF KINGSHIP

THE developed doctrine of kingship of the seven- teenth century has been described by Sir Frederick Pollock as "not rational, not ingenious, not even ancient[1]." Yet the instinct, which it satisfied, is as old as history. In some form the sanctity of kingship has been held from very early times. Although the theory of the seventeenth century was mainly the expression of immediate needs, it is not possible to deny some part in it to a sentiment of loyalty, which is as old as human society. Most primitive tribes seem to have thrown some sort of halo round the person of the chief. Either the mysterious supernatural power of the medicine-man was the basis of his dominion among races, who perhaps had not risen to any definite notions of a divinity; or else he was believed to have been an actual incarnation of the deity. Dr Frazer in *The Golden Bough* has brought together a large number of instances of the prevalence of this notion. He shews also the intimate connection between kingship and priesthood. The maxim, *Rex est*

Early sentiment as to sanctity of Kings.

The King an Incar-nation.

[1] *History of the Science of Politics,* 65.

mixta persona cum sacerdote is the expression of what was once an actual fact; and to this is probably due much common sentiment as to the sanctity of royalty.

The King of Divine descent. With the lapse of time, the belief that a king was a god gave way to the notion, that he was of divine descent. As the Incas claimed to be the children of the Sun, so the notion of divine parentage is the first germ of the theory, which meets us upon the threshold of English History. When the institution of royalty was developed by the circumstances of the Conquest among the communities that migrated to Britain, all the petty monarchs of the early English tribes found it well to strengthen their title by a direct claim to descent from Wodin, thus investing the new authority with something of a supernatural sanction.

Influence of Christianity. With the introduction of Christianity a fresh and more enduring source of strength was given to the notion that obedience was a divine command. Suffering for conscience' sake became a duty. The divine institution of the Davidic kingdom, the mysterious character of Melchisedec the priest king, and the very definite commands of S. Peter and S. Paul could not be, and, as a matter of fact, were not overlooked. The sufferings of the early Christians were an example, which later apologists of resistance might explain away, but they could not well be forgotten. Without crystallizing into a definite theory of the nature of government or of the limits of obedience in extreme cases, there subsisted throughout the middle ages a feeling that

kings and all in authority were the vicars of God, *Obedience*
and that resistance to their commands was, in general, *to Kings*
a damnable sin. An aspiring Pope like Hildebrand *as vicars*
might indeed declare later, that all secular govern- *as a reli-*
ments were of diabolic origin. But there remained *gious duty*
in the common consciousness some sense that the *the middle*
king's power was of God, that obedience to him *ages.*
was a religious duty, taught and practised by Christ
himself and the Apostles. It was not a theory, but
it afforded material out of which a theory might be
formed, if at any time circumstances should drive
men to seek for one. As an instance may be taken
the report of the legates George and Theophylact of
their proceedings in England A.D. 787[1]. They appeal,
as a non-juror might have done, to the fourth of
Daniel, to the thirteenth of Romans, to the words of
S. Peter. They quote the prohibition against cursing
the king even in thought, and speak of all who are
accessory to regicide, as on a level with Judas. It
is evident that the legates are using the common
form of enjoining obedience to civil government.
Clearly they put forward no abstract theory of
indefeasible right or of absolute sovereignty or
even of invariable non-resistance. It must be
remembered, that later royalist writers were only
following in the wake of centuries, when they quoted

[1] Stubbs and Haddan, *Councils* III. 453, Cap. XII., *De ordina-*
tione et honore regum. "Omnes generaliter admonuimus, ut consona
voce et corde Dominum rogent, ut Qui eligit eum in regnum, Ipse
ei tribuat regimen disciplinae sanctae Suae ad regendam plebem
Suam.......In necem regis nemo communicare audeat, quia
christus Domini est. Omnis quisquis tali sacrilegio consensat...
aeterno anathematis vinculo interibit, et Judae traditori sociatus."

Scripture to prove the duty of obedience, or called the king the vicar of God, and employed far-fetched Biblical analogies and forced interpretations to support their contention[1]. All this was old enough[2]. What was new, was the attempt to draw from it a consistent logical theory of the nature of government and of the mutual relations of sovereign and subject.

Early English Kingship.

With regard to early English kingship, that it was not strictly hereditary by the law of primogeniture, is well known. But it must be borne in mind, that, although the right of election[3] and deposition rested with the Witan, they could only exercise their right within the limits of the royal family. The case of

[1] The non-juror Leslie is very angry with Burnet for declaring that the theory of Divine Right was the product of the Reformation. "None knows better than his Lordship, that the notion of Kings having their power from God, was long in the world before either the Reformation or Popery. All the ancient Fathers are full of it. And they took it from the Holy Scripture, where it is abundantly testified" (*The Good Old Cause*, § 2). As to the developed doctrine there is no doubt that Burnet was right and Leslie wrong; but Leslie is quite right as to the notions out of which it grew, as is shewn by the passage cited on page 19. That the Fathers would have been astounded could they have seen their phrases about obedience to the Emperor, taken as proof that they held the theory of the non-jurors, is true enough; that the non-jurors had the least notion that their theory was in any way different from the sentiment of antiquity, there is no reason to suppose.

[2] Cf. for the development of these doctrines in the Fathers and Early Middle Ages, Carlyle, *History of Political Theory in the West*. Mr Carlyle shews by many instances, that the attribution of the origin of kingship to the fall is in no way incompatible with the belief that obedience is a religious duty.

[3] Hotman in the *Franco-Gallia* tries to prove a similar rule of election, but election within one family, as the ancient custom of the Franks.

Earl Harold is quite exceptional, and it is at least not proved that his election was legal[1]. Although the power of the Crown was circumscribed within somewhat narrow bounds, yet in various ways the sanctity of the king was asserted; his peace was of a high nature, above that of other men[2]. In the rise of the law of treason under Alfred we see how important the protection of the king's person is becoming, although as yet it is only as part of the general law, differing merely in degree from treason to a lord, that we discern the germs of the later code of high treason[3].

With the Norman Conquest the royal power received a vast accession of strength. But the doctrine of elective kingship gained additional force from the circumstances of William and his sons. *Effect of the Norman Conquest.* The struggles of the reign of Stephen shew, on the one hand, that considerations of hereditary right are not yet regarded as decisive. On the other, the mere fact of the Empress obtaining a large measure of support indicates, that men are beginning to attach importance to succession by primogeniture.

If the theory of sovereignty had been recognised at this time, there could be no doubt that all theoretical limits upon the royal authority must have been done away with; for the king was immeasurably the strongest power in the state; but no such theory was held, and forms of constitutional checks remained in theory, for a later age to use them in practice.

[1] Mr Round is at issue with Mr Freeman on the point. *Geoffrey de Mandeville*, 8, 437, *Norman Conquest*, III. App. C.

[2] See Stubbs, *Constitutional Hist.* I. § 72; Pollock, *Oxford Lectures*, 65; and Pollock and Maitland, *Hist. of Engl. Law*, I. 22.

[3] *H. E. L.* p. 28, and Stubbs, *Select Charters*, p. 62.

1086.

Again, the action of the Conqueror in compelling all landowners to take the oath of fealty to him against everyone[1], including their immediate lords, tended to widen the generality of the duty of obedience to the central authority, and to form a basis for a complete theory of allegiance. Its significance as guarding against the dangers of an infinitely subdivided sovereignty, the worst evil of feudalism, has often been pointed out.

Primogeniture. Succession to Crown assimilated to inheritance of fiefs.

It was perhaps in another way that the Conquest led most directly to the development of principles, that made up an important element in the theory of the Divine Right of Kings. While withstanding the danger of introducing feudal principles of government, the Conqueror introduced, or, at least, crystallized into system all the influences that made for a complete recognition of feudal principles of land-tenure[2]. The king is now not only the national representative, but also supreme landowner; all land is held of him mediately or immediately. This, " the great generalization that governs the whole of Domesday[3]" led not only ultimately to the conception of territorial sovereignty[4], but assimilated the succession of the Crown to the developing law of the inheritance to fiefs. The Norman kings were far more than

[1] Stubbs, *Select Charters*, pp. 81, 2.

[2] Stubbs, *Constitutional History*, I. § 94.

[3] Pollock and Maitland, *History of English Law*, vol. I. p. 46. Cf. also p. 210: " Every acre of English soil and every proprietary right therein have been brought within the compass of a single formula, which may be expressed thus :—*Z tenet terram illam* de... *domino rege.*"

[4] Maine, *Ancient Law*, 106.

national monarchs. They were lords of a great estate. And the rules which were beginning to govern the succession to fiefs, were held to apply to the Crown. The elective character of kingship began to fall into the background, and the influences, leading to a rigid rule of primogeniture in the case of land, tended to the same result in regard to the succession. Hitherto the Crown had been partially elective, and so far as it tended to become hereditary, there are reasons for supposing that it might have descended, as was so often the case in the earlier mediæval monarchies, by being partitioned among all the surviving sons of the deceased monarch[1]. But the rise of the rule of primogeniture, after the kingdom had become the greatest of estates, ensured that succession should be impartible.   It is only because the notions of public law and sovereignty were as yet undeveloped, that this was possible.   Because men cannot think of the king as other than a natural person, or of the rules governing the succession except as a part of the ordinary law of inheritance, they were driven to assimilate the succession to the Crown to the succession to a fief.   The king was the landowner *par excellence*; his lands must descend by the same rules as those of other men[2].

[1] Pollock and Maitland, *History of English Law*, II. 260 sqq.
[2] *Ibid.* I. 497, 8. " The king is conceived to hold his lands by a strictly hereditary right. Between his lands and the kingship it would be hard to distinguish....The descent of the Crown was not so unique a phenomenon then as it is now."   Cf. also I. 209. " The king, it is true, is a highly privileged as well as a very wealthy person ; still his rights are but private rights amplified and inten- sified."

It has been recently shewn, that it was probably the interest of the overlord, the desire to have one person responsible for the discharge of all the feudal incidents, that led to the developement of primogeniture. For not primogeniture, but equal division is the most natural mode of hereditary succession. But though the holder might well desire that his lands should be partitioned among his children, this would not suit the purpose of the Crown, which stepped in and decreed the rule of impartible succession. And it was owing to the fact, that the notion of hereditary kingship only superseded that of election, when this rule was becoming universal in regard to private lands, that the succession to the Crown, when it became hereditary, went by promogeniture and not by partition[1]. There are grounds for supposing that the Conqueror divided his dominions among his sons, on the same principle that actuated so many Frankish monarchs. And Richard Cœur de Lion refused homage to his brother Henry, because brothers were equal[2]. However, primogeniture triumphed and was applied to the Crown, as to other estates.

Causes of primo-geniture.

The 'case of the king' so often cited by Bracton is a proof both of the incomplete acceptance, as yet, of the rule of primogeniture, and of the entire assimilation of the succession to the Crown with that to a fief. On the one hand, John's succession to the throne in defiance of the strict rule of primogeniture, and the exclusion of Arthur his elder

King John.

[1] Pollock and Maitland, *History of English Law*, ii. 260 sqq.
[2] *Ibid.* i. 505.

brother's son, are evidence that the theory of representative primogeniture was not yet accepted.
On the other hand, this case, until the death of
Arthur's sister in 1241 determined it, was held to
leave the question of right undecided, and to
protect seisin in cases of private lands, as between
an uncle and the son of an elder brother, who had
not himself held the land[1].

John's case is also noteworthy as containing in
the reported speeches of Archbishop Hubert[2], the
strongest possible assertion of the right of election,
and (afterwards at the coronation) of the binding
character of the oath. On the other hand, the
territorial character of kingship was coming into
prominence. John is *Rex Angliae,* no longer *Rex
Anglorum*; while the recent assumption of the style
royal affords an indication of a dawning notion of
the mystical and official personality of the king.

John's reign is further important on account
of the submission to the Pope. So long as the
position accepted by John was, with whatever reluc-
tance, recognised at all, and the suzerainty of the
Pope admitted by the payment of tribute, the statement that the king was under no one save God was
the expression of patriotic aspiration rather than of
actual fact. But the final rejection of the Pope's
demands in 1366, and the protest against Papal claims
with which it was accompanied[3], formed the basis of
the later assertion that ' this realm of England is an

[1] Bracton, *De Legibus Angliae,* ff. 267 *b,* 282, 327 *b.*
[2] Matth. Paris, *Chronica Majora,* II. 454, 5.
[3] *Rot. Parl.* II. 290.

Empire' and contained the germ of that appeal to the grace of God against the will of the Pope, which was the *raison d'être* of the theory of Divine Right.

Further it is to be noted, that in this case as in others the Papacy, though willing to loosen the bonds of allegiance in order to compass its own ends, shewed no preference for constitutional government as such. The tyranny of both John and his son leant largely upon Papal support.

Magna Charta needs no mention, save for the well-known fact, that the sixty-first clause approaches more nearly than any other statute of English History to giving legal sanction to the right of resistance, and making government and obedience truly a matter of compact.

Edward I.'s reign dates from election, not coronation. The accession of Edward I. marks a further step in the developement of hereditary kingship and in the removal of the significance and necessity of the coronation ceremony. The story is well known. Edward was absent upon the crusade at the time of his father's death; the barons, dreading the evils of a lengthy interregnum, elected him king four days after. He reigned from the date of his election, and was not crowned for nearly two years. The crown was claimed by hereditary right, and the will of the barons[1]. Thus coronation, as a necessary element in kingship, sank into abeyance, and the notion, that though kings may die, the authority of the Crown remains undisturbed, began to arise. Not yet will men assert that 'the king never dies';

[1] Rymer, *Foedera*, I. 497.

but the germ of the notion is here, and those who in later ages argued that coronation was merely a ceremony, and that the heir to the throne was ' every inch a king' without it were right in claiming, that they were merely following the precedent of Edward's reign[1].

With the accession of Edward II. election itself *Election disappears.* fell into disuse, and he succeeded his father with no interregnum. Thus the pressure of circumstances and the influence of feudal land law brought about the triumph of the notion, that the right of inheritance is the only essential element in making a king. The right to the Crown was no longer that of election or of coronation, but that of the next heir, whom God alone can make. If we have not yet come to the days when hereditary right was regarded as indefeasible, and no breach was admitted, however short, in the continuity of the succession, yet there were by the beginning of the fourteenth century all the elements of the theory. The Crown had become a birthright.

But the reign of Edward II. had a deeper significance. It has been pointed out[2], that the very *Growth of theory of royal prerogative.* developement of a constitutional system led to a counter-attempt to exalt and liberate from control

[1] *Majestas Intemerata*, p. 45.

[2] Stubbs, *Const. Hist.* II. §§ 247, 273. "On the one side every advantage gained by the parliament is regarded as one of a very limited number of privileges ; on the other every concession made by the crown is made out of an unlimited and unimpaired potentiality of sovereignty.......The theory of sovereignty held by Henry III. is far more definite than that of Henry II., and that of Richard II. than that of Edward I."

the royal prerogative. "For every assertion of national right there is a counter assertion of royal autocracy." The growth of Parliament, as the source of legislative activity, emphasized the distinction between the power of the Crown in Parliament and the personal power of the king. Kings now will insist upon their personal privileges, upon their right to issue ordinances, to misinterpret at their pleasure the petitions of Parliament, in transforming them into statutes. Thus the whole constitutional struggle of the fourteenth century raged round the vexed question of the royal prerogative. On the one hand popular rights had been crystallized into a definite system; on the other the kings exalted their personal position, and tended to regard it as a thing apart, above the constitutional machinery. Before Parliament became an essential element in the state, there was no reason for the king to claim extra-legal authority, save in taxation, for with trifling limitations he was the source of law. He was in his own person not only supreme landowner, but the fountain of justice, the executive authority, and the amender, if not the maker of law. But when Parliament gained the right to petition for new laws, and when in 1322 this right was made exclusive[1], it was natural for the king to distinguish between his rights in his own person and his authority in Parliament. The growth of Parliament, then, is

---

[1] '*Revocatio Novarum Ordinationum.*' It is remarkable, that the Act was passed in defence of the king, not of the people. The object is to secure the king's freedom from any lords ordainers of the future. *Statutes of the Realm,* I. 189.

the origin not only of the immediate struggle around royal prerogative and privilege, but also of the distinction between the personal and political capacity of the king, of which a later age was to hear so much.

Nor was the matter a trifling one at the time. Even in the days of Edward II. it became a matter of controversy. The distinction was apparently one of the arguments for the banishment of Gaveston. The ordinances of 1311 accuse him of "encroaching to himself royal power and royal dignity and lording it over the state of the King and the People," terms which the Long Parliament might have applied to Strafford. Later on, however, in the trial of the De Spensers, the doctrine that there is any distinction between the king and the Crown was condemned[1],

Distinction appears between the personal and political capacity of the King.

[1] The following is the passage condemned:—*Statutes of the Realm*, I. 182. "Homage and the Oath of Allegiance is more by reason of the Crown than by reason of the Person of the King, and it bindeth itself more unto the Crown than unto the Person; and this appears in that before the Estate of the Crown hath descended, no allegiance is belonging to the Person; wherefore if the King by chance be not guided by Reason, in right of the Crown, his liege Subjects are bound by the Oath made to the Crown to guide the King and the Estate of the Crown back again by reason, or otherwise the Oath would not be kept. Now were it to be asked, how they ought to guide the King? Whether by Course of Law, or by Violence? By Course of Law a man will not be able to get Redress, for he will have no judges but such as are the King's, in which case, if the Will of the King be not according to Reason he certainly will have only Error maintained and confirmed; Wherefore it behoveth, in order to save the Oath, that when the King will not redress the matter and remove that which is hurtful to the People at large, and prejudicial to the Crown, it is to be determined, that the thing be removed by Violence, for he is bound by his oath to govern the people and his Liege Subjects, and his

and writers of the seventeenth century were able to point to the statute exiling them, as proving the iniquity of the notion, that it was lawful to levy war against the king's person in defence of his Crown.

No theory of sovereignty in England during middle ages. It was the glory of England, that it was subject not to the ' written law,' but to the ancient customary law of the race, although many modern ordinances, such as the assizes of Henry II., had become a part of it. This fact, perhaps, as much as the prevalence of the theory of feudalism, prevented during the middle ages the growth of any theory of sovereignty, save in the Empire. The doctrine would indeed have seemed ludicrous to an English lawyer of the twelfth or thirteenth century. The feudal idea, despite all the efforts of the central power, was still strong, and *Its formation prevented by feudalism.* there is perhaps no more essential element in feudal theory, than the belief in the infinite divisibility of sovereign power. Doubtless, by the fiction of delegacy, it is possible to stretch even the feudal system on the Procrustean bed of Austinian sovereignty. Yet at least it will be admitted, that no country, in which feudalism was at all a force, whether as forming theory or influencing practice, could possibly have suggested to the acutest mind the conception of an omnipotent sovereign with neither rights nor

Liege Subjects are bound to govern in aid of him and in his default." It will be seen that these ideas were exactly those of the Long Parliament. The author of *Majestas Intemerata* makes much use of the fact that the distinction between the political and personal capacity of the king is a part of "the Spensers' treason." Coke, *Calvin's Case* (7 *Reports*, 11 a) calls it a "damnable and damned opinion."

duties. The relations of the Duke of Normandy, or later of Gascony to the King of France, the Scottish overlordship, the question of the franchises (which it required all the dexterity of the Crown lawyer to get recognised as merely delegations of royal power[1]) must have been fatal to any attempt towards the formation of a theory of sovereignty. Indeed the nature of the feudal tie operated to suggest the notion that government is based upon contract.

Nor again was such a theory needed. So long *The doc-* as custom is regarded as the main source of law and *trine un-necessary.* the province of legislation is restricted, the abstract truth of Austin's doctrine may remain, but its practical applicability is gone. For the idea of sovereignty to arise, there must be a developed state and a considerable measure of legislative activity. Both these conditions were unfulfilled at the time of Bracton. The only sources, from which such a theory might have been drawn, were the civil and the canon law. But, if any writer with a turn for the Roman jurisprudence should have directed his attention thereto, facts would have been too strong for him. The claims of the Pope, recognised and unrecognised, the existence of the canon law, the wide sphere of spiritual jurisdiction, and benefit of clergy would have been a sufficient bar to the formation of any such doctrine[2]. The theory of sovereignty is only of value, when applied to states which are organised; at this time

---

[1] See Maitland, *Introduction to Select Pleas in Manorial Courts*; also *History of English Law*, I. 559.

[2] *Ibid.* I. 160, 1.

the organization of national states was only in the making[1].

Lawyers ascribe almost sovereign rights to the King, yet do not treat him as sovereign.

If, then, it be borne in mind that no theory of sovereignty was or could be held by Bracton, it will not be surprising to find him ascribing to the king rights, which apparently amount to little less than complete sovereignty, while in set terms the king is declared to be under the law. Many passages there are which to modern ears sound inconsistent, such as the statement, that the king is under no one but God, and yet is not above the law. Where then is the source of law? Whence is its sanction derived, if neither the King nor any other person or body of persons are above it? This inconsistency is apparent only to us, because we are unfamiliar with the notion that custom can be truly sovereign. The blunder which a modern reader might be tempted to make on first opening Bracton is that of either charging the author with contradicting himself or of understanding the law, under which the king is said to be, in some fanciful sense as equivalent to no more than moral or natural law. This mistake was actu-

Writers in seventeenth century misunderstood Bracton.

ally committed by the uncritical pamphleteers of the seventeenth century. Circumstances had generated in them the idea that in every state there must be some sovereign. Observing that Bracton and Britton ascribed to the king rights which seemed of the essence of sovereignty, they jumped to the conclusion that in the thirteenth century the power of the Crown was believed to be free from all legal limitations. Unless they were setting forth the moral and religious

[1] See Maine, *Early History of Institutions*, Lectures XII, XIII.

duties of the king, they ignored all that was said
about his being subject to the law ; and this without
conscious dishonesty. They were wedded to the idea
of sovereignty, and seeing that in Bracton's view the
sovereignty, if not vested in the king, was nowhere
to be found, they adopted what seemed to them the
only possible alternative, and inferred that the power
of the Crown in the thirteenth century was legally
unlimited. Once the fact is grasped, that the royalist
writers of the seventeenth century were almost as
deeply imbued with the idea of sovereignty as was
Austin, the course which they took is seen to be
natural. It has been said that " had it [the theory
of sovereignty] been accepted in the thirteenth
century, the English kingship must have become a
tyranny, for nowhere else than in the person of the
king could the requisite sovereignty have been
found[1]." If this be so, it follows that those, who had
no suspicion that the theory was not accepted in the
thirteenth century, must have imagined that English
kingship at that time was an absolute monarchy.

Hence it is not surprising, that royalist writers of *They
thought
that
Bracton
regarded
the King
as
absolute.*
the seventeenth century quote Bracton only less
frequently than the Bible, and, although they must
have read his distinct assertion to the contrary, regard
him with evident *bona fides* as irrefragable testimony
to the truth of their doctrine, that England in the
Middle Ages was an absolute monarchy, tempered
only by (always iniquitous) revolutions[2].

[1] Pollock and Maitland, *History of English Law*, i. 160.

[2] *Majestas Intemerata*, a pamphlet of 50 pages, is crowded with
appeals to the authority of Bracton, Britton, &c. Cf. also *Jenkins*

They had plausible grounds for their view in many phrases of Bracton and Britton.

They found it declared repeatedly that the king is God's vicar[1]; that all persons in the realm are under him; that he is under none but God; that he has no peer: that if he break the law, it is enough that he await the vengeance of God, for none of his subjects may punish him[2]; that no judgment to make void an act or charter of the king is valid[3]; that our Lord the King has ordinary jurisdiction over all in the land; that all (save spiritual) rights are in his hand[4]; that he was created king to the end that he should do justice to all; that the Lord should sit in him[5]; that a jury may be fined for deciding against the king[6]; that none may impose on him without his consent the necessity to amend an injury of his own doing, for necessity may not be imposed on him[7]. They found that Britton regards the whole common law as an emanation from the royal authority[8], that he declares his regality to be inalienable[9], and the king to be the sole interpreter of his will[10].

Redivivus. Cowell quotes Bracton's authority for his assertion that "the king is above the law by his absolute power" (Prothero, *Statutes and Constitutional Documents*, 409, and note).

[1] Bracton, f. 1 *b*.   [2] *Ibid.* ff. 5 *b*, 6, 369.

[3] *Ibid.* f. 34.   [4] *Ibid.* ff. 55 *b*, 412.

[5] *Ibid.* f. 107.   [6] *Ibid.* f. 290 *b*.

[7] *Ibid.* ff. 368 *b* and 389 *b*.

[8] Britton, I. 1.

[9] *Ibid.* I. 221. "Rois aussi ne porrount rien aliener les dreitz de lour coroune ne de lour reauté, qe ne soit repellable par lour successours." This is on the same lines as the arguments of seventeenth century writers, to prove that all the rights of Parliament and people are but concessions, which may at any moment be recalled.

[10] Britton, I. 414.

It is not wonderful that writers of an uncritical *The pas-*
age, imbued with the idea that there must be in *sages in a*
the State some power above the law, should have *contrary*
supposed that the lawyers of the thirteenth century *sense*
explained
regarded the king in that light. It was easy to *away.*
ignore what was said about the king being subject
to law[1], to treat it as a fine phrase, or to suppose that
nothing more was intended than their own distinction between a king, who rules according to the law
of nature, *i.e.* morality, and the tyrant who governs
by caprice.   The seventeenth century royalists were
willing enough to admit the desirability of the
sovereign governing by fixed rules ; only they
denied that he was legally incapable of altering
them.   They no more desired a king to govern
without law, than a modern writer, asserting the
omnipotence of Parliament and its power to abrogate all existing laws, would desire that each suc-
cessive Parliament should repeal all the acts of its
predecessors.   They too wished the king, in obedience to Divine Law, to govern according to the
law of the land ; in this sense they understood

----

[1] Bracton, ff. 5 *b*, 34. The lengthy passage, in which a king
who rules without law is treated as the vicar not of God, but of the
devil, would serve to strengthen the view of the royalists, that
Bracton regarded moral law alone as superior to the Crown. They
must have explained these passages as suggested ; for it was
impossible for any writer, however dishonest, to ignore the strong
phrases about the supremacy of the law used in the very passages,
which they quote as asserting the power of the Crown. Bracton
was a book constantly in the hands of their opponents, and, without
some such justification in their minds, they could not have faced
them. See next note.

Bracton's assertion, that the king was under God and the law [1].

'Only God can make an heir.'   Another notion to be found in Bracton must have contributed much towards generating the belief in the sacredness of primogeniture. The view of the lawyers of the thirteenth century, that *only God can make an heir* [2], although expressed with reference to private inheritance, must have tended greatly to strengthen the sentiment in favour of strict hereditary succession. It led men to regard this mode of the devolution of the Crown, as in some mysterious way superior to the merely human method of election. The birth of an heir is the judgment of God, and has the same sanctity attached to it, as the ordeal or the lot. Men, if they elect, may well make a bad choice; God, though we may not fathom His reasons, will not make an heir without good grounds.

Summary.   To sum up, it appears that Kingship has ever been regarded as in some especial way protected by a Divine authority; that the influence of Christianity has in all ages been held to support this view; that

---

[1] The strongest evidence that this was the common view is the remarkable passage in which Filmer boldly grapples with the most awkward of all Bracton's statements. He declares that the words asserting that the king has a superior in his court of Earls and Barons are to be explained of the king's own consent to this check, which has thus no real authority, for the king's consent may be withdrawn. After boldly sweeping aside this difficulty, he naturally enough declares, that, in saying the king was under the law, Bracton merely meant that he ought to govern by means of it; he is thus under the directive, but not the coactive power of the laws. (*Freeholders' Grand Inquest*, p. 12.) This method of escaping the dilemma is precisely that attributed above to the royalist writers.

[2] Bracton, f. 62 *b*.

English Kingship from being elective in a single family had become purely hereditary by the fourteenth century; that coronation had ceased to be regarded as necessary to the making of a king; and that in the systematic presentment of English law in the thirteenth century there were ample materials for men in a later age, devoid of the historical sense and imbued with the theory of sovereignty, to suppose that the English Kingship towards the close of the Middle Ages was strictly hereditary and unconditioned by constitutional restraints.

CHAPTER III

THE HOLY ROMAN EMPIRE AND THE PAPACY

The Holy Roman Empire embodies mediæval ideal of a state.

THE mediæval notion of an ideal state is embodied in the theory of the Holy Roman Empire. The failure of events to give practical effect to the theory generated controversies, out of which was developed the root idea of the later doctrine of the Divine Right of Kings. The dream was a noble one, of a perfect state with two elected heads, one temporal and one spiritual, working in harmony for the maintenance of peace and for the ordered conduct of life among Christians, in a polity that should combine all that was of lasting value in the system of the Roman Empire with all that was essential to the realization of the City of God. But for the most part it remained but a dream, save for a few fitful intervals of brilliancy under Charles the Great or Otto III. or even Henry III. Yet the controversies of the seventeenth century took the shape they did owing to the earlier struggles between Popes and Emperors. If there had been no Holy Roman Empire, or if there had been no failure to realize the ideal embodied in it, there would have

The theory unworkable.

been no theory of the Divine Right of Kings[1].
The whole standpoint of political thought during *Contro-*
the period of the Reformation is explicable only *versies about*
by being referred to its counterpart in the ideas *Imperial claims*
and the methods of the men, who wrote on *form ex-*
behalf of the Papal or Imperial pretensions to *planation of theory*
sovereignty. One, who has not entered into the *of Divine Right.*
feelings of the earlier age, can scarcely fail to
be hard put to it to comprehend those of the
later. A study of the controversies that raged
around the claims of Pope and Emperor, will reveal
the genesis of most of the notions embodied in
later theories; and will bring us into contact with
the mental atmosphere, in which alone such theories
could take shape.

The Holy Roman Empire, however shadowy *Connec-*
its power, was, so long as men made it an aim *tion of theology*
to work for, a testimony to the most important *and*
characteristic of political thought till the close of *politics.*
the seventeenth century—the belief in the intimate
connection of politics and religion. The ideal of the
Empire, with Christ as its King and His two vice-
gerents upon earth, was that of a theocracy. This
is the explanation of the otherwise strange fact, that
men should ever have believed in so unworkable
a theory, as that of two equal heads of the State.
Christ is the real head of the Empire, and Pope and
Emperor are both conceived rather as executors
armed from above with administrative powers than

[1] " The claim to Divine Right......was first put forward by
Imperialist and Royalist opponents of the Papacy." (Gardiner,
History of England, viii. 182.)

as themselves ultimate authorities[1]. There is no
difficulty in having two superior officials independent of one another, if they are both regarded as
essentially subordinate to a single supreme governor.
It was the vividness with which men realized the
position of Christ as Lord of the Christian commonwealth, that could alone render possible, as an ideal,
a state in which temporal and ecclesiastical jurisdiction existed side by side, and each claimed
' coactive ' power.

That the ideal State is the kingdom of God
upon earth, and that no other can be an object of
veneration to a Christian, is the notion that lies
at the root of the Holy Roman Empire.   It is only
as the immediate character of Christ's Kingship is
lost sight of, and the two subordinate authorities
begin to claim, each for itself, perfect independence
and supremacy, that there is revealed the insoluble
character of the problem involved in the recognised
positions of the Pope and the Emperor.   As this
process continues, first the Pope, as most plainly
the depositary of Divine Authority, afterwards the
Emperor, as called to his office by God's election and
appointment, claims to be the true and supreme head
of the Christian commonwealth, by Divine Right
Lord of the world.   But the notion of an earthly
polity has for neither party disengaged itself as yet

[1] " Opposition between two servants of the same king is incon-
ceivable, each being bound to aid and foster the other : the
cooperation of both being needed in all that concerns the welfare
of Christendom at large."   (Bryce, *Holy Roman Empire*, p. 102 ;
and the whole of Chap. VII.)

from that of the heavenly kingdom. Both Emperor
and Pope are forced to claim Divine Right for their
pretensions, for each believes himself to be head
of something more than a temporal state founded
from motives of human convenience. They are not
merely the directors of an artificial contrivance for
satisfying ephemeral needs; they conceive themselves the chosen captains of the divine organization
revealed by Christ, as part of the eternal order of
the universe.

And thus, whatever claims of supremacy are
made for either Pope or Emperor, it remains that
the theory upon which they are based is essentially
religious. Neither side dreams for a moment of
asserting, that the sphere of theology can be separated
from that of politics, or that the source of political
theory is to be found save in revelation. Neither
side imagines that the views of its opponents can be
discredited, unless their opinions as to religious duty
and the drift of Christ's teaching can be shewn to be
false. Those who deny the political supremacy of
the Pope are heretics, says Boniface VIII. Those
who affirm it are heretics, says Marsiglio of Padua.
Theology can in some way teach men the true
theory of government, the relations between various
powers in the State, and the mutual duties of
sovereign and subjects. No one doubts this, and it
remains, with whatever admixture of philosophical
and historical argument, the fundamental basis of
political controversy, not only throughout the Middle
Ages, but until the theory of Divine Right has
passed away, and men have abandoned the attempt

to defend or controvert a doctrine, which has disappeared.

Position of Emperor bars the way to theories of sovereignty in national States.

Further, the position of the Emperor as in theory, lord of the world, must have had an influence, however slight, in retarding the development of any clear notions of sovereignty in the national states. In England, with its belief in the Imperial position of English kings[1], this influence may have been small or virtually non-existent. Yet the fact that an ignorant writer in the fourteenth century can declare that a statute which he dislikes is invalid, because it has received no confirmation from the Emperor[2], is evidence not indeed of the truth of his statement, but of the existence in men's minds of some lingering belief, a relic from earlier times, in the Imperial claims to universal sovereignty. In regard to France the writings of William of Ockham are evidence of a belief equally untrue to actual fact, that the Emperor in the fourteenth century was still possessed of inalienable rights of sovereignty over the French kings[3].

[1] Cf. Freeman, *Norman Conquest*, I. 132, 3, and Appendix B, 552—556.

[2] *Mirror of Justices*, Lib. v. c. 5, p. 195 : cf. also the passage : "Jurediccion est poer a dire droit. Cele poer dona deux a Moysen, e cel poer unt ceaux qi tenent oreson lu en terre, si com lapostoill e lempereur *e de souz euz tient ore le Roi cele poer en son royaume.*" (L. IV. c. 3, p. 123.)

[3] "Licet Imperator possit multas libertates concedere regi Franciae et aliis; tamen nullo modo potest regnum Franciae vel aliud totaliter ab Imperio separare, ut nullo modo subsit Imperio. Quia hoc esset destruere Imperium, quod non potest Imperator." (*Dialogus*, Pars III. Tr. II. Lib. II. c. 7; Goldast, II. 908.) In the ninth chapter Ockham declares all kings to be subject to

Moreover, in the notion that the Holy Roman *Possibility* Empire was but the continuation of the Empire of *of such a* *theory for* the Caesars, the Flavii, and of Justinian, there was *Emperor.* the material for a theory of sovereignty, which the nations did not as yet possess. But, if the action of any power should operate to lower the prestige of the Emperor and to place kings upon a level with him, so that an English, or French king can speak of himself as Emperor[1], it would be only natural for the pretensions asserted by the civilians on behalf of the Emperor to pass over to them, and to be regarded as of the essence of all kingship that is real, *i.e.* Imperial[2]. The mere use in later times of the phrase Imperial rights as equivalent to sovereignty is evidence of the source, from which the theory was derived[3].

the Emperor, even though he has not commanded it, and they are unaware of the fact.

[1] Richard II. in legitimating the Beauforts speaks of himself as "Entier Emperour de son Roialme." (*Rot. Parl.* III. 343.) Raoul of Praelles declares, "Un chacun Roy est chief de son royaume, et Empereur de son Empire." (Goldast, I. 51.)

[2] Bishop Jewel asserts that what was the Emperor's right "is now a common right to all princes, for so much as kings are now possessed in the several parts of the whole Empire." *Apology.* Works, III. 98.

[3] The Statute of Appeals in the well-known words of its preamble "this realm of England is an Empire" is an instance of this. Here it is plain that rights of empire are equivalent to rights of sovereignty.

Phrases of this sort can only be explained by the fact that there was a belief, that true sovereignty, *i.e.* independence and unquestioned authority, had been derived from an appropriation by each kingdom of rights originally confined to the Empire.

Papacy reduced Emperors to an equality with other Kings.

This work was performed by that power in the Empire, which overshadowed and eventually destroyed for all practical purposes that of its temporal head. It may indeed be doubted, whether the claims of the Emperor as lord of the world, to be universal sovereign and international arbiter[1], could ever have been brought into effect, as the new peoples awoke to the consciousness of national life. As a fact, however, it is certain that this was prevented by the action of the Papacy[2]. In order to establish their own claims to supremacy, the Popes were driven to minimize the prerogatives of the Emperor, and to recognise in him less instead of more authority, than they did in the case of other kings. Thus all monarchies were free to appropriate such rags and trappings of his ancient majesty, as still belonged to the 'ever august increaser of the Empire' in the shape of theories of power that was never exercised and claims of sovereignty that was never effective. In the contest of the Popes with the Emperors was evolved a theory that was destined to play an important part in future anti-papal conflicts, and to perform during the period of the Reformation, the work that was too hard for it, when Pope John XXII. crushed Lewis of Bavaria.

Origin of theory of Divine Right of Kings.

This theory was *the divine right of secular governments to be free from Papal control.* It took shape

[1] See Bryce, *Holy Roman Empire*, Chap. xv. *The Empire as an International Power.*

[2] Wyclif distinctly declares the division of the Empire to be due to the claim of the clergy to secular power. *De Officio Regis,* 252.

in the fourteenth century as the Divine Right of the Emperors. With various additions, of less importance than is commonly supposed, it was to re-form itself in the sixteenth and seventeenth centuries as the Divine Right of Kings.

It is in the gradual rise of Papal claims to *Theory of Papal su-* universal supremacy, that are first put forth those *premacy.* notions which form the basis of all theories of Divine Right; the conception of sovereignty, of the absolute freedom from positive laws of some power in an organized human society; the claim that this sovereignty is vested in a single person by God, and that resistance to the sovereign is the worst of sins. With two powers within the State in the relative positions of Pope and Emperor, it was inevitable that sooner or later there should arise between them a struggle for supremacy. The condition of coordinate *Need of* authority in two diverse but ill-defined spheres *unity in the state a* could not be one of lasting duration. Sooner or *source of* later the desire of power, coupled with a sense *conflict between* of the need of unity in the society, must bring *Popes and Emperors.* either temporal or spiritual head to claim for itself absolute supremacy. There could not fail to be awakened the sense, that the unity of the Christian commonwealth, whether as an earthly state or as a reflection of the Divine order, could be secured only by the recognition of the ultimate authority as vested in one or other of the two powers. Nor was it doubtful which of them had, as a fact, the best claim to superiority. At the best of times, the Emperor was hard put to it to maintain his position, even as king of Germany, against the disintegrating

Emperor weak, Pope strong and possessed of universal authority. tendencies of feudalism; while his authority over other nations as lord of the world, was, save perhaps under Charles the Great, of the most shadowy kind. The Pope on the other hand could allege that with some limitations his jurisdiction was admitted by all western nations; and was effectively exercised. In every nation there was a large class of men subject to his tribunals, and exempt from the ordinary law, while in a number of matters only constructively ecclesiastical, such as testamentary and matrimonial cases, the Canon law regulated the lives of the laity, and drove numbers of them to the *curia* to buy justice. It is not surprising that there was developed against the Imperial claims a complete theory of Papal sovereignty. Later ages might dispute as to whether this sovereignty was direct or indirect, immediate or constructive. But, from the days of Hildebrand to those of Boniface VIII. and John XXII., the theory goes on developing and it is of course a theory of sovereignty by Divine Right. The doctrine of the '*plenitudo potestatis*' is an assertion of the Pope's claim to sovereign power, as a direct grant from God to S. Peter and his successors[1].

---

[1] The views of S. Thomas Aquinas on the subject are comparatively moderate. Yet he declares all kings to be subject to the Pope, and alleges the great authority of the Druids in secular politics as a proof of the natural superiority of sacerdotal power to royal. (*De Regimine Principum*, I. 14.) The author, Ptolemy of Lucca, of the latter part of the treatise goes farther; he proclaims with emphasis the doctrine of the 'plenitudo potestatis' as one of absolute monarchy, vested in the Pope, and quotes the stock instances of Papal jurisdiction over the Empire. S. Thomas, it is noticeable, carefully avoids all debateable ground in his

The canonist could allege the donation of Constantine *Arguments* as evidence of temporal dominion, and with good *for Papal* *claims.* show of justice point to the ' translation of the Empire' from east to west, as proof that from the time of Charles the Great, the Emperor's authority was derived from the Pope.   In support of the Pope's claim to judge of the fitness of the Electors' choice, he could urge the fact that no Emperor was more than Emperor-elect, until he had received coronation at the hands of the Pope.   He could find in Scripture many passages asserting the superior dignity of priestly power to royal ; and could explain away, as he pleased, any which bear at first sight an opposite sense.   The image was ready to hand of the greater and the lesser lights signifying (it was plain) the spiritual and the temporal power ; the two swords which Christ declared to be " enough, not too much " in the hands of His disciples, would form an apt illustration of the Papal authority in temporal as well as spiritual matters.   And so it is proclaimed that the Pope cannot be bound by the Emperor[1], that Imperial laws are void, if they conflict with the Canon law[2], although the Church may

commentary on Romans xiii.; but the position there taken up appears to differ widely from that afterwards assumed by Boniface VIII. (For a fuller account of the political theory of S. Thomas see Poole, *Illustrations of the History of Mediæval Thought*, Chap. VIII. *The Hierarchical Doctrine of the State.*)

[1] " A saeculari Potestate Pontifex prorsus nec solvi nec ligari valet." (*Decret.* Dist. XCVI. c. 7.)

[2] *Decret.* Dist. X. c. 4.   The usual method of argument is that of the next chapter, "Suscipitisne libertatem verbi? Libenter accipitis quod lex Christi sacerdotali vos subjicit

employ the laws of the Emperor to assist her[1], that
the Emperor as the son, not the sovereign, of the
Church is subject to the Pope[2], for did not Constantine give the Crown and all kingly dignity to
Pope Sylvester[3]? Further, the translation of the
Empire is a final proof of the Pope's supremacy
over the Emperor whom he had set up of his
own mere and proper motion[4]. Against the Latin
Emperor of Constantinople urging the command of
S. Peter to obey the secular prince, Innocent III.
can answer, that it applies only to those who hold
their temporalities from him, or else that obedience
is enjoined only for the Lord's sake and may therefore presumably be neglected, if the Lord speaking
through His vicar should order otherwise, or, thirdly,
that the command to obey him is not without
qualification. He can point to the commission of
Jeremiah, "I have set thee over the nations and
over the kingdoms to root out and to pull down, and
to destroy," and, after drawing edifying conclusions
from the lights in the firmament, finally crush his
Imperial disputant with the commission to S. Peter[5].

potestati atque istis tribunalibus subdit? Dedit nam et nobis
potestatem, dedit et principatum multo perfectiorem princi-
patibus vestris. Aut numquid justum vobis videtur, si cedat
spiritus carni, si terrenis caelestia superentur, si divinis prae-
ferantur humana?"

[1] *Decret.* Dist. x. c. 7.

[2] *Ibid.* Dist. xcvi. c. 11, "Si Imperator Catholicus est, filius
non praesul ecclesiae."

[3] *Ibid.* c. 13.

[4] *Decret. Greg.* Lib. i. Tit. vi. c. 34.

[5] *Ibid.* Tit. xxxiii. c. 6. There is a delightful explanation of
obedience being ordered not to 'the king,' but merely 'the king *as*

It is no new doctrine, that the theory of Papal *A theory* supremacy, with the power of releasing subjects *of sove-reignty by* from their allegiance and deposing kings, involves a *Divine* claim to universal monarchy[1]. It is clear, that the *Right.* doctrine of the *plenitudo potestatis* embodies the most important elements of the theory of sovereignty, the notion, that is, that unity in a state is only to be obtained by the unquestioned supremacy of some one authority, whose acts are subject to no legal criticism. Further, it asserts the Divine institution of monarchy, as a form of government. This was the position claimed by the Papacy; men were driven thus to formulate its pretensions by the sense of the need of unity in the commonwealth. They do so by asserting the unity of the Church and of the universe, the claims of the Pope to derive his power immediately from God alone, and to be subject to none other. This is expressed most clearly in the *The Bull* Bull *Unam Sanctam.* There Boniface VIII. after *Unam Sanctam.*

supreme,' " Nec pure sit subscriptum regi praecellenti, sed interpositum forsitan non sine causâ, tanquam."

[1] An instance of the habit of alleging the Papal sovereignty in proof of the superiority of monarchy to other forms of government is the following passage of Barclay:—"Deus enim in suo peculiari populo hunc gubernandi modum expressit, unum illis ducem judicemque praeficiens. Ejusdem sic et Christus typum nobis edidit, sacratissimam illam monarchiam in persona Petri instituens......Neue in tam augusto perfectóque imperio imperfectam regiminis formam post se sineret inolescere; unum omnium hierarcham esse voluit, quem tota ubique Ecclesia principem agnoscat pastorem. Quae res satis declarat, quanto caeteris gubernandi speciebus gratior sit unius principatus, ad quem omnes fere nationes, quantumuis barbarae et feroces, occulta quadam naturae vi, et primorum parentum exemplis incitantur." (*De Regno*, 82.)

asserting emphatically the unity of the Church and of all government and speaking of the unrent coat of Christ, declares that a body politic with two heads is a monstrosity. He employs the illustration of the two swords, declaring that the material sword is to be used for, not by the Church; and goes on to proclaim that the temporal power must be subject to the spiritual, that derelictions on the part of the temporal power may be judged by the spiritual, but that the supreme spiritual power is accountable to God alone. He quotes the commission to Jeremiah as proof that he is invested immediately by God with sovereign authority; and closes by applying to himself the command, "Whoso resisteth the power, resisteth the ordinance of God[1]."

Same method as that of seventeenth century.

Now, here, it is to be noted, are the methods and arguments, which subsist until the close of the seventeenth century. The Pope proclaims for himself a theory of complete sovereignty; he is king, the one true king, accountable to God alone; he asserts that unity is the soul of government, and that every government must have some supreme head as the centre of its unity; that the Christian commonwealth is a monarchy with this supreme authority vested in himself; he denies that there can be two ultimate authorities in the commonwealth, one temporal, one ecclesiastical; one must be subject to the other. He claims that his power comes from God alone, and is derived from no earthly intermediary. He declares that, on no pretence whatsoever, is resistance allowable to this

[1] *Extrav. Commun.* Lib. I. Tit. VIII. c. 7.

divinely ordained sovereign ; while, in order to prove his doctrine of non-resistance to Papal commands, he employs the very text, which a later age makes the bulwark of its defence against the Pope in the claim that resistance to the king as God's vicar is worthy of damnation.

Here then is a theory of government by Divine Right, the exact converse of the theory of the Divine Right of Kings.   It will be strange if the latter doctrine is not found to have its *raison d'être* as a contradiction and a counter-theory to that of Papal supremacy.

Once more, it is to be remarked that the theory described above is essentially one of obedience, and of obedience from motives based upon religion.   It is needful to bear this fact in mind.   In the pursuit of their own aims the Popes were frequently driven to dissolve the bonds of allegiance in communities. Their supporters will speak slightingly of the duties of subjects to their sovereign.   In their zeal for Papal authority, they will be found developing that theory of an original compact, which lies at the root of all theories of popular rights in the seventeenth century. Yet this was but an accident of the Papal position. Of its essence was the claim to the implicit obedience of all men, based upon even stronger sanctions of eternal punishment, than was the Divine Right of Kings. *A theory of obedience, not of liberty.*

Hildebrand indeed may argue that all secular government is of diabolic origin[1].   John of Salisbury may quaintly decide the question as to whether it be lawful to flatter a tyrant, by the suggestion that it is lawful to flatter a man whom it is lawful to kill[2].

[1] Migne, *Patrologia*, 148, 595.   [2] *Policraticus*, III. 15.

With evident leaning to the more lenient view, S. Thomas Aquinas may debate the point as to whether a nation acting in common may restrain the excesses of a tyrant, and declare in an *obiter dictum* that regal as distinct from political power is a consequence of the Fall[1]. Lastly, John XXII., who in the Bull *Si fratrum* takes up a position of complete sovereignty and claims that, the Imperial authority being merely a delegation from the Pope, it reverts to him during an interregnum[2], may seem to ascribe to the Emperor the same merely official position as delegate of another earthly power, as was attributed to kings by Whig theorists. Yet all this is not because these men believe government and obedience to be things of small importance with 'the trail of the serpent over them all.' It is because government is in their eyes a sacred thing, and obedience an integral part of the Divine Law, that they cannot conceive of secular government, as possessing any beyond subordinate authority. All power is of God; therefore the temporal power is only secondary, and must be subject to the spiritual. Obedience to governors is a Divine injunction; therefore in the last resort all men must obey the Pope, the depositary of Divine authority as against King or Emperor, whose position is either, as some say, of merely human origin, or, as in another view, a grant from God through the mediation of the Pope. Men must obey a king, although obedience

---

[1] *De Regimine Principum*, i. 6.   He is quite clear that private individuals are forbidden to resist the sovereign.

[2] *Extrav. Joh.* Tit. v. c. 1.

involves disloyalty to an immediate lord, the king's vassal; but the Emperor is God's vassal, therefore he may be deposed at the bidding of the Pope, whose word is the voice of God. So far indeed were the Popes from claiming on behalf of subjects any general rights against their sovereign, that, as in the case of John or Henry III. in England or of the Spanish monarchy, they ever shewed themselves stern supporters of royal rights, where they felt sure of the king. The very claim to release subjects from their oath of allegiance implies that the oath is binding without such release on the part of the Pope. In essence the theory of Papal sovereignty is a doctrine of obedience, of the Divine institution of all government, 'simply and strictly so called,' and of perfect sovereignty vested in a single head. It is merely an accident that the theory was accompanied by views of the rights of resistance against governors of the secondary order, whose authority is merely delegated. Absolute monarchy deriving its title from God alone, and obedience as a Divine command, are the root ideas of Papal theories of dominion.

Now against these claims it was needful for the Imperialists to manufacture some weapon. The materials were ready to hand. The Pope had claimed entire sovereignty because the common-wealth was one, and two authorities in it are a monstrosity; the Imperialists must do the same. The Pope had claimed rights of jurisdiction over the Emperor as shewn by the donation of Con-stantine and the translation of the Empire; the

A counter theory needed for the Empire.

Imperialists must argue that the donation of Constantine if a fact, was invalid, and that the translation of the Empire had been misinterpreted. They could maintain that, since the Empire was inalienable, Constantine could not have given lasting authority to the Papacy, and that the Pope, far from creating Charles the Great Emperor, had merely assented to a *fait accompli*; that so far was the Pope from possessing a right to review the choice of the electors of the Holy Roman Empire, that the Emperor possessed the right of reviewing the choice of the conclave, and of examining into the fitness of a proposed occupant of the Papal chair; and that, as a fact, this right had been exercised. Lastly, the Pope had claimed Divine Right for his sovereignty, the Emperor must claim it for his. He must demonstrate that the Empire is held of God immediately and not of the Pope; that, since the Emperor is God's vicar, he cannot be the Pope's vassal; that the passages of Scripture alleged in support of the duty of unlimited obedience to the Pope are, if rightly interpreted, evidences of the unconditioned authority of the Emperor; that the words "my kingdom is not of this world" shew the falsity of the pretended Papal supremacy; that the true heretic is not he who denies, but he who asserts that supremacy; that the command to "Render unto Cæsar the things that are Cæsar's," and the words of Christ to Pilate, "Thou couldest have no power at all against me, unless it were given thee from above," prove at once that the Pope has no universal sovereignty and that secular government

is of Divine appointment. In a word, to the Divine *Divine Right of Emperor opposed to Divine Right of Pope.*
Right of the Pope must be opposed the Divine
Right of the Emperor.

Imperialist writers claim in the first place that
"unity, the soul of government" is entirely lost, if
there be two distinct powers with competing systems *Unity needed in a commonwealth.*
of law and jurisdiction claiming authority at the
same time; for "every kingdom divided against
itself cannot stand." This is the burden of a great
part of the *Defensor Pacis* of Marsiglio[1] of Padua, of
the great *Dialogus* of William of Ockham[2], and of

---

[1] *Defensor Pacis*, I. 17; the whole of the second part is taken
up with a demolition of the Papal pretensions, the great cause of
disturbance and discord in the Empire. Cf. Hobbes's *Leviathan*,
Bk. III., "The Kingdom of Darkness," where the Church of Rome
is regarded in the same way as above all things the enemy of peace
in a State.

[2] *E.g.* the following passage : "Non solum illa societas est
propinqua desolationi et ruinae, quae est contra se divisa; sed
etiam illa quae ex modo regendi est disposita ad divisionem et
divisioni propinqua. Sed si communitas fidelium habeat duas
partes quarum una habeat judicem summum, et alia alium;
communitas illa est disposita ad divisionem et divisioni propinqua." Ockham is feeling his way to the notion of territorial
sovereignty, though it was entirely alien from the early theory of
the Empire. "Potestas non solum est impatiens consortis super
eosdem subjectos; sed etiam impatiens est consortis in eodem loco;
sicut enim judex aliquis nollet, quod subditi sui essent alterius
subditi; ita nollet quod aliquis alius haberet potestatem in loco,
ubi subditi sui morantur. Ergo non solum est periculosa societas
fidelium, si sint plures judices super eosdem populos vel subditos;
sed etiam periculosa est societas fidelium, si in eodem loco etiam
super diversos subditos fideles fuerint plures summi judices constituti, et ita non expedit quod clerici habeant unum summum
judicem ecclesiasticum, scilicet papam; et laici unum summum
judicem scilicet imperatorem; cum clerici et laici in eisdem locis
simul commaneant......Nulla communitas simul viventium vita

the *De Monarchia* of Dante[1]. A large section of the work of William of Ockham could have no more appropriate title than "the anarchy of a mixed monarchy."

Need of unity in the State an argument for monarchy.

This passionate sense of the importance of unity in the State is the ground of much of the sentiment not only against the Pope, but also against those who propose any but a single person as head of the State. It cannot be denied that "unity, the soul of government," is theoretically more completely realised in a monarchy than in any other form of government. At least there is no danger of the sovereign power dividing from within and splitting into two hostile factions, as may be the case with government under a representative system. There could be no fear of a schism in Prince or Pope as there might be in Parliament or Council. If this be taken into account, and the reaction against Papal claims be admitted as a ground of the feeling that unity in the State must be secured at all costs, there will be less inclination to blame the men in the seventeenth

politica est optime ordinata, nisi sit civiliter una. Unde fideles sicut sunt unum corpus in Christo (*ad Rom.* i. 2), ita etiam debent esse corpus seu collegium in vita civili : sed communitas illa quae habet diversos summos judices seu diversa capita sive rectores, non est civiliter una; sicut illi, qui non habent unum regem, non sunt unum regnum." (*Dialogus,* Pars iii. Tr. ii. Lib. iii. c. 19.)

[1] Dante argues that God cannot will what is contrary to nature; apparently he means by this that God cannot approve of any competing jurisdiction within the Empire, or of any earthly authority claiming to restrain the acts of "the lord of the world." (*De Monarchia,* iii.)

or the fourteenth century[1], who argued that not only
must there be one sovereign and not two, but that
the sovereign must be one person, or else unity
cannot be secured. The noteworthy fact is that *Similarity*
the arguments employed are precisely the same *of argu-*
ments in
in the fourteenth as in the seventeenth century. *fourteenth*
and seven-
Ockham's long argument to shew that the Emperor *teenth cen-*
is "over all persons and all causes supreme[2]" is *turies.*
on exactly the same lines as those of later times
on behalf of royal authority against Papal interference; save that Ockham treats the Pope as an
authority within the State, while English writers
regard him as a foreign sovereign.

There appear other elements of the theory of *Other*
elements
sovereignty. It is a maxim with anti-papal contro- *of theory*
versialists that sovereignty is inalienable. Thus *of sove-*
reignty.
Dante[3] and Ockham[4] are found arguing that the

---

[1] Dante indeed carries the argument further and makes it the
basis of his proof of the need of a universal monarchy. *De
Monarchia*, Lib. I.

[2] *Dialogus*, Pars III. Tr. II. Lib. III. cc. 16—23. What could
express more completely the claim to be 'supreme over all causes'
than the following passage? "Concluditur ergo, quod communitas
fidelium non erit optime gubernata civiliter, *etiam quantum ad
vitam politicam*, nisi tota et omnis pars ejus habeat unum judicem
et rectorem supremum, de cujus jurisdictione immediata vel
mediata in omni casu ab eo vel à judicibus inferioribus eo omnis
alius pro quocunque delicto debeat judicari." (*Ibid.* c. 20.) The
words I have italicised shew that secular politics are not the
primary consideration of the author. *Supra*, pp. 39—41.

[3] *De Monarchia*, III. 10.

[4] Ockham's argument is that the Empire, not having been
founded by the Pope, could not afterwards have become subject to
him; any action of the Emperor with that object is invalid, for it
destroys the Empire. *Dialogus*, Pars III. Tr. II. Lib. I. c. 18.

donation of Constantine must be invalid, for the Emperor may not destroy the Empire. Ockham declares that sovereignty can neither be divided, nor diminished, nor alienated[1]; although his notions of obedience are not those of later times. In the seventeenth century all these notions reappear. The king grants privileges to Parliament, but sovereignty is inalienable, therefore they may be revoked. He governs by the law, because he is virtuous, not because he is obliged by it. He cannot by diminishing his sovereignty prejudice the rights of his successors.

Contro-versy about corona-tion and unction, as in later times. Even the special points, around which later controversy rages, are discussed. The importance of coronation is insisted upon by Papalists, as a means of proving that the Emperor holds his office from the Pope, exactly as in the later times it is held to be evidence of a compact between king and people. The author of the latter part of the *De Regimine Principum* regards the ceremony of unction, as evidence of the authority over kings vested in the Pope, the interpreter of the Divine Law; the king is the Lord's anointed; and therefore the Lord by means of His vicar may exercise authority over him[2]. Controversialists assert, on the other side, precisely as those of later times, that coronation has no necessary place in conferring royal or imperial power, which exists equally before it[3]. There are

---

[1] "Romanum imperium non potest minui nec dividi, saltem absque consensu tacito vel expresso communitatis mortalium." (*Dialogus*, Pars III. Tr. II. Lib. I. c. 31.)

[2] *De Regimine Principum*, III. 16.

[3] "Omnem gladii potestatem et administrationem temporalem

arguments, quite in the manner of Hickes, to prove that an infidel may be the lawful recipient of obedience ; special stress is laid on the case of Julian the Apostate, just as French writers on behalf of Henry IV. and English opponents of the Exclusion Bill were to argue, that since the primitive Christians were loyal to Julian, the fact of the heir being a heretic could not bar his claim to the succession.

But this was not enough. It was vain to demonstrate the necessity of unity in a stable commonwealth. *More than this needed.* The Papalist was as ardent an enthusiast for unity as the Imperialist. Indeed, had the dream of Papal sovereignty ever been entirely realised in practice, it would not have been of the lack of unity in the governing authority that men would have complained. It was useless to prove the inconvenience of the Papal claims or the utility of the Imperial power. What could avail considerations of expediency and theories of utility against an opponent, who claimed to exercise power derived by a direct grant from God ? The only effective method *Divine Right must be claimed for the Emperor.* of controverting the Papal pretensions was to elaborate a counter theory that the Emperor's rights came direct from God.

Dante perceived the necessity of this more clearly *Dante perceived this. The De Monarchia.* than some other Imperialist writers. This it is, which gives to the *De Monarchia* a value, as a controversial treatise, far above that of other works in many ways more interesting. Dante meets the

habent ante coronationem quam habent post." (*Dialogus*, Pars III. Tr. I. Lib. I. c. 22.) Cp. also the *Octo Quaestiones* of the same writer.

Papal claim to a universal sovereignty by Divine Right with a direct counter-claim on behalf of the Empire. He shews that a universal monarchy is ordained by God, that the Roman Empire won its position through God's grant, and that the Emperor derives his authority not from the Church, but immediately from God. Since all power is of God, if the Emperor's power be lawful at all, the only question is whether it comes from God directly, or through the medium of the Church. Dante occupies himself with a careful demolition of the Papalist arguments, thus proving indirectly that the Emperor holds his crown immediately from God alone; he finally proves this directly. Even had Dante written no other work than the *De Monarchia*, it would be hard to refrain from admiration of the mind, which struck out with such force and lucidity the line of argument, which was to remain for centuries the one effectual answer to all claims of the right of Papal or clerical interference with the freedom of secular governments. By its intellectual grasp and breadth of treatment, the *De Monarchia*, despite its scholastic character, is raised far above the great majority of controversial treatises on the same subject.

Marsiglio of Padua, Defensor Pacis.

It is easy for us to admire the political philosophy of Marsiglio[1], to hail him as the earliest upholder of

[1] *Defensor Pacis*, I. 12, 13. For a further exposition of Marsiglio's philosophy and its relation to modern thought see Poole, *Illustrations of the History of Mediæval Thought*, chap. 9, *The opposition to the temporal claims of the Papacy*: also *Wycliffe and Movements of Reform*, 28—42. On his teaching of religious toleration, see Creighton, *Persecution and Tolerance*, 94—97.

religious toleration and to recognise his acuteness in striking out the notion of representative democracy. Yet it is impossible not to feel that this very fact, the modern character of the *Defensor Pacis*, which renders its interest so great, must have detracted from its controversial value. As a counterblast to the Papal claims, it is far less effective than Dante's short work, and lacks the ring of enthusiasm which vibrates through every page of the *De Monarchia*.

Moreover, both Marsiglio of Padua and William of Ockham are largely, though not exclusively, concerned with utilitarian arguments, and utilitarian arguments must ever appear beside the point to an opponent arguing on behalf of an authority which he believes to be Divine. Again, both these authors allow to subjects some right of resisting the sovereign[1]. Such an admission made immensely in favour of the Papacy. For if resistance or coercion of the prince be justified at all, clearly it must be so in defence of the Divine Law, and who is to interpret the Divine Law save the vicar of Christ? Further, the notion of Marsiglio that the true legislative authority is the people may have the merit of anticipating modern ideas[2]; but it weakened his position as a controversialist. For it detracted from the dignity and authority of the Emperor, the

Utilitarian arguments of Marsiglio and Ockham.

[1] *Defensor Pacis*, I. c. 18. Ockham argues that monarchy is the best form of government, because it is easier to restrain a single head of the State. "Facilius sit populo emendare unum rectorem (si taliter exorbitaverit), ut sit puniendus vel etiam amovendus, quam plures." (*Dialogus*, Pars III. Tr. II. Lib. I. c. 13.) [2] *Defensor Pacis*, I. 12, 13.

only power whom it was possible to regard as upon
a level with the Pope. If, as Marsiglio claimed, the
Emperor was to have coercive authority over the Pope,
he needed every possible accession of dignity and
prerogative. It was absurd to lay claim to this
position, for one who is not conceived as truly sovereign, but is merely an official executing the will of
the true sovereign, the people. So exalted a privilege
as that of judging the vicar of God, asserted on behalf
of a merely representative Emperor, must have appeared supremely ridiculous in the eyes of men, for
whom Canossa was the *terminus a quo* of Papal
assumption, while their theory of ecclesiastical
dominion exceeded the wildest dreams of Gregory
VII. or Innocent III.

William of Ockham. Both William of Ockham and Marsiglio of Padua
assert, that the Emperor's power is from God. But
both of them regard the constitution of the Empire
and even its existence as of human institution[1]; if
in the future it should transgress the principle of
utility, it may be abolished. For both of them it
arises by human, not Divine ordinance. Yet Marsiglio
regards the Emperor as God's vicar in a far fuller
and truer sense than is the Pope. With the rights
of the Electors still effectively exercised, it was
plainly impossible to assert any such claim of immediate investiture by God, as might be claimed
for hereditary monarchs. Although, however, Mar-

---

[1] *Defensor Pacis*, i. 18. *Dialogus*, Pars iii. Tr. ii. L. i. cc. 8,
29—31. Marsiglio expressly disclaims any inquiry into the Mosaic
polity, which was ordained directly by God; he is concerned only
with principalities set up by human law. (i. 9.)

siglio[1] and William of Ockham are aware that some
Divine authority must be asserted on behalf of the
Imperial power, they are far too much governed by
the notion of utility to make this the kernel of their
work. Ockham indeed, in a passage that sounds to
modern ears like an echo of Hobbes, places the
origination of the Empire in the people[2]. The
account, as may be supposed, is far less historically
accurate, than is that of Dante. The latter is so
deeply wedded to the notion that the Empire is held
immediately from God alone, that he regards the
electors, not as themselves choosing the Emperor,
but as merely announcing God's choice[3].

In asserting his claim to supremacy the Pope
came into collision not merely with the decaying
forces of the Empire, but with the rising nationalities
of Europe, which were growing stronger every year,
as feudalism gave way before the central power.
Perhaps the most dramatic achievement of the
middle ages, if the journey of Henry IV. to Canossa
be excepted, was the repudiation by Philip the Fair
of the claim of Boniface VIII. to a position of complete supremacy over all earthly potentates. In the
Bull *Unam Sanctam*[4] Boniface VIII. had carried
Papal assumption to its highest point; and the
ruin, that in consequence befell him, forms the

*Conflict of
the Papacy
with
France.*

---

[1] *Defensor Pacis*, II. 30. Marsiglio is at pains to expound the
true meaning of Rom. xiii., and to declare in strong terms the sin
of resisting the ordinance of God. (*Ibid.* II. 25.)

[2] *Dialogus*, Pars III. Tr. II. L. I. c. 8.

[3] *De Monarchia*, III. 16.

[4] *Supra*, p. 49.

starting-point of all later French argument against
the political claims of the Papacy.

Theory of Divine Right in France.
From this time forth the freedom of France from
Papal interference is the despairing admiration of
Imperialist authors[1]. It is not then a matter for
surprise, that writers in France begin to develope the
same notions of the Divine Right of secular govern-

Raoul of Praelles, 1370.
ments, as are to be found in the Empire. One author
in the fourteenth century asserts with emphasis,
that the French king holds his kingdom immediately
from God alone[2]. Another argues, that, all priesthood
before Christ being merely typical, kingship is the

John of Paris, 1305.
older and therefore the superior of the two[3]. He
declares, that the Papal authority cannot come immediately from God, for in that case the prince would
be the servant of the Pope, as he is of Christ, and this
would be to contradict the xiiith of Romans, where the
king is spoken of as the vicar of God, not the Pope[4];
he goes on to argue in the usual manner from the
words, "Touch not mine anointed" and other texts[5].

Summary.
Thus it appears that from the beginning of the
middle ages politics were conceived as essentially a
branch of theology; that the Popes were gradually
driven by the exigencies of their position to claim
for themselves a position of perfect sovereignty,

[1] Ockham repeatedly alleges the case of the King of France,
who is admittedly free from Papal interference, as an argument on
behalf of the Emperor.

[2] "Il tient et possede son Royaume de Dieu tant seulemen
sans aucun moyen en tele maniere, que il ne se tient de quelque
homme, ne qu'il ne le tient du Vicaire de Jhesu Christ, ne en tant
come homme, ne en tant com son Vicaire." (Goldast, I. 49.)

[3] *De Potestate Regia et Papalia*, cc. 4, 5.

[4] *Ibid.* c. 11.   [5] *Ibid.* c. 14.

sovereignty by Divine Right, disobedience to which
is a mortal sin; that, as against this doctrine, the
supporters of the Emperor formulated a theory of
sovereignty based upon the ground of the necessity
of unity in the state; that they met the Pope's
pretensions to supremacy as God's vicar by asserting,
all of them in some measure, Dante most clearly
and completely, that the Emperor's authority exists
by Divine Right and comes by grace of God, not of
the Pope; that they applied to him the scriptural
injunctions to obedience, which Boniface VIII.
made bold to wrest into a command of unlimited
obedience to the Papacy; and, lastly, that this or a
similar position was taken up by writers on behalf of
the French king. The necessity of unity as the
foundation of sovereignty, and the Divine Right of
secular governments to be free from Papal interference are the root ideas of Imperialist writers.
The Divine Right of the Emperor is asserted not
for its own sake, but against a similar claim to
Divine Right put forward by the Pope. Both sides
recognise that power is of God, both are aware that
there must be in the state some supreme authority
above the law. But in one view the Divine source
of all authority is held to carry with it the supremacy of the spiritual power. These pretensions
could only be met by the assertion, that secular
government was not merely allowed but was actually
ordained by God, and that the secular prince held
immediately of Him with no intervening authority;
or in the words of John of Jandun, *Potestas im-
perialis est immediate a Deo, non a Papa.*

CHAPTER IV

WYCLIFFE AND KING RICHARD II.

English claims of freedom from Papal control. IN the middle ages thought and learning were international, and it would be strange, if the controversies which were seething on the Continent during the earlier part of the fourteenth century found no counterpart in England. Moreover William of Ockham was an Englishman and an Oxonian. England had claimed for long to be an Empire; freedom from Papal interference was more or less an aspiration of English statesmen from the times of the Conqueror and Henry II. Even at the period of completest subjection to the Papacy, the Barons could meet the attempt to assimilate the English law of inheritance to the rules of the Canon law with the emphatic negative "*nolumus leges Angliae mutari*[1]." From the time of Edward I., who outlawed the clergy rather than submit to the bull *Clericis laicos*, there had been passed a series of statutes in restraint of Papal claims. All this might well induce a writer with an anticlerical bias or a monarch with high ideas of his own dignity, to claim complete 'freedom,'

---

[1] *Statute of Merton*, c. 9.

i.e. sovereignty for the English Crown, and to
claim it as coming by Divine Right. This view
finds expression in the writings of Wycliffe, and is
also, so far as we can gather, the basis of the definite
theory of kingship held by King Richard II.

I.

The *De Officio Regis* was written by Wycliffe *Wycliffe's*
rather with the object of asserting the duty of the *Regis.'* 'De Officio*
sovereign to 'assist' the Church by disendowing the
clergy of their temporalities[1] than with any direct
purpose of exalting regal as against Papal authority.
Yet the writer bases his practical exhortations upon a
doctrine very similar to that proclaimed in the Empire
and France[2]. The king is God's vicar in things *Royal*
temporal, as is the priest in things spiritual. But *power* *superior to*
the dignity of the king is superior to that of the *sacerdotal.*
priest, for the king reflects the godhead of Christ,
the priest only His manhood[3]. Thus the spiritual

[1] *De Officio Regis*, 216. The references are to the pages in the
Wycliffe Society's Edition.

[2] *Ibid.* 73. "Non enim est jus humanum nisi de quanto
fundatum fuerit in lege Dei divina." This is the fundamental
basis on which all anti-papal writers ground their theory of
Divine Right. There is no human right except by God's law.
But there are real human rights. Therefore divine authority must
be asserted for them. Starting from the same major premiss the
Pope drew the conclusion that all human rights centred in him;
and thereby would have ultimately dissolved them. Those who felt
the importance of justifying secular governments, were forced to
argue that they have true rights by Divine law independent of
the Papal grant.

[3] *Ibid.* 12—14. "Ex quibus videtur, quod oportet vicarium
Cristi sub racione qua Christus per vicarium Cristi sub racione
qua deus capitaliter regulari."

power is inferior to the temporal in earthly dignity
and authority, although in true dignity the priest
excels the king. The famous decretal of Innocent
III. is explained away, and a theory extracted from
it of the complete sovereignty of the temporal power[1].
The author admits that of the two jurisdictions, the
secular and the ecclesiastical, one must control the
other. But he argues that the more perfect state
has not always the higher authority; Christ's clean-
sing of the temple is an imperial, His submitting to
death a sacerdotal act; hence royal authority is the
higher[2]. There must be one supreme head in a state,
else there will be confusion; the temporal power
is this head, and it is not enough to have the king
supreme in temporals, he must be supreme in all
causes[3]. Wycliffe is not certain, which of the two

[1] *Supra*, p. 48. *De Officio Regis*, 34—36. The argument is less
sophistical than might appear. For Innocent's letter was merely
about a question of precedence, and might be held to imply no
more, than would a claim to give the toast "Church and State."
Compare Cardinal Vaughan's explanation of his giving the toast
"The Pope and the Queen" at the Mansion House in 1893.

[2] *Ibid.* 137. "Unde Cristus quedam fecit ut Imperator, ut
ementes et vendentes in templo flagellando ejecit. i q. iii *Ex
Multis*, quedam ut sacerdos cum se ipsum in cruce obtulit. Cum
igitur prior potestas habet racionem agentis eciam in sacerdotes,
secunda vero potestas habet racionem pacientis eciam ab eisdem
sacerdotibus, videtur quod ex hoc naturali principio 'agens est pre-
stancius passo,' potestas regalis sit prestancior potestate sacerdotali."

[3] *Ibid.* 138, 9. "Item vel oportet illas potestates ex equo haberi
vel unam subordinari alteri. Si enim neutra subordinaretur
alteri secundum leges humanas vergeret ad confusionem ecclesie."
We note here as elsewhere in Wycliffe that the term ecclesia is
used indifferently of commonwealth or church; there is no
thought of two societies.

powers is truly greater, yet the Pope cannot be above the Emperor in the sight either of God or man; for he is his minister[1]. Besides (according to S. Augustine) Adam was the first king, and Cain the first priest[2]. Priests should not refuse to be called the king's priests[3]. The common arguments and illustrations are employed. The Pope was the liegeman of the Emperor before the donation of Constantine, and he can never have ceased to be so since[4]. Emperors have deposed Popes[5]. To understand Romans iii. or 1 Peter ii. of any but the secular power is sophistry[6].

Wycliffe will not allow that the king is subject to positive law. He should obey his own laws but his obedience is voluntary, not by compulsion. For the king is *solutus legibus*; and when law is spoken of as governing him it is moral or Divine and, not positive law that is intended[7]. *The King above the Law.*

For him as for Ockham the necessity of unity in the state is the main proof of the excellence of monarchy[8].

---

[1] *De Officio Regis*, 143. "Unum audenter assero, quod nec clamor cleri nostri nec scriptura faciunt quod papa iste sit majus cesare, vel quo ad seculum vel quo ad deum. Nam ministrare sacramenta non est opus auctoritatis sed vicarie servitutis, sed conducere et precipere taliter ministrare. Quod autem papa sit sic magnus reputative quo ad mundum hoc habet a cesare."

[2] *Ibid.* 144.   [3] *Ibid.* 197.

[4] *Ibid.* 202.   [5] *Ibid.* 128.   [6] *Ibid.* 67.

[7] *Ibid.* 93 sqq. After defining the law of reason or nature, he goes on: "Lex contracta per civilitatem connotat supra talem veritatem ordinacionem et promulgacionem humanam ad civile dominium regulandum, et sic est rex principalis conditor legis sue."

[8] *Ibid.* 246.

Here is a theory of sovereignty, vested in the king by Divine Right and in no way subject to the Pope. It can hardly be supposed, that so great a scholar as Wycliffe wrote his treatise in ignorance of the works of Ockham. Although its method is not quite the same, and the whole book is inferior in grasp and insight to that of the earlier author, yet the conclusions are the same, and it cannot be assuming too much to suppose, that the Imperialist theory influenced English thought in this way.

It need scarcely be mentioned, that with Wycliffe's theory of dominion founded in grace, a bad king has no real dominion[1]. Yet in Wycliffe's system this would be no bar to a doctrine of unlimited obedience[2]. Throughout the greater portion of his work he appears to uphold a theory of this sort, arguing in favour of passive obedience and quoting with approval the examples of the Saviour and the primitive Christians[3]. Yet in other places he contradicts this, first declaring that it is possible to obey by resisting[4] (by which he might mean no more than passive obedience), but going on to inculcate the duty of rebellion and even tyrannicide as possible modes of obedience[5]. It is impossible to

---

[1] *De Officio Regis*, 17. Tyrants have power but not dominion. "Realiter habent potestatem et dignitatem consequentem secundum quam regunt...Sed illa potestas non est dominium."

[2] For expositions of Wycliffe's theory of Lordship, see Poole, *Illustrations of the History of Mediæval Thought*, Ch. x.; Wycliffe, *Movements of Reform*, Chap. vi.

[3] *De Officio Regis*, 6 sqq.

[4] *Ibid.* 82.   [5] *Ibid.* 201.

acquit him of inconsistency in this respect. Indeed, this same inconsistency is found in Marsiglio and Ockham. Both of them emphatically proclaim the authority of the Scriptural prohibitions of resistance, yet in certain cases they seem to approve it.

It is only natural that this should be the case. *Causes of this.* The writers of the fourteenth century were engaged in elaborating an anti-papal theory. In a doctrine, which is only in the making, it is vain to look for the same harmony and consistency in all its parts, as is to be found, for instance, in the developed theory of the Divine Right of Kings. Yet there is no doubt, that this admission of a right of resistance, however qualified, gives away the whole case against the Papacy. Once resistance under any circumstances be admitted, heresy is seen to be a plain case for it, and the Pope on any view is the judge of that. Wycliffe condemns all who resist a tyrant, save on behalf of God's law; he will have nothing to do with utilitarian obedience[1]. Now this is to proclaim a doctrine of complete subjection, so far as civil matters are concerned, while by implication it

---

[1] *De Officio Regis*, 8. " ' Vel illata est iniuria quo ad causam propriam vel pure quo ad causam dei. In primo casu post exhortacionem evangelicam paciencia est optima medicina. Si pure in causa dei cristianus debet, post correpcionem evangelicam, preposito suo usque ad mortem, si oportet, confidenter et obedienter resistere. Et sic utrobique innitendum est paciencie, comittendo humiliter deo judicium iniuriam vindicandi.' Et qui excedit hanc regulam resistit dampnabiliter potestati et dei ordinacioni, ut faciunt hii qui rebellant precipue, id est *affeccione comodi temporalis potestatis.*" *Mutatis mutandis*, Wycliffe's view is that of Bellarmine.

grants to the Pope, as the interpreter of the Divine
Law, the right of interference in all states. Wycliffe
takes away the independence of the prince without
establishing the liberty of the subject; and his
theory, if practically carried out, would have been
used to support both the tyranny of an orthodox[1]
king, and the interference of a meddlesome Pope.
It would have had all the disadvantages of the theory
of the Divine Right of Kings combined with those of
clerical supremacy, and would have been without the
advantages of either doctrine. But this was not
foreseen by Wycliffe, and the main drift of his work
is to inculcate the universal authority of the Crown
and the religious duty of submission to it on the
part of all classes. Until religious toleration should
become an accepted maxim, or the claim of Pope or
clergy to authority in spiritual things be disallowed,
there was no completely effective method of meeting
the Papal claim to political supremacy save by a
theory of absolute non-resistance and Divine Right.
It should, however, be said that both Wycliffe and
Marsiglio are anti-clericalist and Erastian even as
regards religion, and would not have admitted the
final authority of the Pope in questions of faith and
morals.

[1] 'Orthodox' here must be taken to mean orthodox in the
view of the recognized spiritual authority, whether Pope or "poor
priest." The theory really subjects the temporal power to the
spiritual, and would justify all ecclesiastical theories of politics.

II.

Whether the speculations of Wycliffe exercised *Possible* any influence over Richard II. may be doubted. *influences upon* Nor is there evidence that his theory of kingship *Richard II.* was in any way derived from the writings of the Imperialist advocates. Yet at least it is certain that men could not remain unaffected by the great controversy between John XXII. and Lewis of Bavaria, and that the ideas expressed by writers on behalf of the Emperor would be peculiarly welcome to Englishmen. Nor can it be denied that the assertion about this time of the independence of England from Papal interference might easily move a man of Richard's narrowly logical type of mind to claim for himself the position of an absolute monarch by Divine Right. He was the last person to ignore the significance of the preamble to the great Statute of *Praemunire,* which asserts, that "this crown of England hath been so free at all times that it hath been in no earthly subjection in all things touching the regality of the said crown[1]." If this were really *His* so, he would take care to maintain intact the "right *position* and liberty of the crown," and would see to it, that *papal.* no Parliamentary or baronial combination should drive him to abate it one jot or tittle. Although we find him attacked for lowering his dignity before the Pope[2], this is undoubtedly a case of collusion, in which

[1] 16 Ric. II. c. 5, *Statutes of the Realm.*

[2] *Articles of Deposition,* c. 10. Cf. also Walsingham, II. 203; the king and John of Gaunt are regarded as more inclined than Parliament to yield to the Pope in regard to the repeal of the Statute of Provisors.

he sought to obtain the Pope's authority for the great
constitutional changes of the Parliament of Shrewsbury.   When it is his interest, he is willing enough
that Archbishop Arundel should be translated to
S. Andrew's, by Papal authority; yet he complains to
the clergy of the abominable custom of Papal trans-
lations, which in the case of Archbishop Nevill had
been employed as a political weapon against himself;
and he offers his support, if they will make a stand
in the matter against the see of Rome[1].   He cannot
understand why the Pope should demand the repeal
of the "statutes" of *Praemunire* and *Quare Impedit*,
although he is glad to learn that his Holiness has no
desire to diminish the right and liberty of the Crown
of England[2].   When he is on the side of the Pope,
it is for reasons of immediate convenience; at heart
he is as anti-papal as Henry VIII.[3]   Indeed, he was
accused of interfering with the ecclesiastical courts[4].

Richard's theory of absolute monarchy.   But whether or no Richard was influenced by
the writings of Wycliffe and the Imperialist theory,
he certainly believed in the sacredness of his office
and in the 'liberty' of his Crown more strongly than
any of his predecessors, and devoted all his energies

[1] Walsingham, II. 228.

[2] John Malverne in Appendix to Higden, IX. 256.

[3] Walsingham, II. 108; Higden, IX. 26.

[4] *Articles of Deposition*, c. 29.   In regard to a dispute as to an
election of the Abbot of S. Edmondsbury we are told, that "the seide
kynge sende embassiatours to the Pope commawndyng them to saye
to the pope, that his wylle schoeld not be flexible in this matter."
Appendix IV. to Higden's *Polychronicon*, VIII. 452; Walsingham,
II. 68.   Richard afterwards yielded, much to the disgust of Walsingham.   "Sicut Ecclesiae Anglicanae detrimentum, ita Papae et
curialibus magnam peperit materiam insolescendi."   (*Ibid.* 97.)

to the establishment of a despotism. He is ever nervously 'guarding' and 'saving' his Crown and dignity. In the shrill tones of the *doctrinaire* politician, he repeatedly declares that nothing he does shall prejudice his prerogative. On the nobles threatening him with deposition he gives way 'saving the rights of the Crown[1].' The commission of 1386 he sincerely regards as void, as being against the liberty of the Crown[2]. He is the sole source of law, not bound by custom[3]; king by God's grace and right of birth[4], he will not endure that his liberty be touched.

Nor did Richard confine himself to words. He tampered with the Rolls of Parliament[5]; he altered and nullified statutes agreed upon by both Houses of Parliament[6]. He exercised a dispensing power that was liberal beyond the custom of such a king

His practice.

---

[1] John Malverne, Appendix to Higden's *Polychronicon*, ix. 115.

[2] Richard appears to have felt that in assenting to the demands of this commission he was virtually resigning the crown. Walsingham, ii. 152. Cf. also *Rot. Parl.* iii. 224, " Le roi en plein Parlement, devant le fyn d'icell, fist overte Protestation par sa bouche demesne, Qe pur riens qu'estoit fait en le dit Parlement il ne vorroit que prejudice avendroit a lui ne a sa corone ; einz que sa Prerogatif et les Libertees de sa dite Corone feussent sauvez et gardez."

[3] "Rex...dixit expresse vultu austero et protervo, quod leges suae erant in ore suo, et aliquotiens in pectore suo, et quod ipse solus possit mutare et condere leges regni sui." *Articles of Deposition*, c. 16.   [4] *Rot. Parl.* iii. 339.

[5] Walsingham, ii. 227 ; *Articles of Deposition*, c. 8.

[6] Walsingham, ii. 48. "Sed quid juvant Statuta Parliamentorum, cum penitus expost nullum sortiantur effectum? Rex nempe cum Privato Consilio cuncta vel mutare vel delere solebat, quae in Parliamentis ante habitis tota regni non solum communitas, sed et ipsa nobilitas, statuebat." *Articles of Deposition*, c. 17.

*Parlia-
ment of
1397-8.*

as Edward III.; in various ways he shewed that he regarded neither law nor custom as binding his action. But it is in the last years of his reign, that his views found their fullest expression and came near to being embodied in the constitution. In the famous Parliament of 1397-8, he obtained the repeal of the pardon of the Lords Appellant; he procured the ratification of the opinions of the judges at Nottingham, which condemned the Commission of Reform of 1386, declared the proposers of it guilty of high treason, and gave the king power to arrange the order of business in Parliament, a rule that would have entirely prevented the growth of the maxim *Redress of grievances before supply*; finally he persuaded the Parliament to delegate its authority to a perpetual committee of eighteen[1].

*His object
to create a
permanent
despotism.*

There can be no question, that by these measures Richard was attempting to create a written constitution, a *lex regia*, which should save the rights of the English Crown for ever. It is made high treason to attempt the repeal of the statutes; all solemnly swear to keep them. For the future, tenants of fiefs, whether barons or bishops, are to swear to maintain the acts, before obtaining livery of seisin[2]. The king writes to the Pope in order to obtain his confirmation of the measures, an unheard-of thing, made one of the grounds of his deposition[3]. Finally, in his

[1] 21 Ric. II. cc. 1—20. *Statutes of Realm*, ii. 94—110.

[2] *Rot. Parl.* iii. 352 sqq. Even this oath is taken "sauvant au Roi sa Regalie et Liberté et le droit de sa corone."

[3] The articles of deposition are given in Knyghton (Twysden, *Decem Scriptores*, 2746—2756); *Rot. Parl.* iii. 417—427.

will Richard bequeathed his private treasure to his successor, with the proviso that he should ratify and observe the statutes of the Parliament of Shrewsbury. Failing his compliance with the condition, the treasure is left to others, who are to labour even unto death to effect the ratification of the statutes[1].

The import of this is plain. Richard desired to found an absolute monarchy, and to relieve the Crown of all the limitations, with which custom had fenced it about. The principle which animates the king is clear and definite. He acts not from caprice or momentary lust of dominion; but with a settled purpose he asserts the rights of kingship and attempts to render them secure for future ages. The clearest insight into Richard's theory is given by the sermon preached by the Bishop of Exeter at the opening of this Parliament[2].

The text is *Rex unus est omnibus*[3], and the preacher argues that there must be one king, and one governor; otherwise no realm can be governed; in a word, "mixed monarchy" is anarchy. To this end of unity in the state three things are necessary; the king must be powerful, the laws must be kept, and subjects must be obedient. The Crown is possessed of certain privileges, which may not be alienated; any act attempting to do so is void. Parliament is therefore summoned to enquire, whether any such rights have been alienated in the past, that remedy may

Sermon of Bishop of Exeter.

[1] Rymer, VIII. 75, *Articles of Deposition*, c. 31.
[2] *Rot. Parl.* III. 347.
[3] Ezek. xxxvii. 22.

be taken, *non obstante* any ordinance to the contrary. For the king is the source of law and the judges are bound to maintain the rights of his Crown. The same idea comes out in the speech of the Chancellor at the re-assembling of Parliament at Shrewsbury; the object of meeting, he says, is to see that there be not several sovereigns in the kingdom, but one only[1]. All this is on exactly the same lines as the anti-papal arguments of Ockham and others, to prove the omnipotence of the sovereign authority from the necessity of unity in the state.

It may be noticed, that in making Parliament the instrument of the destruction of its own liberties, Richard set the precedent, afterwards followed with better success by Henry VIII. The general pardon which he granted to his subjects[2], is an exact parallel to the famous pardon of the whole realm by Henry VIII. for its breach of the Statute of *Praemunire*. Richard appears also to have been the first king, who saw the advantage of manipulating Parliament; he is accused of packing the House with his own nominees and of bribing members[3].

Richard's views of sacredness of kingship and of unction. Walsingham tells us that after this act the sheriffs throughout the kingdom were compelled to take new and unaccustomed oaths, that they would obey the king's commands whether signified under the Great Seal, the Privy Seal, or even the Signet[4].

---

[1] *Rot. Parl.* III. 357.

[2] 21 Ric. II. c. 20 : the Bishop of Exeter declares the granting of this pardon to be one of the chief grounds of the summoning of Parliament.　　　　[3] *Articles of Deposition*, c. 19.

[4] Walsingham, II. 231 ; *Articles of Deposition*, c. 20.

That Richard was standing up for what he believed to be a principle seems proved by his repeatedly declaring during his troubles, that his wretched condition was an outrage on all kings, and would bring royalty into dishonour[1]. We know, that until the day of his death he regarded himself as king by virtue of unction, despite his deposition, that he regarded this ceremony as conferring a sacramental grace[2], and that he directed in his will, that he should receive a royal funeral. It seems clear, then, that ideas, originally framed into a system of defence against the Papacy, found expression in a doctrine of absolute monarchy held by a self-willed English king, and of the divine origin of kingship, as evidenced by the custom of hereditary succession and by the indelible character of unction.

For the position of Richard as king was itself a *His accession*

---

[1]   "Ce sera pour lui [le roi de France] grant vitupere,
    Voire et pour tous les royz qui nez de mere
    Sont au jourduy;
    Veu loultrage et le tresgrant ennuy,
    La povrete et le point ou je suy."
        (*Histoire du Roy d'Angleterre Richard*: Archaeol. Britann., xx. 339.)
There is much more in the same strain. In speaking of Bolingbroke Richard is made to say:
        "Tous ceulx seront ses ennemis
        Qui aymeront honneur, loyaute, pris
        Et vasselaige."

[2] Walsingham, II. 240. The king had wished to be a second time anointed, with oil from the Holy Land. It was used for Henry IV.; Richard speaks of himself as unworthy *tam nobile sacramentum*. That he desired the ceremony of unction to be repeated is nothing against his regarding it as a sacrament, conferring a grace.

a proof of advance of ideas of primogeniture.

strong proof of the progress of the idea that inherent birthright is the chief title to the regal dignity. Like Arthur of Brittany, Richard was a boy when the throne became vacant; as in the case of Arthur, his father had not himself worn the Crown; while, in both cases, there was living an uncle ambitious and unscrupulous, and one of the most powerful men in the country. Yet while in the twelfth century, the uncle succeeded and the principle of an elective monarchy was affirmed; in the fourteenth, there was no question about the nephew's succession; the principle of representative primogeniture had triumphed.

Appearance of doctrine of legitimism.

Lastly, the speech of the Bishop of Carlisle, which is familiar to us from Shakespeare's version[1], is evidence that the doctrines of unlimited obedience and of legitimism were becoming popular, and that the new dynasty which based itself on the rights of the nation and the choice of Parliament would have to encounter an opposition grounded upon the claims of hereditary right and upon the iniquity of rebellion[2].

---

[1] *King Richard II*. Act iv. Sc. i, ll. 114—149. Shakespeare, who changes the circumstances, took the speech from Holinshed, who got it from Hall. The latter apparently found it in *Lystoire de la traison et mort du roy Richart dengleterre*. (*English Historical Society's* Edition, pp. 70, 1.) Cf. also the speech of the Earl of Warwick in 1386. (Higden, ix. 110.)

[2] The proclamation of the French king against the usurper is further evidence of this. *Lystoire de la traison*, Appendix H.

CHAPTER V

KINGSHIP IN ENGLAND FROM HENRY IV.
TO ELIZABETH

THE claims of Richard II. to found a despotism *Constitu-* were repudiated by the nation. The Revolution of *tional Re-* *volution* 1399 is an assertion of the right of Englishmen to *of* 1399. constitutional government. The articles of deposition in which the charges against Richard are set forth, contain or imply a theory of constitutionalism as uncompromising as the absolutist doctrine of the king. Nor was this all. In elevating Henry of Bolingbroke to the throne the English nobles passed over the nearest heir, and asserted the right of Parliament to elect the fittest person from within the royal family. Yet the position is not quite clear. Henry paid homage to the principle of legitimism by his claim to be the nearest heir to Henry III. The fiction was transparent enough; no one believed *Henry's* Henry's ancestor Edmund Crouchback to have been *claim to* *hereditary* older than his brother Edward I. Yet the more *right* ridiculous the fable appears, the stronger is the *evidence* *of popular* evidence it affords of the hold upon the minds of *sentiment.* Englishmen of the principle of strict hereditary succession. Men will not bolster up a claim by a transparent falsehood, save to satisfy some really existing sentiment. However, constitutionalism triumphed for a time, and the theory of government propounded by an English lawyer[1] at the close of the period is as emphatic in its repudiation of despotism and preference for 'mixed monarchy,' as were the doctrines of Wycliffe and Richard II. upon the other side. Yet the new dynasty was a failure; strong government was needed, and the country "perishing for lack of it" called the legitimate line to its assistance[2]. It is as a reformer, not as a pretender, that Richard Duke of York first comes into prominence. Yet it was only owing to his position as the legitimate heir of Edward III. that he gained the leadership of the reforming party. From the position of popular leader clamouring for good government he quickly passed to that of the dispossessed heir demanding his rights. It is now that the notion of indefeasible hereditary right first appears in English history[3]. On no theory of the

Inde-feasible hereditary right a Yorkist doctrine.

[1] Fortescue, *De Laudibus Legum Angliae* (1468–70); *The Governance of England* (1471–6).

Accounts of Fortescue's theory are given by Mr Plummer in his introduction to the latter and by Dr Stubbs, *Constitutional History*, § 365.

[2] *Ibid.* § 372. Parliament thus sums up the grievances of the nation under the Lancastrian dynasty, "In whose [Henry's] time not plenty, peace, justice, good governance, policy, and virtuous conversation, but unrest, inward war and trouble, unrighteousness, shedding and effusion of innocent blood, abusion of the laws, partiality, riot, extortion, murder, rape and vicious living have been the guides and leaders of this noble realm of England." *Rot. Parl.* v. 464.

[3] It is an extension to the succession of the doctrine *Nullum tempus occurrit regi*. Some of the arguments employed are noticeable: The Duke of York answers the objection raised

State can a rightful heir be greatly blamed for heading a revolt against a usurper. But after the original usurper is dead, and his dynasty to all appearance established, the dispossessed line will not obtain any general support, unless there be prevalent a strong sentiment of legitimism, a widespread belief that, so long as the rightful heir is to be found, nothing can bar his claim. Thus the nominal occasion of the Wars of the Roses, however little it may have been their real cause, is a proof of the influence, which the principle of legitimism had gained by the middle of the fifteenth century. Men will not profess to take up arms in support of a doctrine, that is not popular and widespread. And the principle triumphed. Not *The principle triumphant.*

against his claim, that allegiance had been sworn to Henry VI. with the assertion that no oaths are binding if they conflict with the law of God, i.e. hereditary right. He claims to be "right inheritor of the said crowns as it accordeth with God's law and all natural laws." (*Rot. Parl.* v. 377.) In the first year of the reign of Edward IV. Parliament condemns the treatment of Richard II. "king anointed, crowned, and consecrate," as "against God's law, man's legiance, and oath of fidelity." There is no act upon the Statute book granting the crown to Edward, as in the case of Henry VII. and even James I. Parliament merely declares that he took to him the right on the death of his father. It speaks of the Duke of York claiming the crown as "using the benefice of the law of nature, not having any Lord then above him but God." (*Ibid.* 464, 5.) It would be impossible to express more strongly the notion of inherent right, as the one title to the crown; questions with regard to the succession are already acquiring a mystical character, and lawyers refuse to meddle with the *arcana imperii.* The judges on being asked to discuss the validity of the Yorkist claim, declared that the "matter was so high and touched the king's high estate and regalie, which is above the law, and passed their learning, wherefore they durst not enter into any communication thereof." (*Ibid.* 376.)

only was Edward IV. able to oust those who were
"Kings in deed and not in right[1]"; but his opponents
themselves put forward pretensions to hereditary
right. Abandoning the claim that Henry IV. was the
nearest heir to Henry III., they advanced the plausible contention that the Yorkist line was barred by its
descent from a woman. Thus in one way or another
the validity of the hereditary test was admitted.

Nor are the breaches of the principle before the
reign of Henry VIII. as important as might appear.
Richard III. may have been a usurper, but at least
he claimed to succeed by the best right. He alleged
that Edward V. was illegitimate, and that the young
Earl of Warwick's claim was barred by the attainder
of the Duke of Clarence. If this were so, he was
the undoubted heir of Edward IV. Anyhow, the
titulus regius said he was, and gave him the Crown
for that reason[2].

Heredi-tary succession under the Tudors.

Bosworth field put an end for a time to the
claims of strict right, and the Crown was won by
an adventurer, who probably had a better title
to be regarded as heir of Welsh princes than of
English. Yet even for the hereditary claim of Henry

[1] *Statutes of the Realm*, II. 380.

[2] *English Historical Review*, VI. 260 sqq., 453, and Gairdner,
Life and Reign of Richard III. Chapter III.; Speed's *History*,
717—25. The author of *Majestas Intemerata* is well aware that "the
first of Richard III. bastardizes Edward the Fourth's posterity to
flatter a tyrant; but what historian since ever fixed a truth upon
this act?" The Act professes merely to resolve the doubts by
declaring the succession not granting the crown, to which the title
of Richard III. is "just and lawful *as grounded upon the laws of
God and nature* and also upon the ancient laws and customs of
this said realm."

Tudor something might be said. The legitimation
of the Beauforts might be held to extend to the succession. It could be pretended that the titles of all
other claimants were barred; that of Elizabeth of
York as a woman, that of Richard III. as a usurper,
and that of Warwick as scion of an attainted house[1].
At least, by marrying Elizabeth Henry endeavoured
to secure for his dynasty the hereditary title, which he
must have felt flimsy in his own case[2]. Henry VIII.
reigned as the unquestioned heir of Edward III.
These facts shew that, if the principle of hereditary
right was not allowed to prevent title by conquest
or choice, it was at least felt desirable to pay to it
the decent respect of ingenious falsehood. On the
other hand, a curious contrast to the sentiment is
the statute, which gives protection to all supporters
of a *de facto* king[3], and even attempts to prohibit
future Parliaments from attempting its repeal.

The next reign exhibits the most startling breach
of the principle of hereditary succession. The peculiar matrimonial relations of Henry VIII. necessitated continual changes in the succession, which could
no longer be regarded as a sacred thing. When
Henry was empowered to choose his own successor,
absolutism had triumphed at the expense of legitimism[4]. Certainly a king, in whose hands are

[1] On the claim of Henry VII., see Stubbs, *Lectures on Mediæval and Modern History*, 392—4.

[2] For the pains, which Henry VII. took to destroy all evidences
of the early marriage of Edward IV. see *English Historical Review*,
VI. 265.

[3] 11 Henry VII. c. 1.

[4] 28 Hen. VIII. c. 7, and 35 Henry VIII. c. 1.

placed the control of the succession, is more completely sovereign in theory, than even Louis XIV. whose will might indeed be law, but he would never have been recognized as competent to alter the succession. Henry named his own children in the order which appeared to follow most closely the rule of primogenitary succession: in that order they succeeded. Doubtless it is true that Mary and Elizabeth could not both of them be lawful heirs; one of them must be illegitimate; yet at least the succession of Edward VI. and his sisters followed the natural order; if the dissolution of the marriage with Catharine of Aragon be regarded as merely a divorce, it is even possible to maintain, that the sentiment of hereditary right had not been violated.

Position of Elizabeth. Yet Elizabeth's case, which was the most doubtful of the three, certainly aroused controversy. It does not appear, that she was regarded upon the Continent as a legitimate sovereign. From the outset, Mary Queen of Scots claimed the Crown by hereditary right. This right she undoubtedly possessed, if the divorce of Catharine were invalid. Elizabeth's irritation at Mary's quartering of the arms of England, her vain attempts to obtain from Mary the ratification of the treaty of Edinburgh, in which her present and future claims to the throne were renounced, were the inevitable result of her own doubtful title. They shew how deeply Elizabeth was penetrated with a sense of the insecurity of her position, and testify to *Claims of Mary Stuart.* the strength of Mary's claim and of the sentiment in its favour. Doubtless other and more potent causes led to the insistence upon Mary's rights; yet

these alone would not have been sufficient to render
Mary a dangerous competitor, had not a defective
hereditary title been felt to be a good handle against
a sovereign, who was for other reasons objectionable.
Upon no other grounds were Mary's claims formidable; for not only had Henry VIII. been at pains
to exclude the Scotch line from the succession, but
this disposition had been ratified by Parliament in
the first year of Elizabeth's reign[1]. It appears,
then, that, as in later times, there was some popular
sentiment that hereditary right was indefeasible, a
'fundamental law,' which no Act of Parliament could
override.

Additional evidence of this is the statute 13 Eliz. *Import-*
cap. 1[2], which makes it high treason to question *ance of the*
statute
the right of Parliament to alter the succession. This *13 Eliz.*
Act is evidence both ways. In the first place it *c. 1.*
proves, what indeed is clear on other grounds, that
neither Elizabeth nor her ministers regarded themselves as bound by the rules of primogenitary succession, and that they claimed for Parliament absolute
freedom of choice; clearly, hereditary succession is no
'fundamental law' to them. On the other hand, the *Popular*
doctrine of indefeasible hereditary right would not *sentiment*
as to
have been condemned, had it not been prevalent *hereditary*
among a considerable section of the nation. Thus, *right.*
then, in the theory of the Tudor period assertions of
indefeasible hereditary right are not to be expected;
actual facts are against it. Probably, however, the

[1] 1 Eliz. c. 3, § 2.
[2] *Statutes of Realm*, IV. 52 : also printed in Prothero's *Statutes
and Constitutional Documents*, 89.

notion was widespread, but its utterance was unsafe.
The sentiment must have been general, or the
unanimity which welcomed James I. to the throne
would have been impossible; for James had no title
save that of inherent birth-right, and succeeded in
spite of the two Acts of Parliament excluding his
house.   On the other hand the existence of these
statutes and that discussed above is alone proof that
the Crown is far the most important power in the
State, and that theories are prevalent which exempt
it from all restraints in regard to the succession.

Nature of Tudor despotism implies theories of universal obedience.   The causes and character of the Tudor despotism
need not be here discussed.   Yet one point must be
noted.   The exaltation of the royal authority was
due to the need of a strong government.   The crime
of the Lancastrian dynasty had been, not that it
was capricious or self-seeking or oppressive, but that
it was weak, that law and order were not maintained
and private war was once again becoming prevalent.
It is as 'saviours of society' that the Yorkists and
afterwards the Tudors win their position.   In the
statutes of liveries and in the Star Chamber is to
be found the *raison d'être* of Tudor despotism.
Government must be effective, private oppression
must be punished, great offenders must be forced
to submit to the authority of the Crown.   That
is the general sentiment.   In a word, obedience
must be enforced.   The very causes, which drove
men to support the Tudors at all, drove them also
to insist on the paramount importance of obedience,
and to proclaim the iniquity of rebellion.

But, if the Tudor dynasty was essentially a

dynasty of rulers, the Reformation gave to them a *Result of* vast accession of power.   One aspect alone is impor- *the Re-formation.* tant here.   In the series of statutes enacted in the years 1529—1534, culminating in that of the royal supremacy, another stage was reached in the long struggle, for centuries waged by the English kings against clerical immunities and the political claims of the Papacy.   What had been little more than an aspiration under Henry II. or Edward III. or Richard II. was at last an accomplished fact. England was free from Papal interference, if only she could maintain her position.   The battle was *The inde-* not won yet, and in this fact lies the justification *pendence claimed by* of men's passionate faith in the Divine Right of *Henry* Kings.   We are too apt to think that, from the time *VIII. has yet to be* of Henry VIII. or at least of Elizabeth, the success *made* of the English Reformation was assured.   The per- *good.* sistent efforts of foreign powers to convert England, the dreams of so able a man as Gondomar[1], and the overtures to Charles I. and Laud[2], are alone sufficient proof to the contrary.   If all danger of England's submitting to the Papal yoke were over, certainly the fact was unknown at the time either to English statesmen or to Papal diplomatists.   England in the time of Henry VIII. asserted her claims to inde- pendence.   A century of statesmanship and conflict was required before they were finally made good. Thus a theory was needful which should express the national aspirations.   It was impossible to assert the sovereignty of the English Crown and its

[1] Gardiner, *History of England*, II. 218, 19, 252—4.
[2] *Ibid.* VIII. ch. LXXIX.

A theory needed to justify the position taken up against the Pope. independence of Papal control without some grounds being given. It was necessary to meet the Pope's claim to allegiance and his pretended right of deposing kings, with some counter claim. There is no need to investigate afresh the causes, which determined the nature of this counter claim. They were at work in the earlier struggles between the Empire and the Papacy. Clearly, the Pope's claim to a universal monarchy by Divine Right, and to implicit obedience on pain of damnation, must be met in similar fashion, whether in the sixteenth or the fourteenth century. The English State must assert a claim to Divine appointment. Obedience must be demanded as due by God's ordinance, and all resistance must be treated as sin.

Need of a single central authority. Now it is to the conception of a single supreme authority in the State, that men are inevitably driven in seeking to formulate an anti-papal theory. Wearied of quasi-feudal anarchy and disgusted with ecclesiastical interference, Englishmen felt the need of relying upon one central power and of asserting its universal jurisdiction. Nor could it seem doubtful at that time, who was vested with the sovereignty. *The king naturally regarded as 'sovereign.'* The king was immeasurably the most important element in the State; in the case of Henry VIII., especially after the Act of 1539, the idea of sovereignty was almost completely realised in his person[1]. It is far easier to arrive at the notion of sovereignty,

---

[1] 31 Henry VIII. c. 8. It is thus described by the Bishop of Oxford. "Here was a 'lex regia' indeed; a dictatorship, which with all conceivable limitations, left the 'king master and only master' in his own house." *Lectures on Mediæval and Modern History*, 303.

if it be seen to be vested in a single person, than if
it belong to an assembly or to a body such as Parliament, made up of more than one assembly.   Only
under the form of monarchy does the notion of
sovereignty readily lend itself to popular exposition.
Further, the Reformation had left upon the statute *Act of*
book an emphatic assertion of unfettered sovereignty *Supre-macy.*
vested in the king.   And the supremacy of the
Crown constituted a new prerogative, which, since
Parliament could allege no precedent for controlling
it, might be claimed as the personal right of the
head of the State.   Lastly, the king had the name
of sovereign.

That complete sovereignty is to be found in
some person or body of persons in the State is a
necessity of effective anti-papal argument.   If during
the Tudor period it was not to be found in the
Crown, where was it?   Sir Thomas Smith might
indeed write of the power of Parliament[1], but if the
directing will is the supreme power in the State,
Elizabeth was sovereign far beyond any despotic
Premier or 'uncrowned king' of our own day.   If
we take into account the powers of arbitrary jurisdiction exercised by the Privy Council, the infre-
quency with which Parliament sat, and its lack of
independence when sitting, there can be no doubt
that Elizabeth was the person 'habitually obeyed' by
the majority of Englishmen throughout her reign.

---

[1] *De Republica Anglorum*, II. 1.   Cf. Maitland's Introduction
to Mr Alston's edition of this work.   Therein it is shewn how
Sir Thomas was halting between two opinions in the matter of
sovereignty.

Whether based upon authority or influence, the supreme power could be more truly conceived as belonging to the queen alone than as shared with anyone else. Some theory of uncontrolled secular authority is needed to meet the Papal claims; some power must be called into play to overthrow them. The most natural theory of sovereignty is that of monarchy. The only authority which could for an instant match itself with the Pope was that of the Crown. For the purposes of theoretical consistency and practical efficiency alike, a doctrine of sovereignty vested by Divine Right in the king was the indispensable handmaid of a national Reformation.

Obedience to law the governing thought in the sixteenth century.

For a time, the thought will suffice of the universality of law and of its absolute claim on the conscience. Men must assert the power of the Crown and the duty of obedience to it, not so much because they have framed any general notions of its majesty and dignity, as because it is the one effective authority. Royal power must be exalted as against that of the Pope. If phrases slip in which grant to kings an unconditioned omnipotence, which few of them ever dreamed of exercising, that is rather because no one as yet is concerned to deny them, than because they are construed strictly or regarded as of much importance. Against the Papal supremacy the unlimited jurisdiction and authority of kings is asserted. That these positions were destructive of popular rights, which nobody claimed and nobody exercised, is not as yet seen. Monarchy will only come to be defended for its own sake when

Bellarmine and Suarez have elaborated a theory of popular sovereignty as a weapon against recalcitrant monarchs, and when Knox and Goodman have proclaimed the lawfulness of resistance (when the Presbyterian clergy command it) and the duty of deposing 'idolatrous' kings. Meanwhile it is of kings and their appointment by God as necessitating obedience that men will talk. This is the position *Divine authority of kings.* most easily proved from Scripture and forms the natural antithesis to the Papal monarchy. Unlimited authority must be claimed for the law or the king; as yet there seems no difference. The king is the source and interpreter of law; men have no fear that he will seek to change existing arrangements or to overstep the boundaries set by custom. The only authorities which claim unlimited allegiance are the king and the Pope; there is no question as yet between Crown and Parliament. Obedience is essential. To give it to the Pope dissolves 'the political union.' It must therefore be due to the king.

Thus it is obedience, rather than a theory of government, that writers in the sixteenth century insist upon. Nor did they repeat the error of Wycliffe and Ockham, and leave a loophole for Papal interference by admitting the possibility of resistance in extreme cases. While claiming, as the writers of the fourteenth century, Divine sanction for secular governments, they dwell further upon the absolute duty of non-resistance in all cases. *A theory of obedience not of the State. In the sixteenth century no case of resistance is admitted.*

In Tyndall's work, *The Obedience of a Christian Man,* passive obedience is inculcated without any *1528.*

qualification. No terms could be stronger than those
in which the writer enforces the duty of non-resistance. Written to demonstrate the groundlessness
of the charge of anarchism levelled at the Reformers,
the book asserts that the Pope is the true anarchist,
and declares that under Papal dominion "kings are
but shadows, vain names and things idle, having
nothing to do in the world, but when as the holy
father needeth their help[1]." Robert Barnes in his
1534. *Supplication to the most gracious prince Henry VIII.*
and *Men's Constitutions bind not the Conscience,*
declares most emphatically in favour of Passive Obedience. Another work of 1534 carefully expounds
regal authority as against Papal, and claims God's
ordinance on behalf of kings[2]. Bishop Gardiner in
1535. his Oration *On True Obedience* developes completely
the notions of absolute subjection to the sovereign,
of the King's power being God's ordinance, and of
the sinfulness of resistance ; and infers from this the
weakness of the Papal claims[3]. More clearly than
other contemporary writers, he sees that the real
question is not as to the religious duty of obedience
in general, but of the limits of obedience in extreme cases[4]. For only then does the Pope enjoin

----

[1] *The Obedience of a Christian Man,* 114.

[2] *Opus eximium de vera Differentia Regiae Potestatis et Ecclesiasticae.* Goldast, III. 22.

[3] The argument is as follows : "If he [the king] be the head
of the people, and that by the ordinance of God, as no man
sayeth nay," the Pope's claims to supremacy must fall to the
ground (58). I quote from the reprint of Heywood's translation
of 1553.

[4] "It is certain that obedience is due, but how far the limits

disobedience; but he denies that any limits to obedience are to be found in Scripture[1]. Like Wycliffe, he repudiates the notion, that the thirteenth of Romans can refer to the Pope. The distinction between the greater and lesser lights is declared to be a "blind distinction and full of darkness[2]." He is at pains to assert that the royal supremacy is no new doctrine, but runs through English history and implies no more than that "the Prince is the whole prince of all the people and not of part[3]." The central idea of the book is the same as that of all effective antipapal treatises; that obedience is due to the king, as a divinely appointed governor. Papal precedents of royal subjection are brushed away by a development of the doctrine *nullum tempus occurrit regi.* "Time may not prescribe against God's truth," and kings cannot alienate a God-given right. His contention, that examples are needless, for God's law is constant, and man's precepts variable, implies the whole force of the sentiment, that led men to frame a theory of the Divine Right of Kings[4]. A stable bulwark was needed against the Papal attack. Obedience must be absolute and immutable, or the Pope will find it possible to make good some part of his claim. This can only be if the power of the Crown be regarded

of requiring obedience extend, that is the whole question that can be demanded." *Ibid.* 59.

[1] "What manner of limits are those that you tell me of, seeing that the Scripture hath none such?" *Ibid.*

[2] *Ibid.* 63.

[3] *Ibid.* 72. "It appeareth that the thing itself which was expressed by the name was not only true but ancient."

[4] *Ibid.* 80, 81.

as God's appointment and non-resistance as a Divine ordinance[1].

1543.   *The Necessary Erudition of a Christian Man* is another early work, which authoritatively asserts the Divine authority of Kings and the iniquity of all resistance[2]. In more than one of Latimer's Sermons[3] and in the two famous Homilies, that of the reign of Edward VI. entitled *An Exhortation concerning Order and Obedience,* and that of Elizabeth's collection directed *Against Wilful Rebellion,* the religious basis of non-resistance is asserted. Doubtless it is true, as the popular party afterwards claimed, that it is non-resistance to law which is here set forth in general terms; and that no guidance is given by the Homilies for the case of a monarch, like James II., arbitrarily violating the laws.

In the reign of Elizabeth there are the strong assertions of Jewel that "obedience is due to princes and magistrates though they be very wicked[4]," that

[1] Gardiner declares that his purpose in writing is "to move all men to obedience, which only in the commandments of God and for God's sake maketh us happy and blessed." (*Ibid.* 101.)

[2] *The Necessary Erudition of a Christian Man,* the Fifth Commandment. "Scripture taketh princes to be as it were fathers or nurses to their subjects." "By this commandment also subjects be bound not to withdraw their said fealty, truth, love and obedience towards their princes, for any cause whatsoever it be, ne for any cause they may conspire against his person, ne do anything towards the hindrance or hurt thereof." The terms of the following passage are significant. "And furthermore by this commandment they be bound to obey also, all the laws, *proclamations, precepts and commandments* made by their princes and governors except they be against the commandment of God."

[3] Latimer's *Sermons,* 148, 496.

[4] *Apology for the Church of England.* Jewel's *Works,* III. 74.

the "Pope ought to acknowledge and call the Emperor Lord and Master," and that "we ought so to obey princes as men sent of God[1]."

The arguments of Jewel's *Apology* are evidence of the direct connection between the theory of the sixteenth and seventeenth centuries and the earlier Imperialist doctrine. Further evidence is the translation of Marsiglio's great work which was published in 1535, the chapter on the modes of restraining a bad prince being significantly omitted as not "pertaining to this realm of England." Bilson's work, *The True Difference between Christian Subjection and unChristian Rebellion* is important, as not merely containing a theory of non-resistance, but also as covering almost the whole ground of the historical argument against the Papal claims. The relations of Popes and Emperors form the subject of many a page of anti-papal argument, which must seem to modern readers pedantic and unimportant. But the independence of the Emperors was the necessary ground on which to rest the later claim to the independence of all states. Without this, it was impossible to prefer for national independence any claim founded on right as distinct from force. If the King was or had been supreme and free from Papal control, nothing of course could alter the fact. But it was no more than a fact. The Pope claimed a Divine Right for his position, and this could only be met by a counter claim not of fact, but of right. The historical question depended entirely upon the relations of Popes and Emperors, Eastern as well as Western. If it

Contro-versial importance of early Imperial history.

1585.

---

[1] *Apology for the Church of England.* Jewel's *Works*, III. 76.

could be clearly proved, that in early times the Pope
had submitted without a murmur to the authority
of the Emperor, the fact would go far to justify
the assertion that the political claims of the Papacy
were of modern growth, and rooted in nothing better
than the false decretals and acts of power. In the
view of the defenders of the Act of Supremacy the
position of the Pope was that of a usurper. The
Protestant writers were maintaining the claims of
the genuine heir. It is true that their contention
could not be demonstrated by shewing that Papal
interference was of recent growth ; yet such a proof
would raise a strong presumption in their favour.
Thus the position of Constantine, the rights of
Julian, the acts of Theodosius, the powers of Justinian, the claims of the mediæval Emperors were
of vital importance in the controversy. Unless the
Imperialist position were tenable, the Pope's claims
were unassailable historically, and there would be
small ground for the oft-repeated assertion of the
freedom of the English monarchy. If the Pope
had always claimed and exercised the powers he
now pretended to, there was good reason for supposing them given of God. If on the other hand
they were originally vested in the Emperor, his power
must be of God, and the cause of secular governments
in general was justified. Thus that Paul of Samosata
or the Donatists appealed not to the Pope, but to
the Emperor, is no mere academic point, but a
necessary step in an argument of incalculable practical importance. This fact may account also for the
leaning some shew in the direction of Erastianism.

Bilson, for instance, appears thoroughly to approve the conduct of the Eastern Emperors in regard both to Popes and Patriarchs. His desire to demonstrate the political supremacy of the secular power carries him to extremes.

Bilson's book is further noteworthy, in that it contains not merely the customary announcement that the King's power is from God and subject to him alone, but also a demonstration that God especially prefers hereditary monarchy. From the example of the Davidic kingdom the author infers that "succession in kingdoms hath not only the consent of all ages and nations; but the manifest subscription of God himself; that it is His special favour and blessing to continue the successions of godly princes[1]." *Bilson on Heredi- tary Mon- archy.*

The last instance of anti-papal argument that need be considered here is Bullinger's reply to the Bull of Pope Pius V. excommunicating Elizabeth. In this the anti-papal character of Tudor theories of obedience is fully exemplified. The author declares that the Pope usurps the rights granted to Kings by God, but regards (naturally enough) these rights as equally attributable to the supreme power in a republic[2], and equally granted by God in that case. With Mary Stuart still alive he is at pains to declare that the succession to the Crown goes by election[3]. One phrase of this book expresses the whole senti- ment at the root of the theory of the Divine Right *1571.*

---

[1] *True Difference*, 515.
[2] *Bullae Papisticae Refutatio*, 44.
[3] *Ibid.* 69.

of Kings: *The bonds of political society are not
dissolved, but strengthened by the word of God*[1].

*Need of a
theory of
the Divine
Right of
Kings.*

It is the occasion of this treatise which marks most
completely the necessity of a theory of the Divine
Right of Kings. So long as the Popes were content
with a general claim, or dreamed of converting
Elizabeth, an uncompromising royalist doctrine was
scarcely needed. But, when it was attempted to put
the theory into practice, and all good Catholics were
bidden to become traitors on religious grounds, it
was necessary that a theory should appear of the
religious duty of obedience to the established
government. Loyal and patriotic feeling under
the circumstances must inevitably lead to the
exaltation of the dignity and authority of the
Crown. Its complete independence of the Pope, its
institution by God, and the duty of non-resistance
must now be emphasized with wearisome reiteration,
if the State was to retain the allegiance of those
large numbers who were gazing with longing and
regret at the old order. From the year 1570 of the
Bull of excommunication there is a king 'across the
water' claiming allegiance, threatening and sometimes
organizing descents upon the coast. Every patriotic
Englishman must henceforth affirm, that his own
princess is the lawful recipient of obedience, with
as good or better title than that of the Pope; in
a word that she is Queen by Divine Right. If the
Pope had excommunicated Council or Parliament,
men might have urged the divine authority of

---

[1] "At politica vel civilis gubernatio confirmatur, non dissolvitur
verbo Domini." *Bullae Papisticae Refutatio*, 71.

the Sanhedrim or God's favours to the chosen
people. But since it was the Queen who was
deposed, the Queen must be defended, and the
rights of the Crown shewn to exist by a Divine
decree.

Lastly, it may be observed that the position of *Effect of the death of Mary Stuart.* affairs in respect of the succession had undergone
a change towards the close of the reign. It was no
longer necessary to speak of hereditary right with
bated breath. So long as Mary Stuart lived, to
enforce the claims of strict right might be to
countenance immediate rebellion; certainly it would
pave the way for a Papal reaction that was likely
to prove more lasting than that under Mary Tudor.
But now that the young King of Scotland was
heir according to strict rule, there was nothing to
prevent the national sentiment in favour of legi-
timism exerting its full force. Besides, it is the *Papalists now oppose doctrine of hereditary succession. 1593.* Roman writers who now begin to attack the doctrine. Doleman's *Conference about the Next Succession
to the Crown of England* (written by the Jesuit
Parsons) proclaims in strident tones the new alliance
between Papal sovereignty and popular rights. The
author repeatedly declares that "Propinquity of birth
or blood alone, without other circumstances, is not
sufficient to be preferred to a Crown[1]"; that forms
of government are variable and may be established

---

[1] *A Conference about the Next Succession*, 1; cf. also 11, "It
[that any prince hath his particular government or interest to
succeed by institution of nature] is ridiculous, for that nature
giveth it not, but the particular constitution of every commonwealth within itself."

and changed according to the will of the community[1]; that "the succession to government by nearness of blood is not by Law of Nature and Divine, but by human and positive laws only of every particular government, and consequently may upon just causes be altered by the same[2]." The basis of the author's political theory is frankly utilitarian; Doleman asserts that "the Commonwealth hath authority to dispossess them that have been lawfully put in possession, if they fulfil not the Laws and *Conditions* by which, and for which their dignity was given them[3]." He upholds the right of resistance, although, with a shrewd eye to the Papal supremacy, he forbids it to be exercised by "private men," who are inferior to the Prince; whereas the Commonwealth is superior to him[4]. The importance of the Coronation oath as implying the conditions of allegiance is insisted upon.

In this book there is found the complete expression by an Englishman of the doctrines of the right of resistance, of popular sovereignty, and the merely official character of kingship. These are proclaimed purely in the interests of the Papal monarchy, without the smallest enthusiasm for liberty. The book appears to have been widely circulated, as the ability with which it was written deserved. Doleman is the most frequent subject of attack by supporters of James, and his work is

[1] *A Conference about the Next Succession*, 10. "The Commonwealth hath power to choose their own fashion of government, as also to change the same upon reasonable causes."

[2] *Ibid.* cap. I. title.

[3] *Ibid.* 26.   [4] *Ibid.* 58.

evidently regarded as the most salient exposition of
the treasonable character of the Papal aims.   Speed, 1611.
in describing the peaceful accession of James, goes
out of his way to make a thrust at this treatise in
particular.   "Let Doleman therefore dote upon his
own dreams, and other like traitors fashion their
bars upon the People's forge; yet hath *God and
his right* set him on the throne of his most lawful
inheritance[1]."

By the irony of fate the work was not only *Use made
of the book
in later
times.*
hashed up in the interests of the Puritan party in
1647; but had the fortune to be reprinted by the
supporters of the Exclusion Bill as the best com-
pendium of arguments against the doctrine of
inherent right[2].   It was strange that a work written
to exclude a Protestant prince from the throne of
England should have exercised its most effectual
influence in all but causing the exclusion of a
Papist[3].

[1] Speed's *History*, 911.

[2] Halifax charges the author of the *History of the Succession*
with plagiarism from Doleman, from whom he asserts all his
arguments to have been drawn.

[3] Cardinal Allen's *Defence of the English Catholics* is based
upon a similar theory of popular rights to that of Parsons.   The
purpose of the book, however, is to justify the deposing power, and
the succession is not discussed.   Yet Allen's insistence on the
importance of the coronation ceremony as conferring rights
upon the Pope is interesting.   Once more it is in the necessities
of Papalist controversy that originates the theory that the coronation oath proves the existence of a compact between king and
people.   " Upon these conditions [the oath to preserve the Catholic
faith] therefore, and no other, kings be received of the Bishop that
in God's behalf anointeth them; which oath and promise not being

Anti-Roman writers henceforth strong supporters of absolute monarchy.

From this time forth anti-papal writers will feel bound to attack the notions of popular sovereignty put forward by the great Jesuit controversialists in order to serve the occasion. Doleman, Bellarmine and Suarez are the *bêtes noires* of Anglican divines. Against them, as the preachers of resistance and inventors of the theory of original compact, the heavy artillery of the royalist pamphleteers is always directed. The attempt of the Jesuits to manufacture anti-monarchical sentiment in the interests of the Papal claims could not but have as its main result the effect of causing orthodox English churchmen to attach an increased value to kingship and to emphasize the peculiar importance of hereditary succession.

cir. 1600.

Heywood's *Royal King and Loyal Subject*[1] reaches perhaps the high-water mark of sixteenth century loyalism. The plot and general development of this play have no other object than that of illustrating the virtue of absolute obedience under oppressive and tyrannical treatment. To the King of England is attributed arbitrary and unlimited authority. Loyalty could hardly go further than the unbroken submission of the Earl Marshal, nor could caprice ever make more unreasonable demands, than the King in this play. The author evidently

observed, they break with God and their people ; and their people may, and by order of Christ's supreme minister their chief Pastor in earth, must needs break with them ; heresy and infidelity in the Prince tending directly to the perdition of the Commonwealth " (113).

[1] For the probable date of the play see J. Payne Collier in Introduction (p. vi) to the reprint by the Shakespeare Society.

wrote his work with the one aim of inculcating this
lesson of royal omnipotence and perfect obedience.
Nor is the play evidence of Heywood's sentiments
only; its success testifies to those of his audience.
Assuredly no other motive but that of loyalty could
have led to such a play being 'acted with applause,'
as we are told that it was. Despite the recent
panegyric on the author by a republican critic[1], it
may be questioned whether this production is not
too deficient in dramatic power and poetic interest
to have afforded pleasure to an audience that
was not steeped in royalist sentiment. Of *The
Maid's Tragedy*, which was a little later, the same
cannot be said. Yet that also proves how strong was
the popular belief in the mystical nature of kingship and in its claims to unquestioning obedience.

Thus, then, it appears that by the close of
the sixteenth century events had done much to
strengthen the monarchy, and to generate notions
of its Divine institution; and that there had been
elaborated a theory of the unlimited jurisdiction of
the Crown and of non-resistance upon any pretence,
which was not to be brought to the test of popular
criticism until the next century. These notions had
all arisen out of the necessities of the struggle with
the Papacy, although the Civil Wars of the previous
age had doubtless produced by way of reaction a
sense of the necessity of securing strong government

[1] Mr Swinburne in *Nineteenth Century*, Oct. 1895 (400), *The
Romantic and Contemporary Plays of Thomas Heywood*. It is
fair to say that *The Royal King* is not placed on a level with most
of the author's works.

and universal obedience to the law.   English controversialists, in answering the theory of the Papal
supremacy, were driven to propound a doctrine of
the Divine Right of secular governments, which is
in its essential meaning no other than the Imperialist
theory of two centuries and a half before.   To the
Empire ancient and mediæval they go for the
historical justification of their position, and for the
rest build up their argument with texts and
illustrations from Scripture.   Theories of inherent
rights of birth as governing the succession are latent
rather than expressed.   But the sentiment in favour
of indefeasible hereditary right has been steadily
growing, and will appear triumphant, so soon as
" England's Empress " shall have left the way free
for a successor, reigning by right of birth alone.

CHAPTER VI

HENRY OF NAVARRE AND THE SALIC LAW

THE political and religious questions which occu- *Similarity*
pied the minds of Englishmen in the seventeenth *of political*
century find their counterpart in controversies evoked *contro-*
during the French Wars of Religion[1]. In the theories *England*
of Huguenots, Lorrainers and *Politiques* appear most *and*
of the ideas, of which we hear so much in England a *France.*
little later. France indeed was a soil peculiarly suited
to the development both of Regal and Papal theories.
From the position of the King, as eldest son of the
Church, men might demonstrate his subjection to
the Pope. The deposition of Childeric by Pope 752.
Zacharias was the earliest exercise of the deposing
power, and was alleged by the supporters of the
league against both Henry III. and Henry IV. as
conclusive proof, that this power had been recognized in the past. In no other country is the
connection of politics and theology more intimate
and vital. Of pure politics there is even less than
there is in England in the next century. Political
theory is rarely developed, save with the object of
strengthening some theological position.

[1] On this point and the position of Henry IV. see the remarks
in Seeley's *Growth of British Policy*, i. 68.

The pretensions of the Huguenots to be taking up arms against their prince by the authority of God exemplify the fact, more patent later in Scotland and England, that the Presbyterian and the Papal theories of politics have common elements. The essence of both is the claim put forward by an ecclesiastical organization to control and direct the action of the State, although in the case of Presbyterianism the acceptance of the doctrine of the 'two kingdoms' makes for liberty (cf. Appendix III—Jus Divinum in 1646). Huguenot Preachers and Presbyterian Disciplinarians are like their Papalist enemies in this, that they would place the secular power under the heel of the spiritual, or else would claim the exercise of sovereign rights for a portion of the community. It was as a danger to the State, claiming for themselves an *imperium in imperio*, that the Huguenots as a political power were finally crushed by Richelieu, while religious liberty was preserved to them.

Again, in the position assumed by the League with regard to Henry III., there is much that is parallel to the relation between Charles I. and the Long Parliament. Henry is lawful king; no one doubts it. Yet he must be restrained and coerced by force of arms in the interests of the Crown which he wears. The distinction between the personal and political authority of the Crown first arose, as has been shewn, in England under Edward II., and will reappear during the Great Rebellion. But the conception of their office entertained by the ultra-royalist rebels of the League is precisely similar.

They too claim to be taking up arms against the person of their king in support of his authority.

Lastly, the reign of Henry IV. is the supreme triumph of legitimism, and far outdoes in importance the accession of James I. to the English Crown. James I. had the sentiment of the whole English nation at his back; and the very few disloyal Catholics were a negligible quantity compared with the League. Henry of Navarre, with almost everything against him save his right as legitimate heir by the Salic law and the grant of God, yet made good his claim to the Crown. His success finally disposed of any claims of the right of election or of the Papal sanction, and testified to the depth of the sentiment in favour of hereditary succession by rule of law. Yet the issue was in one respect different from any possible question of English politics. The strength of Henry's position was not as that of James I. or Charles II., the indefeasible right of the heir according to the rule of primogenitary succession. It was the Salic law, as commonly understood, that gave him his claim, and its inviolability is of the essence of all arguments in his support. He was not the heir by primogeniture, and had the Crown descended, as in England, the Duchess of Savoy[1] must have worn it.

Hence there will be an important difference

---

[1] Catharine, who married Charles Emmanuel the Great, was Philip's elder daughter by Elizabeth of Valois. The claim to the throne of France was however put forward on behalf of Isabella, the second daughter. The reason apparently was that she was as yet unmarried.

between French and English theories of Kingship. The inviolability of the succession "as by law established" will play a much greater part in French controversy. Supporters of Henry IV. can hardly develop such a theory as that of Filmer, for the Salic law is an artificial institution; and it can scarcely be claimed, that it has the author of Nature on its side. At least, the Divine Right of the law of succession is less plausible a doctrine in France than in England. We must expect then to find French theory more legal than English. The Salic law is "the peculiar institution" and especial glory of France; but universality cannot well be claimed for it. In Filmer and Leslie we have what purports to be a universal system of politics. This will be less possible in France. French theory is in many respects identical with English, but in this matter it must differ from it. French thought will be less theological, less transcendental, more legal and local than English.

Position of France in regard to the Pope. But against the claims of the Pope, Gallican doctrine will be as uncompromising as Anglican. Its historical justification is indeed stronger. French authors can look back to a long series of triumphs over Papal aggression, they can point to conflicts no less acute and more successful than any which England had witnessed in pre-Reformation days. The triumph of Philip the Fair over Boniface VIII. is the most impressive event in the relations between France and the Papacy[1]; whereas in power to strike

[1] King James remarks, "Most notable is the example of Philip the Fair, and hits the bird in the right eye" (*Works*, 412).

the imagination the submission of John to Innocent III. far outdoes any of the successful efforts of the English kings. A Frenchman can detail with pride the relations of Charles VI. to Benedict XIII., or of Louis XII. to Julius II.[1], and can even point to the recent refusal of Henry II. to admit the validity of the Tridentine decrees[2]. Whereas in England the Popes had constantly protested against all legislation directed against their autocracy, their partial recognition and reluctant endurance of the Gallican liberties[3] may be adduced to prove, that in the case

[1] See especially Toussaint Berchet, *Pium Consilium super Papae Monitorialibus*, Pars I.

[2] *Apologia Catholica*, 186, 7. "Interea vero dum legitimum illud concilium expectatur neque Rex Francorum neque supremae ipsius Curiae Concilii illius Tridentini decreta unquam in hoc regno mandari voluerunt, nec nisi ab Ecclesiasticis, qui Pontificiae Monarchiae subsunt, fuerunt recepta. Contra Rex Henricus II. piae memoriae certam legationem misit, qua huic Concilio (prout Concilium esse volunt) obsisteret et renuntiaret se nullo pacto id probaturum esse. Etenim revera illud accipi non potest, quin eadem opera corrumpantur et jura authoritasque Francorum Regis, et vetera decreta in summis Regni Ordinibus constituta pragmaticae sanctionis nomine et sanctissimae libertates Ecclesiae Gallicanae, quibus florentissime hujus regni dignitas conservatur."

[3] On the Pragmatic Sanction, see Creighton, *History of the Papacy*, II. 198, 9 and 423 sqq. "It was a memorial of national opposition to the theory of the Universal Church. It expressed the claim of a temporal ruler to arrange at his pleasure the affairs of the Church within his realms." Louis XI. first abolished the Pragmatic Sanction and afterwards restored its provisions by royal ordinance. "The Pragmatic Sanction rested on the basis of the power of General Councils, of an inherent right of self-government in the Universal Church, which was independent of and superior to the Papal monarchy" (*Ibid.* IV. 231). Although the Pragmatic Sanction was superseded by the Concordat of

of France all claims to political supremacy have
been expressly renounced by the Pope.

Yet there were difficulties in the position of
French Catholics, to which neither Imperialists nor
Anglicans were exposed. For they admitted the
spiritual claims of the Papacy, and it is far from easy
to do this, while denying *in toto* .its pretensions to
political supremacy. It was impossible for the supporters of the King to take the line of the Imperialists
and boldly to claim that the Pope was amenable to the
jurisdiction of their master. To admit, as did French
Catholics, that the Pope is a sovereign prince, and that
he further has spiritual authority over the orthodox in
every nation, is to grant him a power of interference,
out of which very little ingenuity is required to con-
struct a theory of universal supremacy. Nor on the
other hand can the *politiques* boldly cut the knot in
the Anglican method, by denying that the Pope is head
of the Church. The inconsistency of their position
necessarily affected their theory. Since it was hard
for French writers to reconcile the liberty claimed for
the French king, with the authority allowed to the
Pope, they may be expected to be less clear than either
Englishmen or Imperialists in their statement of the
necessary unity of the sovereign power. Save in the

Francis I. with the Pope, yet the sentiment it enshrined was
preserved: the new arrangement gave no further rights to the
Pope, but relieved the Crown from the fear of being thwarted by
the leaders of the Gallican Church. So to say, the Pragmatic Sanction had affirmed the independence of the nation, the Concordat
secured the supremacy of the Crown. On this aspect of the
Concordat see Kitchin, *History of France*, II. 182, and Armstrong,
French Wars of Religion, 122.

case of writers with a Huguenot bias, this notion is far less prominent in French than in English or mediæval opponents of the Papal claims. A little want of harmony and consistency in this matter was to be expected from the circumstances of the case. With this brief account of the causes which led to the growth in France of a theory similar in its main scope, though different in certain details from the English doctrine, the study of the chief controversialists may be approached.

In the *Vindiciae contra Tyrannos* and the *Franco-Gallia* are to be found the ideas at the bottom of all theories of popular rights until the eighteenth century. The doctrine of an original compact appears full-blown in the *Vindiciae,* although it is worthy of remark that the compact between King and people is here regarded as not the first, but the second contract involved in the institution of civil society. The first compact is that between God on the one hand and King and people on the other, as contracting parties; this was discarded by later writers. The second compact is the ordinary contract of government, and is identical with that of Hooker or Locke. From it are drawn the usual proofs that the right of resistance is vested in the people and may be exercised upon a breach of the contract by the sovereign. This compact may be express or tacit, but it is inviolable and unchangeable in its terms; no oath or consent of either party or of both can abrogate it[1]. The basis of the argument

Theories of popular rights.

---

[1] "Inter regem et populum mutua obligatio est, quae sive Civilis sive Naturalis tantum sit, sive tacita, sive verbis concepta,

throughout the book is the principle of utility[1]. It is contended, just as in the manner of Locke, that the King can have no power over either the life or the property of his subjects, for it is contrary to *the principle of utility* for men to give power over their life or property into the hands of another[2]. For such a purpose men, who are naturally free, would never have set up a King. There are the very same erroneous beliefs in the artificial nature of government, and in the possibility of limiting the 'sovereign,' which Locke was afterwards to render famous. The author shares with the great Whig philosopher the inability to see that in any developed state there must exist some ultimate supreme authority, to whose action no legal limits can be affixed. Both Locke and Languet think they can "put a hook into the nose" of the Leviathan[3]. The law is for them endowed with Divine Right, eternal and immutable, the breath of

nullo pacto tolli, nullo jure violari, nullo vi rescindi potest." *Vindiciae contra Tyrannos*, 147.

[1] "Hic considerandum est imprimis certissimum totius huiusce disputationis fundamentum, quo reges utilitatis publicae causa constitutos fuisse statuimus. Eo enim posito tota lis finita est." *Ibid.* 112. The author repeatedly has recourse to the principle of utility as the final proof of his position.

[2] *Ibid.* 112 sqq.

[3] It is hard to overestimate the resemblance between the ideas of Locke and the author of the *Vindiciae*, e.g. "Primum sane palam est, homines *natura liberos*, servitutis impatientes et ad imperandum magis, quam ad parendum natos, non nisi magnae cuiusdam utilitatis caussa imperium alienum ultro elegisse, et suae quasi naturae legi, ut alienam ferrent, renunciasse." *Vindiciae contra Tyrannos*, 98. The question as to whether the *Vindiciae* should be attributed to Languet or Du Plessis Mornay need not be here discussed.

God rather than man, controlling sovereign and subject alike[1]. This of course is to miss the conception of sovereignty, for the argument will apply to any form of government. Locke saw and boldly admitted, that his theory was as fatal to Parliamentary omnipotence, as it was to royal prerogative, but the author of the *Vindiciae* appears to confine his views to kings.

In another respect the author of the *Vindiciae* is as curiously at one with Whig Englishmen of the seventeenth century, as he is at variance with modern feeling. He is emphatic in his rejection of

---

[1] "Rexne, inquam, a lege an Lex a rege pendebit? * * * Itaque est quod reges legi ipsi pareant, eamque tamquam reginam agnoscant. ......Quis vero ambigat, quin legi, quam regi parere, id est, homini utilius et honestius sit? Lex est boni regis anima; per hanc movet sentit vivit Rex Legis organum, et quasi corpus, per quod illa suas vires exerit, sua munera obit, sua sensa eloquitur. Animae vero, quam corpori, parere, justius est. Lex est multorum prudentum in unum collecta ratio et sapientia. Plures autem oculatiores et perspicaciores sunt, quam unus. Tutius itaque est Legem, quam hominem, quantumuis perspicacem, ducem sequi. Lex est ratio sive mens, ab omni perturbatione vacua, non ira, non cupiditate, non odio, non studio mouetur, non precibus, non minis flectitur. Homo contra, quantumuis rationis particeps sit, ira, vindicta, aliove subinde appetitu vincitur rapiturque, et ita variis affectibus perturbatur, ut sui ipse compos non sit: nempe, quia ex appetitu et ratione constat, quin hic interdum vincat, fieri nequit. * * * Denique lex est mens, vel potius mentium congruata multitudo: mens vero diuinae aurae particula, ut qui legi paret, Deo parere, Deumque arbitrum quodammodo facere videatur. Contra vero, quia homo ex mente divina, et anima illa belluina constans, sibi saepe non constat, saepe dementat, et insanit: cum vero ita afficitur non jam homo sed bellua est; qui Regi parere mavult, quam legi, belluae quam Dei imperium malle videatur." *Vindiciae contra Tyrannos*, 103.

the right of private individuals to resist the prince on any pretence whatsoever[1]. Passive obedience is their duty, prayers and tears their one resource. Only to corporate bodies, integral parts of the kingdom, does the *Vindiciae* grant the right of resistance. To private individuals Christ's patience is held up as an example; and the precedents of tyrannicide in the Old Testament are explained away, as the result of direct Divine inspiration. Anyhow, the view is closely parallel to the English doctrine, that resistance is unjustifiable on the part of private persons, but lawful, when commanded by the "inferior magistrate." Probably the doctrine is a relic of feudal theory. Its appearance in Huguenot theory, with its strange exaltation of municipal and provincial authority, seems to carry us back to the days of provincial sovereignty and semi-sovereign *communes*. Certainly under any form of government great dangers would arise, if the rights ascribed by 'Brutus' to the municipal organizations were admitted. His theory would reduce the State to a confederation of semi-independent bodies and would give rise to scenes like those so vividly depicted in Mr Chesterton's *Napoleon of Notting Hill*. It would be quite in accordance with the doctrine, if the London County Council were to direct an insurrection in favour of

[1] *Vindiciae contra Tyrannos*, 65 sqq., 178 sqq. No supporter of Passive Obedience could be more emphatic in his denunciation of any general right of insurrection than is this upholder of popular liberty. If the aristocracy lend their support to a tyrant, it is by God's command, and the only lawful weapon is prayer. This notion is of course exactly similar to the royalist contention, that kings are frequently "given in wrath."

the principle of betterment, or the Leicester Board
of Guardians to organize rebellion against the Vac-
cination Statutes. There would be less unity, but
greater freedom.

There are some points of similarity to Papal
theory in this book. God is the true king, and
therefore must be supported against the earthly
king, who is merely God's vassal. Just as a single
city of the empire would be within its rights in
supporting a duly elected Emperor against a usurper,
so a city of France may support God against a king[1].
Moreover, kings hold their dignity by Divine right,
therefore they are amenable to God's authority, and
in support of God's truth they may be resisted[2].
The author argues that if the maxim *Nullum tempus
occurrit regi* be true, it is *a fortiori* evident that no
prescription can touch the inalienable sovereignty of
the people[3]. Indeed the notion that sovereignty is

---

[1] *Vindiciae contra Tyrannos*, 57 sqq. [2] *Ibid.* Qu. 1.

[3] *Vindiciae contra Tyrannos*, 96. The following passage, summing up the whole argument, may be quoted: "In summa, ut hunc
tandem tractatum concludamus, principes eliguntur a Deo, constitu-
untur a populo. Ut singuli principes inferiores sunt : ita universi,
et qui universos repraesentant, regni officiarii, principe superiores
sunt. In constituendo principe intervenit foedus inter ipsum et
populum, tacitum, expressum, naturale, vel etiam civile, ut bene
imperanti bene pareatur, ut reipublicae inservienti omnes in-
serviant.......Huius vero foederis seu pacti regni officiarii vindices
et custodes sunt. Qui hoc pactum perfide et pervicaciter violat,
is vere exercitio tyrannus est. Itaque regni officiarii ipsum et
secundum leges judicare, et renitentem vi coercere, si alias non
possunt, ex officio tenentur. Hi duorum generum sunt. Qui
regni universi tutelam susceperunt, quales Comes stabuli,
Mareschalli, Patricii, Palatini et caeteri singuli per se caeteris

inalienable finds expression on all sides, whether
the doctrine advocated be the ultimate authority of
Pope, of King, or of people. Nor is this surprising.
Practical necessity rendered it essential for each
side to insist much upon the doctrine. For neither
party could shew such an unbroken series of precedents, that they could make their position secure
without asserting that, while examples might support
their own view, precedents against them will avail
nothing.

*Hotman's
'Franco-
Gallia.'* The *Franco-Gallia* of Hotman is a work of a
different order. It is a purely historical argument to
prove that the Frankish kingdom was, in the earliest
stages of its development, a limited monarchy. The
inference is that the present autocratic power of the
Crown is an usurpation and may justly be abolished
in favour of a return to the old state of things.
The notion that governs the whole course of the
argument, is the same as that held by English writers
of all schools in the next century. Constitutional
arrangements, whether they consist in the sovereign
rights of the Crown or in the power of the people, are
believed to be unchangeable, a 'fundamental law'
which no lapse of time or developement of circumstances can abrogate. Thus the primitive system
of government, whatever it be, is the only rightful

conniventibus aut colludentibus, tyrannum coercere debent; qui
alicujus partis, regionisve, quales duces, marchiones, comites,
consules, maiores tyrannidem tyrannumque ab ea regione urbeve
arcere jure suo possunt. Porro singuli sive privati adversus
tyrannos exercitio, gladium non stringent; quia non a singulis,
sed ab universis constituti sunt" (*Ibid.* 182, 3).

ono. Whatever powers originally belonged to the people, they still possess, however long be the period since they were recognized as effective. Whatever rights were vested in the Crown at the beginning, it still has, and no amount of constitutional develope-ment can check them. Hotman's conclusions are similar to those of the *Vindiciae* and of Whig writers. To him the King is a mere official created by the people for their own behoof[1]. Like Locke and Rousseau, he will allow omnipotence to no adminis-tration, and would apparently, like Rousseau, regard all forms of constitution as liable to change at the will of the sovereign people. The basis of the argument, where it is not historical, is utilitarian, and Hotman has frequent recourse to the maxim *Salus populi suprema lex*[2].

Here, then, are the same ideas, as were at the bottom of English theories of popular rights in the seventeenth century. Proclaimed first of all by Huguenots, they passed over to the ultramontane supporters of the League, when the death of the Duke of Alençon left Henry of Navarre the heir

Compari-son with English theories of resistance.

[1] "Deinde cum illi populi Regem sibi crearent, (sicuti et jam prius dictum est et postea dicetur) perabsurdum est existimare populum a Rege potius, quam Regem a populo denominatum" (58).

[2] It is noticeable that Hotman adduces in proof the limited character of the French monarchy, the admitted fact that the Salic law was unalterable, and that the treaty of Troyes was invalid for that reason. It is curious how completely this weak point in their position escaped the notice of most supporters of the Divine Right of Kings. In one and the same breath they assert that the succession is fixed by a fundamental law, and that the king is absolutely sovereign.

to the French Crown. Henceforward they become identified with Papal pretensions. The great treatise of Barclay, *De Regno*, is directed against Buchanan, Brutus, and Boucher, the Scotch, the Huguenot, and the Papalist opponents of the rights of the Crown and of the inviolability of the Salic law[1].

Theory of Divine Right of Kings. It is now, in the later years of Henry III. and the earlier of his successors, that there appears a well-defined theory of the French monarchy. Against the Papal claims to interfere with the internal politics of France and to alter the succession as by law established, the Divine Right of Kings and the fundamental character of the Salic law are emphatically asserted.

Similarity to English doctrine. The main arguments are similar to those employed by English controversialists. Kings are of Divine appointment, all resistance to them is therefore sin[2]. The Pope has not and never had authority to depose princes[3]. Since the King's rights come directly from God, the Pope can have no power to take away what he never granted[4]. The deposition of Childeric was merely the formal ratification of a change, that had long ago taken place and affected the name, not the reality of kingship. It was effected with the consent, not by the authority of the Pope. Perhaps the deposition was not quite

---

[1] For a complete account of Huguenot and League politics see Armstrong, *The Political Theory of the Huguenots* (*Eng. Hist. Rev.* IV. 13) and *The French Wars of Religion.*

[2] Barclay, *De Regno*, 113.

[3] E.g. Toussaint Berchet, *Pium Consilium*, Pars I.

[4] Berchet (Goldast, III. 163).

justifiable and were better forgotten; it was a case of
doing a little wrong, that a great right might result[1].
The instances of royal repudiation of Papal interference are duly recorded; and the usual Scriptural
passages and illustrations are brought into play[2].
The position of the Emperor in regard to the Pope
is affirmed to be one of superiority.   This is an
important element in the controversy; for the
Carolingian monarchs are regarded as kings of
France.   The translation of the Empire is thus invested with significance, from the French, as from
the Imperialist standpoint, and the treatment of
Julian by his subjects receives, as usual, its meed of
attention[3].   It is not easy to single out any one
name as pre-eminent, in the case of a doctrine so
widespread.   Yet the fact that the theory of the
Divine Right of Kings was in its origin a weapon of
anti-papal controversy, is made plain by the treatise
of Berchet in favour of Henry IV. and comes out in
the collection of Gallican writings made by Pithou[4].

Special points, for comparison with English theory, *Points of*
may be indicated.   In the first place comes the *difference between*
difficulty (before alluded to) inherent in the circum- *English*
stances of French Catholic writers.   Barclay and *and French*
others are clearly hampered by the necessity of *doctrines.*

[1] Masson, *Responsio in Franco-Galliam*, 126.

[2] The following is a specimen of the mode of argument : "Nec
enim solum propter iram, id est metu poenae, illis [regibus] obedien-
dum est, sed propter conscientiam, quia nimirum omnes scire
oportet, id est divina voluntate et constitutione fieri debet."
Servin (Goldast, III. 200).

[3] Barclay, *De Potestate Papae* (Goldast, III. 635).

[4] *Les Libertez de l'Eglise Gallicane.*

admitting the spiritual claims of the Pope and his title
to the obedience of the clergy. Barclay is unable to
take the same line as Imperialist or English writers
and to affirm the absolute necessity of unity in the
sovereign authority.   He is content to admit that
the Papal and Regal power are equal, and must
respect one another[1]. At bottom he holds the notion,
also held by Presbyterians, that Church and State are
two separate kingdoms, each a 'societas perfecta.'
He will allow no exemptions to the clergy from the
operation of the ordinary law, and even hints a wish
that excommunication should be unaccompanied by
civil disabilities[2].

Other writers, such as Du Moulin[3] and Servin[4],
are found arguing like Ockham or Marsiglio, that
Christ's kingdom is not of this world, and that the
whole doctrine of Papal sovereignty is based upon a
fallacy.   But all alike are clear, that the prince is to
be obeyed, although he be excommunicate or a
heretic. All affirm that kings are accountable to God
alone, and above the restraints of civil law; only
natural law can lay commands upon a king, says
Servin[5]. All are agreed that subjects must obey
for conscience' sake, and not merely for wrath.
1592. Servin also has a lengthy argument to prove
that coronation and unction are mere ceremonies
and no essential part of the regality, and that
the coronation oath gives the people no rights

---

[1] Barclay, *De Potestate Papae* (Goldast, III. 645).
[2] *Ibid.* c. xxxiv.   [3] Goldast, III. 63.   [4] *Ibid.* 241.
[5] His argument is strange; the Pope is *solutus legibus*, therefore
a fortiori the king is also. Servin, *Vindiciae* (Goldast, III. 197).

against him. It is a pious custom only; it will not affect Henry's authority, though the Archbishop of Rheims refuse to crown him, as a heretic[1].

In regard to the Salic law more than one line is taken. Du Moulin finds in it evidence of the perfection of the French monarchy, as founded on the model of the Davidic kingdom[2]. Bodin seeks a philosophical justification for it as the ideal mode of succession[3]. Most writers content themselves with the declaration that the custom is a fundamental law and may not be violated by the King. They do not, as a rule, lay claim to any special Divine sanction for it, but declare that the law of succession in all kingdoms is of merely human origin; obedience to the lawful successor is a Divine ordinance[4]. The *Apologia Catholica* is clearest in its exposition of the point. There can be little doubt, that the stress necessarily laid on so plainly artificial a rule as that of the Salic law, gives to the French theory a far more legal aspect than had the English. Past

The Salic Law. 1561.

---

[1] Goldast, III. 209 sqq. Cf. also *Apologia Catholica*, 100 sqq. Bodin takes a similar view, supporting it by the maxim *The king never dies*. This aphorism, as a proof of inherent right, is a favourite argument of French, as of English writers; it is the most effectual way of disposing of any claims, that kingship is elective or founded on compact.

[2] Du Moulin, *De Monarchia Francorum* (Goldast, III. 51).

[3] Bodin, *De la Republique*, VI. 5.

[4] "*De jure divino est servare veram fidem et religionem; de jure autem humano est, quod hunc aut illum habemus regem.*" Barclay quotes these words from Bellarmine, and says that he ought to have added, "Ubi hunc vel illum regem semel habeamus, de jure divino est, ut ei in civilibus causis cum omni honore et reverentia pareamus." *De Potestate Papae* (Goldast, III. 659).

struggles and present necessities alike rendered necessary this emphatic assertion of the binding character of the Salic law. Not only was it the ground of Henry's claim, but it was the source of the independence of the French monarchy. For Edward III. was undoubted heir to the French Crown, had there been no such rule. Thus the sentiment in its favour had to strengthen it every feeling of patriotic pride at the successful issue of the Hundred Years' War[1]. It is a commonplace with French writers that the treaty of Troyes was invalid, for it gave to Henry V. and his heirs the reversion of the Crown, and a treaty to violate the Salic law is void[2]. The vividness with which men realized the distinctive character of the rule of succession, as giving to the French monarchy a perfection lacking to other kingdoms, made it the more impossible for them to claim universality for so peculiar a system. There is no such attempt as that made by Filmer, to seek for hereditary monarchy

---

[1] Du Moulin thus describes the close of the Hundred Years' War: "Tandem vero Angli spe sua frustrati, *a lege antiquissima Salica* dejecti sunt." Goldast, iii. 51.

[2] Servin, whose main source of inspiration is hatred of Spain, declares that even if the League could make good its point, there would be no advantage gained by Spain, for England's claims would have been valid, if the Salic law were not binding. "Sed ista dicentes non animadverterunt se non tam Hispaniam et Guisianam causam, quam Anglicam defendere" (Goldast, iii. 206). It was no wonder that the Salic law awakened such passionate enthusiasm; for if the Hundred Years' War be taken into account, it seems true to say that it was the salvation of France. The claim of Edward III. was far better than that put forward by Philip II. for himself or for his daughter.

a foundation in the natural constitution of society.
It is of Nimrod, rather than Adam that we hear as
the founder of kingship.   Certainly we come across
comparisons of a kingdom to a family, and of kings
to fathers.   But they are never the basis of the
theory, as in the *Patriarcha* or *The Rehearsal.*   If
agnatic kinship had been regarded as primitive or
universal, there would have been stronger grounds
for a French patriarchal theory of kingship, than
there were for the English.   But it does not appear
that the possibility of such a theory ever suggested
itself.   Besides, it would not have been easy to
derive the doctrine of the French succession from
the common rules of inheritance.   Henry IV. was
not heir of Henry III. at private law; and much
pains is taken by the author of the *Apologia Catholica* to demonstrate that, although the Bourbon
prince was too distantly connected with the Valois
to inherit their private property, he was yet the
lawful heir to the throne[1].   The Crown is regarded as
something different in its nature from mere property;
and a peculiar custom is needful to regulate the
succession to the mystical position of a king.   Bodin
is at pains to declare that the King succeeds not by
right of inheritance or by gift of God, but solely
through the rule of law.   It is easy to see how
different is this view from the English conception of
succession, which is always regarded as mysteriously

---

[1] *Apologia Catholica,* 20.   "Hoc quidem jus regni, inquiunt
Doctores nostri, revera non est hereditarium, sed ad familiam
pertinet, etiamsi nemo in ea existeret, qui succederet in defuncti
bona."

above positive law, founded by God and Nature, and followed in all rightly regulated families.

*Bodin, De
la Re-
publique,
1577.*

To other French writers Bodin stands in somewhat the same relation as does Hobbes to the English supporters of Divine Right. Nominally scientific, his treatise has really the same practical aim as those of Servin and Berchet. All his acuteness and philosophical grasp of the nature of government are directed to one end, that of securing the Crown to the next heir, Henry of Navarre. More clearly perhaps than any previous writer French or English does he realize the nature of sovereignty[1]. Of the conception of a 'mixed' or limited monarchy he is as contemptuous as Hobbes or Filmer or Austin[2]. Quite in the manner of the last, he describes the notes of sovereignty, and defines law as a command of the sovereign generally binding. Sovereignty he declares to be indivisible and inalienable, and upon the question of customary law comes to conclusions similar to those of Austin[3].

[1] *De la Republique*, i. 8, 10.

[2] *Ibid.* ii. 1. Speaking on a 'mixed form of government' he says:—"Je respons qu'il ne s'en est jamais trouué, et qu'il ne se peut faire ny mesmes imaginer, attendu que les marques de souveraineté sont indivisibles." p. 263.

[3] "La coustume prend sa force peu à peu, et par longues années d'un commun consentement de tous ou de la plus part; mais la loy sort en un moment et prend sa vigueur de celuy qui a puissance de commander à tous; la coustume se coule doucement et sans force; la loy est commandee et publiee par puissance et bien souvent contre le gré des subjects; et pour cette cause Dion Chrysostome compare la coustume au Roy, et la loy au tyran: *dauantage la loy peut casser les coustumes et la coustume ne peut deroger à la loy* * * * la coustume ne porte loyer ny peine; la loy emporte

In depth and accuracy of thought his treatise far surpasses the *Leviathan*, and Bodin escapes the pitfall, into which Hobbes fell, of seeking the origin of sovereignty in a contract. Even a *lex regia* is according to him an impossibility in France, for the people never having possessed sovereign authority cannot have transferred it to the Crown.

The practical part of the treatise is much the same as that of other writers. The authority of the Pope is repudiated, although little is said on the subject[1]. The power of the prince is asserted to come from God, and the usual texts are employed to inculcate the duty of absolute non-resistance[2]. Monarchy is shewn to be the best form of government, in an argument of similar character to that of Ockham[3]. But Bodin is more emphatic in his contention, that since the members of a "sovereign number" may disagree, sovereignty should be vested in a single person[4]. Finally, a philosophical

---

tousiours loyer ou peine, si ce n'est une loy permissiue qui leue les defenses d'vne autre loy: et, pour le faire court, *la coustume n'a force que par souffrance, et tant qu'il plaist au Prince souuerain, qui peut faire une loy y adjoustant son homologation. Et par ainsi toute la force des lois civiles et coustumes gist, au pouvoir du Prince Souverain*" (*De la Republique*, 222).

[1] *Ibid.* 190 sqq.

[2] " Qui mesprises son Prince souuerain, il mesprise Dieu duquel il est l'image en terre." *Ibid.* p. 212.

[3] *Ibid.* vi. 4.

[4] *De la Republique*, p. 968. " Il n'est pas besoin d'insister beaucoup pour monstrer que la monarchie est la plus seure [forme de gouvernement], veu que la famille qui est la vraye image d'vne Republique ne peut avoir qu'vn chef, comme nous avons monstré, et que toutes les loix de Nature nous guident à la monarchie, soit que

justification is sought for the rule of the French succession, and the Salic law is alleged to be in harmony with the teachings of nature[1].

Summary.   Thus it appears that in the writings of French controversialists there was developed a theory, which with slight modifications is identical with the English theory of the Divine Right of Kings.   The essential notion is that the King owes his position directly to Divine appointment and is therefore accountable to God alone, and not to the Pope.   From this naturally arises the sense of the absolute duty of non-resistance upon religious grounds.   The King is regarded as above the restraints of positive law, save in the matter of the succession.   This, like the English custom of hereditary succession, is regarded as a constitutional or 'fundamental' law, which may not be violated by King or people or both together.   In English theory the notion appears as indefeasible hereditary right, in the French as the inviolability of the Salic law.   The legendary antiquity of the latter further strengthens the sentiment in its favour, although when Hotman pointed out the true meaning of the passage supposed to prescribe the rule, Servin is content to say, that whatever the origin of the rule, it is a custom of long continuance

nous regardons ce petit monde qui n'a qu'un corps, et pour tous les membres un seul chef, duquel depend la volonté, le mouuement, et sentiment, soit que nous prenons ce grand monde qui n'a qu'un Dieu souuerain; soit que nous dressons nos yeux au ciel nous ne verrons qu'un soleil: et jusques aux animaux sociables, nous voyons qu'ils ne peuuent souffrir plusieurs Roys, plusieurs seigneurs, pour bons qu'il soyent."

[1] *De la Republique*, VI. 5.

and may not be broken[1]. Bodin completely developed the theory of sovereignty, but the position
of French writers, as loyal subjects at once of Pope
and King, renders many of their utterances on this
subject less clear than those of Englishmen far
inferior in ability.

How far, then, was English political thought *Influence of French upon English theory.* actually influenced by these writings? It is impossible to say. It is however plain that the
English theory of Divine Right was a plant of
indigenous growth. However much French writers
may have done to influence English thought, or to
render general a sentiment in favour of Divine Right,
yet assuredly English theory did not arise out of
French. On the other hand the position of England
as an ally of Henry III. and Henry IV., the unpopu-
larity of the Guises including Mary Stuart, and the
hatred of the Spanish monarchy and of all schemes
for advancing its power would tend in various ways
to attract English sympathy to the side of those who
were defending the French monarchy from Papal
aggression and Spanish intrigue. Further, there is
some evidence of direct influence. The treatise of
Bodin in particular largely formed men's notions of
government in the next century. It was translated
into English and made a text-book at Cambridge.
There is no question of the great effect of Bodin's
writings upon those of Hobbes and Filmer and
Leslie; and he is quoted by various other writers.
There can hardly be any doubt, that the comparatively thorough understanding of the doctrine of

[1] Goldast, III. 207.

sovereignty evinced by some of the least able among English writers was due to Bodin rather than to Hobbes, who was hated as an 'atheist' and despised as a believer in the original compact[1].

France and Scotland. A further source of influence is to be found in the relations of France to Scotland. The close connection between the two countries led to the migration to France of some Scotch Catholics, who would look with unfriendly eyes at the attempts of the Presbyterian leaders to dominate the politics of their country, whether by deposing Mary Stuart or menacing her son. The theory of popular govern- *Apologia pro Regibus.* ment propounded by Buchanan was met by a reply from Blackwood, a Scotsman settled in France. Buchanan was again one of the chief objects of attack *De Regno.* in the *De Regno* of Barclay, another Gallicised Scot. That Barclay should have announced upon the title-page that his book was a reply to a Scotch Pres-byterian, a Huguenot, and a French Papalist writer is evidence of the connection between the political ideas of France and Scotland. This book was dedi-cated to Henry IV. But Barclay never forgot that

---

[1] It is worthy of note that Bodin in more than one place expresses himself in the strongest terms on the subject of the sovereignty being vested in the English king. In the coexistence of the privileges of the English Parliament and of the unlimited authority of the Crown, he finds evidence of his contention, that conciliar assemblies, whatever their power and antiquity, are no legal check upon the 'sovereign.' From Elizabeth's treatment of the House of Commons in respect to the succession he infers that Parliament has no real power to control the action of the Crown. *La Republique*, I. 8, pp. 139 sqq. "La souueraineté appertient pour le tout sans diuision aus Roys d'Angleterre, et les estats n'y ont que voir."

he was a Scotsman and that James I. needed to be
defended in the exercise of his Divinely granted
authority. Had it not been for the latter making
it a condition that Barclay should renounce Catholicism, he would probably have returned to Scotland,
there to find a new field for controversy in the sacred
cause of monarchy[1]. But the influence of both
Barclay and Blackwood upon the mind of James is
unquestionable, and through this channel, if no other,
they must have influenced English thought. Filmer,
indeed, singles them out along with Heywood as
his chief forerunners, and regards their utterances
as a complete expression of the rights of kings.
Barclay's treatise *De Potestate Papae* was translated
into English in 1611, a proof that his influence was
not confined to France. Thus there is a chain of
connection between the English and French theories
of Divine Right. French theory and practice must
certainly have influenced these Scotch writers. They
could hardly enter into the controversy against
'Brutus' or Boucher, without taking account of
French writings in support of monarchy. Nor could
Scotsmen, living in France, remain unaffected by
what was going on around them and by the circumstances which led to a large body of French Catholics
supporting the Divine Right of Henry IV. There
can be no doubt that the earlier struggles of
Huguenots, Leaguers, and *Politiques* all contributed
to the developement of English political thought in
the seventeenth century, whether in the direction of
Divine Right or of the original compact.

[1] *Dict. of Nat. Biog.*, III. 173.

Blackwood's two works, *De Vinculo Religionis et Imperii* and the *Apologia pro Regibus*, are instances of the double aspect of the theory. The former treatise was written in order to emphasize the connection between the true faith and the doctrine of non-resistance. Its first two parts published in 1575 are written to shew that Calvinism involves a theory of resistance and is therefore false. The book is a protest from a strong Roman Catholic against the clericalism of the Presbyterian system. Exactly as Anglican divines affirm the Papal claims to be heretical, because they tend to dissolve the bond between sovereign and subjects, so Blackwood contends that Calvinism is proved to be false by its teaching of resistance[1]. He complains that the new system takes away all freedom from states: whereas true religion is ever the support of government, and forbids resistance even to tyrants[2]. The inference is that religion is the only security of states,—that there will be an end of law and order if false sects are permitted to exist. It is a sense of the political danger involved in toleration that prompts the author to write. The aim of most writers is to

---

[1] "Religio quae semper hucusque regnorum conservatrix fuit, nunc temporum in reges armatur. Ex quo apparet *veram non esse religionem,* sed larvatam hypocrisim et perfidiam personâ religionis indutam, eo detestabiliorem, quo meliore se auctore jactitat." (*De Vinculo,* 261.)

[2] "Quae, vestram fidem, conscientiae libertas quae in effraenam progressa licentiam, nihil imperio, nihil reipublicae, nihil moribus, nihil legibus liberum reliquit?" (*De Vinculo,* 262.) "Jamne religione perfidiam velabant suam? At religio servat ac tuetur, non labefactat, non evertit imperia." (*Ibid.* 289.)

inculcate the religious duty of obedience, that of Blackwood is to assert the political necessity of persecution.

The third part of the book was not published until after the assassination of Henry IV. and is notable as containing a very strong condemnation of the League. The author is nearly heartbroken to think that any Catholic should have borrowed the maxims of Protestants. The interest of this treatise is great, for it affords complete justification for the manner in which Anglican divines identified Papist and Dissenting principles of governments. Blackwood makes the same identification from the opposite point of view. His argument is that no true Catholic can approve resistance, therefore all who profess to approve it in defence of the Catholic cause are in reality on the side of the Protestants. The Anglican view is that no true Protestant can approve resistance, and therefore that those Dissenters who allow it in the cause of Protestantism are Papists in disguise.

The *Apologia pro Regibus* is interesting in a different way. Whether or no it be out of compliment to the reputation of Buchanan, as a classical scholar, the inspiration of the book is largely classical[1]. Although Scripture is sometimes cited, the

---

[1] Blackwood's position as at once a strong royalist and a devoted Papalist is remarkable. In the last part of the *De Vinculo* he extols the Pope's power, but avoids all reference to the deposition of Childeric or any disputed case; he is careful to confine himself to the perfectly harmless instances of royal reverence for the person of the holy Father. But in the

bulk of the illustrations and arguments are from classical history or philosophy. Appeals to Roman law are frequent and the secular tone of the whole is remarkable. Perhaps Blackwood thought that his former work said enough upon the religious side. Or it may be, that the cause lay in the position of the writer as a Roman Catholic defending against Presbyterian subjects a King who was known to be a heretic. The book is further interesting for its references to England, which to Blackwood as to Bodin, is a clear instance of undiluted absolutism. Certainly if the derided principle of a mixed monarchy were proved to have no force in England, it would hardly be thought to exist in France or Scotland. Blackwood, who is a strong Anglophobist, declares that neither in England nor certain other countries can the people be admitted to share the sovereignty, even with the consent of the King[1]. He denies the validity of Henry the Eighth's testamentary devolution of the Crown; for the succession descends by an immutable law to the next of kin,

Apologia pro Regibus his views come out more clearly. He cannot understand why Buchanan should object to the Pope doing what he approves in his own ministers (121). The deposition of Childeric was done not at the bidding, but with the consent of the Pope, and therefore implied no popular rights against the prince (197). He ascribes sovereignty to the Pope and declares him to be as far superior to other monarchs as they are to their subjects. Yet he admits an ultimate power in the council to depose for heresy. But since this power is never exercised, save in cases of Papal heresy, no inference of popular sovereignty can be drawn from it. The people are no judge of truth (201—4).

[1] *Apologia*, 6.

not as his father's heir, but as the legitimate ruler
of the kingdom[1]. Blackwood's theory of sovereignty
is complete with this exception. Monarchy may not
be divided or shared in any way. Yet he regards
force as the origin of kingship, a view curiously unlike that of other writers, while Nimrod is clearly
the first king[2]. He is so anxious to assert that the
king is above the law, that unlike Justice Berkeley
he denies that he is *lex loquens*. He declares that
all laws only retain their force through the tacit
assent of the sovereign at his accession[3], while in
regard to local laws and customs he approaches the
Austinian maxim, "Whatever the sovereign permits,
he commands[4]."

---

[1] *Apologia*, 73 sqq. "Reges non regum sed regni sunt heredes"
(112).

[2] *Ibid*. ch. VII.   [3] *Ibid*. ch. XI.

[4] "Neque tamen eam vim ac firmitatem habent, ut a principe
mutari non queant, cuius tum in leges, tum in homines potestas
nulla ratione definiri potest" (*Ibid*. 110). Buchanan desired a mixed
form of government, in which the King should have the supreme
executive, the judges interpretative, the people legislative power.
Blackwood ridicules this, and pertinently asks, "Non attendis
legis interpretationem legis vim obtinere?" (ch. XIII.). He shews
that there could be no supreme power in Buchanan's ideal state
with its three ultimate authorities independent of one another.
"Regem populo subesse iubes, quem populo vis inuito legem im-
ponere. Populo summam rerum attribuis, quem reluctantem et
inuitum regis imperio subiicis. Sed qui fieri potest ut idem
patiatur et agat? idem dominatur et serviat?" (295). The whole
of Chapter XXXIII. is an argument in favour of monarchy as the
expression of the principle of unity in all states. It is noteworthy
that he regards this as the supreme effort of art, not nature;
he apparently regards the family as an artificial organization.
He finds it necessary to point out to his opponent that all states

Previous enquiry necessary to the understanding of seventeenth century controversy.

This long preliminary investigation has shewn the causes at work in mediæval England, in the conflicts within the Holy Roman Empire, in the French Wars of Religion, and in the circumstances of the English Reformation, which contributed in various ways to the development of a theory of kingship more uncompromising, narrow, and absolutist than had yet been prevalent in England.

It is now possible to approach the political controversies of the seventeenth century with some prospect of understanding why they took the shape they did. The ideas have arisen of Divine Right, of a 'fundamental law' of succession, of sovereignty, and on the other hand of the original compact, and of the duty of resistance at the bidding of the Church. It remains to view these notions welded into harmonious theories, to trace the process by which they were superseded, and to estimate the practical effect upon later ages of their once having been prevalent.

contain some supreme authority, that the Roman or Athenian democracy or the Venetian oligarchy ruled with exactly that 'regal,' i.e. sovereign power which Buchanan thinks it possible to eliminate from the commonwealth (193).

CHAPTER VII

FROM JAMES I. TO THE JACOBITES

THERE were many reasons why James I. should *James I.*
hold the doctrine of the Divine Right of Kings in *and the*
Theory of
its strictest form. His claim to the throne of *Divine*
England rested upon descent alone; barred by *Right.*
two Acts of Parliament, it could only be successfully maintained by means of the legitimist
principle. Further, it was disputed by the Roman
controversialists, who had not sufficient hope of
converting James to make them love his title.
Doleman's attack on the hereditary principle is
written from the Papalist standpoint. But it was not
only from the Roman side that the position of James
was threatened. Presbyterianism in Scotland, as
expounded by Knox or Buchanan, and inwoven with
politics by Murray and Morton, was a system of
clericalism as much more irritating and meddlesome,
as it was stronger and more popular in its basis than
that of the Papal sovereignty. Even had there been
no question of the English throne, there was enough
in the position of a king, thwarted and insulted on
all hands by the ministers of an upstart and narrow
communion, to bring him into approval of a theory,

which asserted against Papist and Presbyterian alike
that every soul without benefit of clergy is subject
to the royal authority, for the secular power is ordained by God alone and may not be controlled by
Pope or minister.   Nor could the influences at work
also in England and France, which led to the theoretical exaltation of monarchy, have been devoid of
effect upon the mind of James.   Thus it is no matter
for surprise, that at a time, when the sons of Zeruiah
were too strong for him, and he felt his authority a
mockery before the insolent representatives of ecclesiastical bigotry, James should promulgate with
logical completeness and grasp with the tenacity of
a narrow, but clear-sighted intellect the theory of
the Divine Right of Kings.   In the *True Law of
Free Monarchies*, which saw the light five years
1598.   before the death of Elizabeth, is to be found the
doctrine of Divine Right complete in every detail[1].
On his accession Parliament passed a statute which
purported not to give James a title, but merely to
declare his inherent right[2].   This would seem evidence that the theory of Divine Right was by this
time generally prevalent.   Yet though, as was shewn
above, approaches had been made to it in more ways
than one, it does not appear as yet to have taken

[1] There is an error on this point in the article in the *Dictionary
of National Biography*.   There it is stated by Gardiner that 1603
was the date of its appearance.   But it was published anonymously
in 1598.

[2] 1 Jas. I., c. 1.   See Appendix A.   Cf. also Coke's *Reports*,
VII. 10 b: "The king holdeth the kingdom of England by birthright inherent, by descent from the blood royal, whereupon
succession doth attend."

much hold of the popular imagination or even to have been fully grasped by those who professed to believe it. *Inconsistency of popular opinion.*

Evidence of this is to be found in Overall's *Convocation Book*. This was avowedly intended to be an authoritative exposition of the doctrine, but it exhibits a curious inability to understand what it actually involved, and is very different from the perfectly harmonious system of the royalists of the Restoration or of James himself. The Canons are emphatic on the Divine authority of *de facto* governments[1]. The language of the book on this point so greatly alarmed the King that he wrote irritably to Archbishop Abbot, bidding him not to meddle in matters too high for him[2]. James was justified in declaring that, should Philip of Spain succeed in conquering the country, his right to the throne would be Divine on the principles of the *Convocation Book*, and Englishmen would be precluded from ousting the usurper in favour of the lawful king. The compilers were so deeply imbued with the root idea of the theory of Divine Right, that secular government is lawful without Papal or clerical confirmation, that they were unable to attach due importance to the ' organic details ' of the

[1] Canons XXVIII—XXXIII.

[2] The letter is printed in the edition of the *Convocation Book* in the Library of Anglo-Catholic theology. The book was, on account of this, not published until 1690. There is a strange inconsistency in the letter of James ; for he complains of the Canons as not affording a justification of England in assisting the United Provinces.

doctrine, or to distinguish between claims founded on force and the right of conquest.

The theory not yet generally accepted. James on the other hand met with a rebuff, when he attempted to expound his views of the inalienable character of sovereignty. The irritation of Parliament at his assertion, that, since all its privileges were originally granted by the Crown, they were liable to be revoked by the same authority, may be taken as fairly representing the general sentiment at this time. Further, the answer of Coke to the King's request that he might sit as judge in the courts of law, is a precursor of the coming breach between the supporters of the sovereign rights of the Crown and the upholders of the Common Law. However, in Calvin's case the personal character of allegiance was asserted to the full[1], and the decision of Bates's case[2] affirmed the doctrine that no King may materially

[1] The unanimous opinion of the judges decided that allegiance is due by the law of nature and God and may not be altered, and is due to the person of the King, not to his politic capacity. It was greatly to exalt the position of the King to declare that the mere fact of his being King of England and Scotland so united the countries that henceforward no one born in one of them was an alien in the other. And the language in which this is declared still further exalts the Crown: "Whatsoever is due by the law or constitution of man may be altered: but natural legiance or obedience of the subject to the sovereign cannot be altered; *ergo* natural legiance or obedience to the sovereign is not due by the law or constitution of man. Again, whatsoever is due by the law of nature, cannot be altered, but legiance and obedience of the subject to the sovereign is due by the law of nature; *ergo* it cannot be altered." Coke's *Reports*, VII. 25 a.

[2] Prothero's *Statutes*, 340—353.

diminish the rights of sovereignty, therefore that the statutes of Edward I. and Edward III. prohibiting unlimited customs did not bind their successors.

Mainwaring's *Sermons* published in 1628 are evidence at once of the prevalence of the doctrine and of its slow progress. The preacher asserts the Divine basis of royal authority and the right of the King to satisfy his necessities as seems good to him. Laud, however, thought the publication of these sermons inexpedient and endeavoured to prevent it[1]. When the character of Laud's own opinions as to royal authority are taken into account, this fact is significant of the popular attitude on this subject. As yet the country would not swallow the doctrine that was so palatable to it during the latter half of the century. Not that there was much disloyalty. Up to a much later date the nation as a whole was profoundly loyal to the monarchy. But it was not until extreme theories of popular rights aroused the antagonism of the large class who held to the old order, that counter theories of a royal sovereignty uncontrolled by custom became at all widely prevalent.

From the time however that the conflict between King and Parliament entered upon its acute stage there grew up a passionate sentiment of loyalty to the Crown, which would be satisfied with nothing less than the doctrine of Divine Right in its extremest form. As a popular force in politics the theory

The doctrine grows into popularity during the Civil War.

---

[1] See Gardiner, *History of England*, vi. 208, 9.

hardly exerted much influence until the time of the
Long Parliament.   Henceforward Divine Right becomes the watchword of all supporters of the rights
of the Crown, at least until the Revolution.   The
most servile Parliament of Henry VIII., or that
which recognized with such fulsome redundance the
flawless title of James I., would scarcely have suffered
the employment of such terms, as those which in
1640 gave expression to the sentiment of the great
majority of the clergy :—

"The most high and sacred order of kings is of
Divine Right, being the ordinance of God Himself,
founded in the prime laws of nature, and clearly
established by express texts both of the Old and
New Testaments.   A supreme power is given to
this most excellent order by God Himself in the
Scripture, which is, that kings should rule and
command in their several dominions all persons of
what rank or estate soever, whether ecclesiastical or
civil. * * * For any person or persons to set up,
maintain or avow in any their said realms or territories respectively, under any pretence whatsoever,
any independent coactive power, either papal or
popular, (whether directly or indirectly,) is to undermine their great royal office, and cunningly to overthrow that most sacred ordinance which God Himself
hath established ; and so is treasonable against God
as well as against the king.   For subjects to bear
arms against their kings, offensive or defensive, upon
any pretence whatsoever, is at least to resist the
powers which are ordained of God ; and though
they do not invade, but only resist, yet S. Paul tells

them plainly they shall receive to themselves damnation[1]."

It will be observed that there is no mention here of indefeasible hereditary right. None was needed. So long as Charles I. was King and his right to reign undisputed, there was no cause to linger over any question of hereditary right. Only, when the notion is expressly rejected by an influential section of the community, will it become necessary to reaffirm it. It is a truism that dogma never takes definite shape, save as a result of its denial by some thinker or leader. Thus the enthusiastic attachment to the notion of Passive Obedience was due to the Civil War and to the anarchy and tyranny that followed it.

Before that time men might well have misgivings about the duty in extreme cases. But henceforward all who had suffered through the war entertained no doubt but that obedience to the most oppressive of regular authorities would lead to less misery than would resistance. So with hereditary right. It was the execution of Charles and the exclusion of his heir that led men to dwell upon the distinction between a *de facto* and a *de jure* authority. The logical mind of James I. would have found nothing to shock it in royalist pronouncements of this period. The confusion apparent in Overall's *Convocation Book* had now disappeared from the popular mind. No one now, whichever party he favours, but has a clear enough sense that it is possible to assert Divine Right for the lawful heir without predicating it of an usurper.

[1] Cardwell's *Synodalia*, i. 389.

There was now present every condition necessary for awakening men to the sharp distinctions between *de jure* and *de facto* authority and between passive obedience and active resistance however slight.   On the one hand there were the recollection of the arbitrary rule of Charles I. and the general hatred of the methods of Strafford and the Star Chamber.   These would serve to keep men in mind that a lawful government might be intolerably oppressive, and that therefore complete or active obedience would not always be a duty.   On the other hand there was the existence of an upstart military autocracy, claiming to be the inheritor of the secular traditions of the English constitution and demanding universal allegiance, as though there were no question about the legality of its acts.   This would sufficiently ensure that every royalist and every opponent of Cromwell and the Major-generals should realize, that an usurper can have no moral claim to obedience, and that it may be a sacred duty to restore the dispossessed heir.   Passive Obedience and Indefeasible Hereditary Right were no new conceptions; they had long been in the air, and the necessity of combating Papal claims had brought about a doctrine of which they were merely the logical expansion.   But as a force in English politics they owe their importance largely to the Civil War and the successful usurpation of Cromwell.   The horror which was awakened by the execution of Charles, and the melancholy reverence which *Eikon Basiliké* won for the Martyr, would tend to deepen in men's minds their sentiment in favour of royal power, as clothed with mysterious sanctity, and separated by a gulf from all other forms of government. Thus, while the origin of the theory of the Divine Right of Kings is earlier and due to other causes—for no real additions are made to the doctrine expounded by James,—its widespread prevalence was certainly due rather to the Civil War than to any more remote causes. It is the sentiment that brought back Charles II. to his father's throne, and finds expression in the Act of Uniformity[1].

In the Tudor period the doctrine is seen in the *Three* making. It is forged as a weapon in the great con- *stages of the* flict with ecclesiastical aggression. The character *doctrine.* given to it by that controversy remained ever its 1. *Reli-* most essential quality. But the theory of govern- *gious in sixteenth* ment was developing at the same time and partly *century.* through the same causes. In the seventeenth century 2. *Poli-* the real value of the theory in the development of *tical in seven-* political thought appears. Retaining still its anti- *teenth* papal character, it yet exhibits itself more completely, *century.* as the form in which was expressed the discovery of sovereignty. The controversies which rage round the origin of law become now prominent. And the supporters of the doctrine of Divine Right are constantly found fighting for their contention, that law cannot exist independently of some lawgiver, and

[1] Declaration to be made by schoolmasters &c.: "I A.B. do declare that it is not lawful upon any pretence whatsoever to take arms against the king, and that I do abhor that traitorous position of taking arms by his authority against his person or against those that are commissionated by him," 14 Car. II. c. 4. 13 Car. II. c. 1, makes it an offence to declare that either or both Houses of Parliament have any legislative power without the king.

that the ultimate legislative authority in any state is necessarily above all positive law. The value of the theory as a political force is due not to this purely scientific element, but to the testimony it bears to the need of continuity in national life and to the paramount importance to a state of a law-abiding habit. It is easy to deny the doctrine. But those, who do this, should bear in mind that the singularly orderly character of English constitutional development, its freedom from violent changes, would not have been obtained but for the influence of this doctrine.

In contemplating the earlier stages of the Reformation, we are driven to regard with gratitude the men, who alone made possible a justification of the position of independence assumed by the English monarchy against the Pope. But the Divine Right of Kings is more than the effective expression of Gallicanism. It has a purely political side, which comes out most strongly in the middle of the seventeenth century. From the writings of that period we learn how it has stamped upon the English mind the conception of sovereignty, and thereby rendered a service which can hardly be overestimated by all who value the writings of John Austin. Further, in contemplating the Restoration and the period of the Exclusion Bill and the Revolution, we are driven to express the debt of modern times to the faith, through which alone men weathered the storm of political change and achieved the ends of freedom and good government with less of bloodshed and anarchy than has been the lot of any other nation. This passionate sense of the need of continuity in national institutions is perhaps the dominant note of the pamphlets and sermons which poured forth in a deluge, when men were debating the question of a Popish successor to Charles II., and weighing in a balance the risks of persecution and the advantages of an unbroken succession.

A further impulse to enthusiasm was afforded by the Exclusion Bill. The controversy, which raged round that ill-fated measure, was the source on the one hand of the most emphatic expressions of belief in indefeasible hereditary right and passive obedience, and on the other of the clearest exposition of the theory of popular rights. Doleman's pamphlet was reprinted. The theory of original compact and of the purely official character of the kingly dignity was elaborated; while the discussion on the position of Julian the Apostate reveals the similarity of the arguments employed to those of French and Imperialist thinkers, and is evidence that the popular party had no fault to find with the dialectic method of their opponents. *The Exclusion Bill.*

In *Julian the Apostate* Johnson argues that the inference commonly drawn from the obedience of the Christians to an unbelieving Emperor is false, for as a matter of fact they did not recognize his authority, and S. Gregory Nazianzen had fears that his father the Bishop would have kicked the Emperor[1]. To this it is replied in *Constantius the Apostate,* that the assertions are unfounded and are a libel upon Christians; further, that if *Johnson and his opponents.*

[1] Johnson's *Works,* p. 21.

they were true, it would not affect the argument, for Christians recognized Constantius and obeyed him, although he was an Arian. Thus the duty of obedience to a heretic sovereign was demonstrated. The acknowledged dangers to be apprehended from James lead men to emphasize the duty of *passive* obedience. Tears and prayers are repeatedly declared to be the only lawful weapons against a tyrant. It was felt that there might ere long be need of them. The Doctrine of the Cross, as it is called, is written up with much enthusiasm in a host of pamphlets and sermons.

1681.
Filmer's
'Patri-
archa.'

It was shortly after this time that Filmer's *Patriarcha* was first published. The work won great and deserved popularity as the ablest justification of the extreme royalist doctrine. Filmer had the acuteness to see that of the two modes of argument, that of relying upon a medley of Scripture texts, forbidding resistance and asserting Divine sanction for kingship, and that of claiming that monarchy is in accordance with the teachings of nature, the latter rested upon a far more solid basis. It is always possible to explain away single texts of Scripture. Indeed no one nowadays but knows that, when S. Paul and S. Peter enjoined obedience to established government as a religious duty, they were far from considering the question of men's duty in extreme cases, and had no notion of discussing the right of insurrection. Whether or no Filmer was aware of this may be doubted. Probably he was not, as in another place he founds an elaborate argument on the thirteenth

of Romans[1]. But he was instinctively conscious
that this was not the best method of establishing
his position.   In his treatise the textual method
of argument falls quite into the background before the prominence given to the conception that *Changed
monarchy is founded in nature. The idea is not *mode of
argument.*
new. It was introduced with more or less of completeness by most of the supporters of Divine Right.
Indeed Harrington alludes to it as a recognized
argument. But with them it is rather an illustration
or a figure of rhetoric than the basis of an argument.
Filmer rests his whole system upon it. He attempts
to find the origin of kingship in the natural constitution of society, and bases it neither on force nor on
popular sanction, but on human nature, as formed
by the Creator.   Most writers regard the fact that
kingship is founded by Divine ordinance, as proved
by the institution of the kingdom of Israel or by
isolated phrases in Daniel or Proverbs; to this proof
they are content to add that kingship is indeed
natural, as may be seen in a family or the animal
kingdom among geese or sheep. Filmer on the other
hand contends that kingship is natural, and that
therefore it must be ordained by God, the author
of nature. His whole argument depends on the
identification of the kingdom with the family, and
of royal with paternal power. That the King is
the father of his people was a metaphor frequently
employed by writers in favour of monarchy. Filmer
expands the metaphor into an argument, and founds
upon it the only rational system of absolutist

[1] Preface to *Observations on Aristotle.*

Many writers do not make the patriarchal theory the basis of the doctrine. politics. The patriarchal conception of society is far from being of the essence of the theory of the Divine Right of Kings; it is merely the best argument by which it is supported. Some supporters of the theory scarcely refer to the idea, most however do so, but employ it very loosely, and clearly without the notion that it was a far better justification for their opinions than the phrase, " By me kings reign, and princes decree judgment." King James uses the analogy avowedly as a metaphor. Sir Dudley Digges declares that the King is " without a metaphor the father of his people," evidence that the comparison is commonly regarded as a mere figure of speech. Like other authors he regards the marriage tie, as equally typical of the bond between King and people, and is ready with the argument against resistance, " What God hath joined, let no man cut asunder." Sanderson, like Bodin, declares that kings have more powers than parents, and that a monarch is " a brother and something more." Mainwaring regards the bond between King and people as fourfold, consisting of the ties that bind (1) The Creator and the Creature, (2) Husband and Wife, (3) Parents and Children, (4) Masters and Servants[1].

These are only a few instances of the general view, which is merely that allegiance is the strongest of all bonds and includes all other human ties. Of any general patriarchal theory of kingship there is little evidence before Filmer[2]. It is his merit to have

[1] *Religion and Allegiance*, 3.

[2] S. Thomas Aquinas, who regards the family as something similar to the kingdom, is the type of most thought. Sanderson

discovered that the common metaphor contained
within it the germ of a system far more substantial
in its basis than the ordinary hotch-potch of quotations from Scripture. The popularity of the book is
further evidence that the idea came to most men
with the force of a discovery. For its sole contribution to the theory is the careful elaboration of the
patriarchal conception of kingship. If the notion
had previously been regarded as a necessary element
of the doctrine, it would be hard to account for
Filmer's reputation. Men clutched at the chance,
given them by the *Patriarcha,* of grappling with
their opponents on better terms than were afforded
by the weapons with which they were familiar. At
the same time Filmer can hardly be said to have
been the discoverer of the conception. His book was

says "the master or *paterfamilias* is a *kind* of petty monarch
there" (*Judgment in One View,* p. 106), and argues that "what
power the master hath over his servants for the ordering of his
family no doubt the same at the least, if not much more, hath the
supreme magistrate over his subjects for the peace of the Commonwealth, the magistrate being *Pater Patriæ* as the master is *Pater
familias*" (p. 108). And again, "A governor is a brother too and
something more; and duty is charity too and something more.
If then I may not offend my brother, then certainly not my
governor" (p. 112). *Vox Populi,* a pamphlet against Spain of
1624, is an instance of the loose way in which the patriarchal
power is regarded, even by a writer who seems to approach Filmer.
"Amongst all nations the rule of a family or country was *conferred*
upon the eldest. Until there were kings they were instead of such,
and when there were kings, either they were *chosen out* of these,
or these were their substitutes in such families and places where
they resided" (7). *The Royal Charter granted unto Kings* regards
the Divine origin of kingship as proved by the case of Melchisedec,
who was "without father, without mother" (6).

certainly the occasion of its prevalence, but so wide-spread a metaphor as that of the King being *pater patriae* is sure to be pressed to its full extent by some writers. The arguments of Bodin in favour of monarchy and the phrases employed by Williams, Bishop of Ossory, in a little pamphlet, *Jura Magistratus*, are an indication that men were feeling their way to a system akin to that of Filmer[1].

The importance of Filmer in the history of the doctrine is indeed great. But he deserves to be remembered, less as the most perfect exponent of the theory, than as the herald of its decadence. It is an easy transition from the conception of government as directly established by Divine command to the notion that, since God is the author of nature, whatever is natural has His sanction. Yet the change is great. For direct Divine Right has been substituted a constructive theory of Divine approval. The theological conception of politics is giving way before what may be termed the naturalistic. In this disguised form the theory of Divine Right, as the only possible justification for any political system, lingers on until with the present century the notion of natural rights has fallen into discredit. In a sense it may be said, that Filmer paved the way not only for Locke, but for Rousseau. It is plain that the theory of natural rights, whether vested in King or people, is the next stage of

The constructive theory of Divine Right.

Transition to natural rights.

1644.

---

[1] *Jura Magistratus*, 15: "Every master of a family that ruleth his own household is a *petite* king"; and again, "A kingdom is nothing else but a great family where the king hath paternal power," 22.

developement to the conception that all political systems must find their sanction in the Bible, as the complete Revelation of the Divine Will. Whether the theory be one of Divine Right in the older sense, or of natural rights as a proof of Divine sanction, the motives which lead men to adopt it are the same. It is the desire to find some immutable basis for politics and to lift them above considerations of mere expediency, that prompts men to elaborate systems of Divine or natural rights. They are haunted *Motive to believe in a theory of Divine or natural rights.* with the hope of finding a universal system, superior to time and circumstance, untrammelled by considerations of historical development or national idiosyncrasy. And to both schools, that of the believers in Divine right, whether of Pope or Presbytery or King, and that of the upholders of natural and inalienable, i.e. Divine rights of nations or individuals, the same objections apply. No system of politics can be immutable. It is impossible in framing a doctrine of government to lay down *Fallacies of theories of natural rights.* eternal principles, which may never be transgressed. A universal theory of the state is a chimæra, for historical development and national character are the most important of all considerations in investigating the laws of political development. The arguments, with which Burke encountered the system of the Revolutionary idealists, are equally applicable to the theories of Bellarmine on behalf of the Pope, or of James I. or Filmer in favour of monarchy. The theory of natural rights is the old theory of Divine Right disguised.

Yet it was disguised. There is no denying the

great transformation thought has undergone, when controversialists have abandoned the habit of uncritically compiling a cento of Scripture phrases for arguments. No longer is the Bible regarded as the sole source of political theory. Instead of this, an attempt, however imperfect, is made to seek in the nature of man and the necessity of human society the changeless principles of civil government and inviolable laws of political duty. Once the project of finding an immutable system of politics be granted as worthy of undertaking, it is certainly more reasonable to seek it in the teachings of nature, than in the doubtful import of a fortuitous concourse of Scripture texts. At least it is one step further towards a utilitarian or a historical system of politics, for nature certainly would seem to approve the principle of utility, and it distinctly indicates the importance of developement according to the law of an organism. The first fact, that utility is in accordance with the law of nature, was recognized by Locke and Sidney, while Filmer has certainly more of the historical spirit than any of his opponents, or than some of his predecessors, such as Blackwood. In any case it is the merit of Filmer to have seen, that a natural system of politics was more likely to prove well-founded than a purely theological scheme; or rather to have regarded theology as pointing to nature as the teacher of political philosophy.

Filmer's change of front really gives up the ground. Yet the credit due to him as a political thinker, is not clearly his as a supporter of his own theory. His method paved the way for its overthrow. The older mode of arguing from Scripture texts, as direct Divine injunctions, had this advantage, that it was impregnable to the assaults of criticism, and that neither natural law nor the principle of utility could avail aught against it. In partially deserting the old method of argument Filmer has in reality surrendered the case for Divine Right. In appearance his position is far stronger than that of his predecessors. The reason of this is that his argument approaches more closely to those with which we are familiar. Filmer's theory of Divine Right was expressed in a syllogism:—

What is natural to man exists by Divine Right.
Kingship is natural to man.
Therefore Kingship exists by Divine Right.

This is a sounder mode of procedure than that of collecting a few texts and illustrations from the Bible and ignoring or emptying of their meaning any that make for the contrary view. Yet Filmer's position is far more open to attack than that of the older controversialists. The verse " they that resist shall receive to themselves damnation " is apparently of unmistakeable import, which can only be evaded by sophistry. No arguments from expediency, no fresh reading of history could affect the elaborate accumulation of texts made by Mainwaring in support of his doctrine. The only possible way to meet him was to deny the interpretation or the applicability of the passages quoted. In fact, considerations of utility or historical circumstances could not affect the ordinary argument for Divine Right. But with Filmer's arguments this is not the case. For the whole question of what constitutes the law of nature is involved, and it is easy to argue as did

Locke for the principle of utility, the instinct of self-preservation, as of natural and therefore Divine origin. Both Locke and Sidney, indeed, elevate their own principle of natural rights above any considerations of temporary expediency, and would not allow that the legislature in a state is sovereign, even though it were manifestly expedient that it should be so. But the principle of utility governs much of their thought, and they are justified in regarding its dictates as being every whit as much a law of nature, as the necessity of obedience to government. The theory of natural rights and original compact propounded by the Whig opponents of Filmer is less well-founded and more artificial than the Divine Right of Kings. But the speculations of Locke and Sidney have this of value, that they recognize to some extent the importance of considerations of utility in framing a practicable theory of politics. It is the failure to see this, not the elaboration of an absolutist system, that is the real ground of the puerilities of the royalist school. But in appealing to natural law Filmer was paving the way for the use of this principle of utility to overthrow his idealist system. With those of the old school it was useless talking of utility. They regard the Bible as containing in set terms an emphatic prohibition of resistance, and they put this in the forefront of their argument. Against such a contention no argument from the inexpediency of absolute non-resistance can have any hope of success. The arguments drawn from isolated texts seem to modern readers the most absurd part of the theory of Divine

Right. They are in reality the strength of the
position. If the arguments were absurd, it was not
easy to prove it. But for Filmer the Bible is no
mere storehouse of texts, though he will be ready so
to employ it on occasion. It is the one historical
document which gives authentic information as to
the nature of primitive society. In the early
chapters of Genesis he finds evidence, that society is
as old as humanity, that kingship is an expansion of
family life, and that monarchy is the inalienable
natural power of the father. The value of the
conception is great; it is far less unhistorical or
artificial than the Whig idea of the state, and
contains by implication the pregnant truth that the
state is an organism, not a machine. Yet the
Divinity claimed for kingship is, as has been pointed
out, purely constructive. The protection afforded by *Filmer's*
direct Divine injunction is abandoned; the inspira- *position open to*
tion of the Bible is of service, only so far as was *attack.*
needed to authenticate the account of society given
in Genesis. The truth or falsehood of Mr McLen-
nan's theory of primitive society would have been
a vital matter for Filmer. Had the theory of the
former been accepted, the system of the latter would
have fallen like a house of cards. But the *mutterrecht*
would have had no bearing on the common arguments. Nothing was easier than to meet Filmer
on his own ground, and Locke did so. He asserts
that Filmer has misconceived Genesis, that, as a
fact of history, no such kingly power as was claimed
for him, was ever held by Adam, that, if it had
been, it could have no possible reference to the

power of modern kings. Locke then interrogates his own consciousness, as to what are the natural instincts of men, and infers, on the same ground of natural law as Filmer, a totally opposed conclusion. Filmer's political theory is in brief this. Natural rights are Divine rights. There is one natural right only, the authority of the father. This is preserved in the sovereign power in all states. All men are born slaves. Locke on the other hand asserts, that all men are born free and equal, with inalienable rights granted them by God; that states are founded upon compact from motives of utility, and are not given unlimited authority, for that would be to contradict the law of self-preservation. The point of view of both Locke and Filmer is in reality identical. Both believe that there existed a state of nature, and that true principles of politics may in some way be discovered by investigation into it. Both believe that whatever rights belong to man living in a state of nature are inalienable and may not be taken from him by any form of organized society. Filmer believes that the one inalienable right is the power of the father. He saw what Hobbes and Locke and all believers in the original compact failed to see, that political society is natural and necessary to men, and is no artificial creation of their choice. But his method of proving this is by finding the state of nature in the patriarchal society described in the Bible. He, indeed, believed that there was irrefragable evidence to prove that his state of nature was a historical fact; while Locke and Hobbes were content to urge on *à priori* grounds that theirs must have existed, although there was no evidence to shew it.

In both cases there was the same impassable gulf between the present condition of society and what was believed to be the primitive state. The theory of compact is Locke's method of bridging the gulf. Filmer in this point is less successful. He admits that the heir of Adam is not now to be found, and only escapes the difficulty by means of the principle that possession gives the best right, where none else is to be found. But, as with Locke the rights of man in the state of nature still subsist to be the foundation of political liberty, save in so far as they have been partially surrendered to the civil government, so with Filmer the rights of the father are the foundation of all political society and of the title of every government to the obedience of its subjects.

Gulf between actual society and the state of nature.

Locke of course had no difficulty in pointing out, that it is a strange proceeding to argue Divine appointment for a number of monarchs, who are admittedly the descendants of usurpers, merely on the ground that their ancestors were less scrupulous than those of other men. Locke's destructive criticism is completely effective, owing to the slender bond of connection between the primitive family and modern political society. Thus Filmer's work forms the transition stage between the older views and those of Locke in more ways than one. Not only does it afford the necessary link of developement between theories of Divine and of natural right; but it approaches the schemes of Locke and Rousseau in its singular idealism. It is almost grotesque to treat political theory as though all its problems could be solved by an appeal to the primitive family. The attempt to find in patriarchal authority the sole source of all political rights, and to derive the modern state directly from the Adamic society gives to Filmer's work an air of unreality, which is not shared by that of earlier writers. While Filmer's method was sounder, his system was more artificial than that of his predecessors. The same might be said of Locke with reference to Filmer. His system is as much more unhistorical in its basis, as it is more reasonable in its conclusions, than that of Filmer.

Stages in the development of the theory and subsequent ideas. The change which had thus come over the royalist method of conducting the controversy is significant. The theory of the Divine Right of Kings took its rise as a doctrine of the right of secular governments to be free from clerical interference. In its essential idea the doctrine had been at work in English politics from the days of Henry VIII. So long as there was much to be apprehended from the side of those who claimed a Divine right to control the state in the interests of an ecclesiastical organization, it was necessary to lay stress on the religious side of the argument for kingship. But as this danger tended to disappear, and the doctrine had begun to do its work, secular politics were free to develope on their own lines. Theological systems of politics and purely theological arguments were no longer needed to meet the claims of Pope or Presbytery, and politics entered upon the modern stage. The theory of natural rights is inevitably the next stage of developement. It abandons the attempt to discover in Scripture the sanctions of civil society, and its direct institution by God. Yet it retains the conception of an immutable system of politics, rooted in the nature of man, and not to be changed through motives of mere expediency. Like the theory of Divine Right, the doctrine of natural rights is an attempt to determine à priori the nature of government, the limits of obedience, and the principles which should govern state action. Less even than the theory of Divine Right does it take account of circumstances or historical causes. It proclaims a system of politics, clear, universal, and unalterable, based not on the uncritical study of Scripture, but on what are believed to be the teachings of nature and the dictates of pure reason. Many supporters of Divine Right confined their view to special states, and peculiar circumstances, whatever their system might claim of abstract truth and universality. The supporters of natural rights in most cases paid no regard to racial characteristics or external conditions, but proclaimed a doctrine that should last for all time and be valid for all stages of civilization. Yet if they erred greatly, in seeking an eternal system of rights and duties to govern the fleeting arrangements of political constitutions, at least their plan of seeking political theory in nature had this merit: that they could not altogether ignore the principle of utility. Thus they were one step nearer to modern political theory.

At this point considerations of utility will begin
once more to be of importance, while a further stage
will be the abandonment of the attempt to find an
immutable political theory; and politics will become,
as they are at the present day, purely utilitarian or
historical. It was the work of the supporters of the
Divine Right of Kings to make this possible. It
was impossible for the state to develope its principles,
so long as its very existence, as an independent
power, was constantly threatened by clericalism.
To set it free from ecclesiastical control it was
needful to claim Divine institution for its head.
But when this purpose was realized, and independence attained, the state, secure in its new-found
freedom, may develope principles of politics without
reference to theology. Before, it would have been
at once dangerous and useless so to do. The main
work of the theory of Divine Right was drawing to
a close, although a little remained to be accomplished. It was natural that its supporters should
alter the basis upon which their theory rested.
Men do not desert a belief, until some time
after its main purpose is fulfilled. As has been
seen, there were still potent causes to attach
men to the doctrine. So long as the recollection
was vivid of the martyrdom of Charles and of
the tyranny of Oliver, men would continue to
assert the theory. Besides, all danger from Rome
or Scotland was scarcely over as yet. But the
latter had sufficiently diminished in magnitude, to
admit of the transition from the purely Scriptural to the sociological argument on behalf of

Divine Right[1]. It is also a note of the more general
change from the theological age to the rationalist,
which marked the latter half of the seventeenth
century, and may be discerned in Baxter.

The changed method of conducting the con- *Nalson.*
troversy appears in a work written later, though
published earlier than *The Patriarcha,* Nalson's
Common Interest of King and People. The title 1678.
of this book sufficiently indicates the main line of
argument employed. The author begins with an
elaborate account of the principle of self-preservation
and of the desire of happiness, as the ruling motives
of human nature. No terms could be stronger than
those in which the writer sets forth the universality
of this law of nature, and, were it not for the excellence of the style, the first few pages might have
been written by Bentham. The basis of the theory,
unlike that of Filmer, is utilitarian, although other
proofs are not discarded. There is a short exposition
of the patriarchal theory, but this is not made the
foundation of the system. Monarchy is proved to
be the most perfect form of government by reason
of its antiquity, its universality, its conformity with
human nature, and of the fact that it satisfies the

---

[1] A proof that this was the case is afforded by the writings of
Bellarmine. The Cardinal repeatedly allows to kingship the con-
structively Divine character of being rooted in natural necessity.
But he declares that the Pope has an immediate commission from
God, which kings have not. Their right is indeed Divine, for it is
natural, but it is not, as the Pope's power is, founded on direct
Divine injunction. Against Bellarmine the older writers assert
that the king does hold his power by a direct Divine grant. But
Filmer partially abandons this argument.

great ends of all action, the instinct of self-preservation and the desire of happiness. So far the tone
is strangely modern. Then in a short passage the
writer reverts to the older mode of argument, and
adduces the fourth of Daniel as clear evidence of the
Divinity of Kingship. The book is remarkable for
its lucidity and grasp of principles. It is further to
be observed, that it contains an elaborate demonstration of the incompatibility, not merely of the
Papal sovereignty, but of the Presbyterian system
with the independence of the secular authority and
with the liberty of the subject. Nalson is convinced
that Presbyterianism, if allowed a free hand, is destructive of the freedom of Crown, Parliament, and
individual alike. Here again with all his ability,
which invests the work with an interest lacking to
the usual hash of texts in royalist pamphlets and
sermons, the author has yet surrendered his whole
case by his adoption of the utilitarian standpoint.
In a case like that of James II. will it be possible
seriously to maintain that his continued reign would
be agreeable to the principle of utility? Doubtless
it might be the case, for, as Hobbes thought, the
evils attendant on the most peaceful Revolution may
outweigh every benefit attained thereby. Luther
also had taken the view, that no price was too high
for the peace secured by the power of the prince.
But such a view could never become popular. Unless
the doctrine of non-resistance has something higher
than considerations of utility to recommend it, it
cannot hope to hold its ground. The mass of mankind will never be convinced, that it is useful to

maintain in power a government, which is oppressive beyond limit. But they may be persuaded that it is their duty to do so. If acuter minds have come to the conclusion that a revolution is always inexpedient, the only method of making their opinion practically effective will be by inducing the vulgar to believe that it is always iniquitous. This was the great source of strength to the upholders of Passive Obedience, as the plain teaching of the Gospel. If Christianity be indeed a doctrine of the Cross in their sense, and every kind of tyranny is to be endured by true Christians, there will be no use demonstrating the inexpediency of non-resistance. The more foolish it is from a common-sense point of view, the more clearly is it the duty of those who look beyond this world. What has convenience to do with God's direct command? But with Nalson's system these considerations lose their force, and in his book, even more than in that of Filmer, we see the beginning of the end. But Filmer's patriarchal theory was the necessary transition to the next stage of developement, that represented by Locke and Sidney, while Nalson's thought rather looked forward to a yet further day, when natural rights themselves should be scouted as ridiculous, and political theories be constructed on utilitarian principles alone.

Both Filmer and Nalson were a little in advance *Yet the old* of most contemporary writers. They do no more than *method is still* foreshadow the decadence in store for the old modes *popular.* of thought and argument. Meanwhile, these remain with little diminution in popularity for some time

to come.   The majority of the supporters of Divine
Right, even after the Revolution, use arguments that
differ but slightly from those of the time of the
Commonwealth.   Indeed, one effect of the Revolution
was to turn the eyes of all who did not love it on
the past and to deepen for a time the sentiment
Third in favour of the purely Biblical method of political
stage of theory.   The non-jurors had been beaten by accom-
the theory:
romantic. plished facts.   Like all supporters of "lost causes and
forsaken beliefs," they draw their main inspiration
from the past.   The very fact that men are beginning
to discredit their modes of reasoning as obsolete, will
cause them to cling to them with greater tenacity, as
the loved relics of the order which has passed away.
The *raison d'être* of their party is the sentiment of
romantic attachment to old modes of thought and
feeling, to outworn theories, and to ideals which
practical men have forgotten.   The Jacobite will be
more, not less inclined to lay stress upon the religious duty of Passive Obedience and upon the direct
appointment of kings by God, than was the controversialist of the Restoration, who had, as he hoped,
not merely to justify the past, but to carve out the
future.   To the one Divine Right was a force of
practical value, and its employment part of the
business of life.   To the other it was a memory
and a vain regret.

Prevalence The Revolution and the Act of Settlement
of the
belief even disposed for ever of the doctrine of indefeasible
after the hereditary right, and made it all but impossible
Revolu-
tion. to maintain the theory of non-resistance.   Yet
these results were by no means immediate, so far

as the bulk of Englishmen were convinced. The doctrine indeed could not die out all at once. And the existence of a widespread feeling in favour of the Stuarts is evidence that it did not do so. The Revolution threw on to the side of the Stuarts the whole latent sentiment in favour of all institutions or beliefs of which the life is decaying. The great practical reason for supporting the theory of Divine Right no longer existed. At last all danger to the state from clerical interference was at an end. It became moreover increasingly clear that the doctrine as a pillar of government had done its work, and that the leaders of thought and action, with whom rested the future, had far other aims in view than the conduct of politics in accordance with theological theories of kingship and obedience. But all this tended to beget a sentiment, that was to invest the Stuart line with a dignity, which it never had when in possession, and to bestow upon it a charm, to which no reigning dynasty can lay claim. From 1688 the Stuart cause is the expression of the 'passion of the past'; and the theory that supports it suffers a like change. All men's hatred of what is new because it is new, their dislike of conquering ideas because they are winning, their love of the antique for no reason than that it is not modern, will draw them to the side of the 'king over the water.' The Divine Right of Kings has reached its last stage. At first a method of meeting in argument a foe, whom it was impossible to conquer by force, it grew in weight and efficiency, until it became one of the chief means whereby men justified to themselves the rejection of that Papal supremacy that threatened to retard the free developement of the national states. The deep sentiment of anti-clericalism which it enshrined saved men from the danger of submitting to another and a yet more blighting tyranny of ecclesiasticism, that threatened to suck the life out of state and people with a network of inquisitorial jurisdiction and with a narrow code of life and morality. In the political conflicts of the seventeenth century, in which religion played so large a part, the Divine Right of Kings had been the form in which expression had been found for men's reverence for tradition and for their instinctive sense that progress can never come by trampling on old institutions. Thus the theory was the bulwark of the restored monarchy, by rallying sentiment round the King, as the ancient centre and symbol of national life. It had preserved the continuity of the constitutional system, and was probably a main cause of the tranquillity, which marked the English alone among the Revolutions

Effect of the theory in maintaining the continuity of the English state. of history. By a fiction, as expedient as it was transparent, the sentiment in favour of obedience to law was prevented from receiving any shock, and those who smile at the falsity of the assertion that James II. 'abdicated the throne' would do well to bear in mind that it is far easier to shake the law-abiding sentiment by an admitted break with the legal system of the past, than it is to repair it by any improvement in the constitution. But, if with a certain amount of ingenuity the doctrine of non-resistance might still be maintained to be a principle of English constitutional life, it was not so with

indefeasible hereditary right, which, after suffering
a shock at the Revolution, received an irretrievable
blow in the Act of Settlement. Nor was it possible
any longer to contend that the King was absolutely
sovereign, and accountable to God alone. Henceforward the Divine Right of Kings is the expression
of regretful aspirations, and in no sense of actual fact.
From a practical force it has become a romantic
sentiment. Pity for the unfortunate and loyalty to
a forlorn hope were now the main elements in the
faith. Its true character is to be found in that burst *The*
of lyrical lament, that echoed with pathetic melan- *Jacobite Songs.*
choly of tone the longings of men, who were ever
"looking backwards." It is in this rather than in
sermons or treatises that we must seek the source
of such lingering vitality, as still remained to the
doctrine. No fresh developement in argumentative
method was possible, and the writings of Leslie are
in many respects little more than an expansion of
Filmer. But perhaps in the very brilliancy of the
non-juring controversialist, in his pungent satire and
acute criticism we may have an indication, that the
defence of the doctrine is becoming rather a *jeu
d'esprit* than a serious labour. Once an intellectual
weapon against the assaults of Rome, the by no
means contemptible expression of a very practical
determination to ensure for the state a free hand,
the doctrine in losing its value as a force has acquired a certain æsthetic interest. The feeling which
keeps it alive is partly artistic, partly sentimental, and
becomes vivid to us in the song for the blackbird,
and the legendary halo surrounding Bonnie Prince

Charlie. This phase of the belief is enshrined for ever in the novels of Sir Walter Scott. The use, which more recent writers of romance have made of the Jacobite sentiment, is a further proof that the main interest of the belief after 1688 is æsthetic. This aspect of the doctrine is indeed so familiar to us, that it is hard to realize that it ever possessed any other. We find it easy enough to regard with a certain tolerance a faith, which is to us a mere romantic pose. But it is not so easy to recognize, that this was only the latest phase in the history of a theory, which had been a force of great practical importance, the expression (in obsolete forms) of deep truths of political philosophy and of a necessary stage of political developement. That all this was the case there is ample evidence to prove. But the practical work of the doctrine was done before the Revolution, and it is well to realize that the tendency to hold it was the inevitable feeling, that touches all dying causes with a sunset charm. It is those, who find artistic gratification in contemplating with half-simulated regret an order which is no more, who will more and more make up the diminishing band of Jacobite enthusiasts.

It is worthy of remark that Swift and Boling-broke, the two most brilliant practical politicians on the Tory side, have neither of them anything but contempt for a doctrine which they regard as absurd and as emptied of all effectual influence. Swift's pamphlet, *The sentiments of a Church of England man*, save in the assertion that the supreme legis-lative power may never be resisted, is utterly unlike

the work of earlier royalist writers. Nor does Bolingbroke like the theory any better. Indeed his criticism
is far more modern in its tone, than that of any other
writer with views resembling his own. His assertion
that " a divine right to govern ill is an absurdity;
to assert it blasphemy[1] " might have been written
a hundred years later, and exhibits the same sort
of ignorance to be deplored in most criticisms of the
doctrine. The real point of it is entirely missed, and
a faith, which had at least in the past exercised great
influence, is exhibited as though it had never been
more than antiquarian pedantry.

Just in so far as for practical men the theory is
ceasing in the reign of Anne to have any interest,
it begins to have a value for all who with whatever
motive are in love with what is antiquated, and is
passing into tradition. There is always a sense of
attachment to a dispossessed house, and some men
still cling to Divine Right as investing with a certain
glamour of mystic import the ancient line and its
God-given title. The Divine Right of the Stuarts
becomes the symbol and the sacrament of the contrast between right and might, between the favour
of men and the justice of God, between the romance
of the past and the sordid turmoil of the present,
between the ideal of a state and the reality of politics.
Perhaps it is not too much to say, that the doctrine
yet survives as an influence through the peculiar
melancholy interest, that is still felt to surround the
ill-fated race, whatever be the light in which their
rule is regarded.

[1] *The idea of a patriot king.*   Bolingbroke, *Works*, II. 379.

Yet the theory had still some vitality.

Yet even as a practical force the doctrine was by no means dead for some time yet. In this connection, the non-jurors may perhaps be disregarded as a small body of idealists. But the insecurity of the new order, the constant intrigues with the court of S. Germains, the perpetual fears of Jacobite risings are a proof that the feeling in favour of the dispossessed dynasty, as alone possessing a lawful title, has by no means spent its force. The incidents of the Sacheverell case are alone evidence that the nation had not as yet made up its mind on the question. Mr Lecky[1] is of opinion that the Revolution was brought about by a small minority of men far in advance of the general body of their countrymen. Had Bolingbroke been the victim of an idea, and proclaimed the Pretender, as Atterbury wished, there would in all probability have been a peaceful restoration of the Stuarts. On the other hand, the failure of the rebellions of 1715 and 1745 shews how little of practical vitality there was about the Jacobite creed. Yet it may well be, that if a great leader had arisen, he might have brought about a successful reaction. Men may follow a statesman in carrying to a successful issue a cause, for which they will not move a finger in doubtful circumstances. Yet it is something that the belief in hereditary right should have been strong enough to cause the only High Church schism in the history of the English Church. At the Sacheverell trial Divine Right is clearly a popular sentiment. Even as late as 1747

[1] *History of England*, I. 19.

a pamphleteer is found lamenting its continued prevalence.

It must not be forgotten, that the English clergy claimed the phraseology of the Bill of Rights in support of their contention that the Revolution did not transgress the principle of non-resistance. The strength of popular belief in the principle is attested by the very insertion of the word "abdicated" in that document. Again, the fiction of the supposititious birth of the Pretender is a proof of the influence the Whigs felt it necessary to counteract. Further, it was possible by skilful omission for the clergy to continue to preach the duty of passive obedience to the established government. Sacheverell was able to allege in his defence that the Revolution was not a case of resistance[1], and that those who brought it about have grossly lied, if they claim that it was. Many, then, even of the loyal clergy are still found maintaining the doctrine of non-resistance. Of the non-juring controversialists Leslie and Hickes are the most interesting.

Berkeley's *Discourse of Passive Obedience* is worthy of note as a specimen of the later method of argument. Nothing is said therein of hereditary right, which cannot well be defended by a supporter of the Act of Settlement. The argument is that government is natural and necessary to the

Berkeley, 1709.

---

[1] Speech of Dr Sacheverell, 4: "My Lords, the Resistance in that passage by me condemned is nowhere by me applied to the Revolution, nor is it applicable to the case of the Revolution, the Supreme Power not being then resisted": cf. also Leslie, *The Best Answer* and *The Rehearsal, passim.*

wellbeing of mankind, that obedience is a natural law, that to natural laws there is never any exception. If once hard cases be admitted as a ground for disregarding the rule, it will be as easy to prove the convenience of murder in certain circumstances, as it is to justify resistance to a tyrant. Thus the transformation of method, which Filmer was found beginning and Nalson carrying a little further, was completed by Berkeley[1]. He deliberately drops the old mode of argument, because, as he plaintively remarks, men will no longer suffer it. He hopes, however, to prove his case by employing the law of nature to endow with immutable and inviolable authority the principle of passive obedience.

At the close of this enquiry may be quoted Bishop Butler[2], whose speculations on government and subjection shew what was the residuum left by the doctrine of Divine Right. Human society and government are in his view part of the constitution and course of nature, and therefore Divine. Obedience is also a part of the law of nature and has therefore Divine sanction. He contends that government, as distinct from mere force, necessarily implies reverence in subjects, and that reverence will be liable to disappear, if it be not founded on the sentiment that authority is the ordinance of God. The duty to obey the prince rests however on the same footing as all other general obligations, which are none of them absolute or without

[1] Berkeley's theory applies to the supreme power in all governments.

[2] Butler, *Sermons on Special Occasions*, III. and V.

exception.   Butler is clear that the possibility
of exceptional cases arising ought to be as little
brought to mind as may be.   Rather there should
be inculcated the duty of Christian subjects to obey
not only for wrath, but for conscience' sake.   This
view, similar to that held by Hooker[1], is a fair
specimen of the point of view of the eighteenth-
century divine.   It is evident that by this time all
sense of the original purport of the theory has been
lost, and, since its work is done and facts render it
impossible of support by any loyal subject, its edge
has been taken off.   Yet, whittled down to a few
harmless truisms, it still remains to stimulate the
sense that obedience to law has some sanction higher
than mere personal convenience.

To sum up: out of the sentiment common to all *Summary.*
Christians that subjection to lawful authority is in
general a religious duty, since authority is part of
the natural and Divine order, the Papacy developed
a claim to complete supremacy, as the only Divinely
ordained government.   This claim was met by a
counter-claim to Divine Right on behalf of the Imperial dignity.   In the sixteenth century the doctrine
was elaborated with greater rigidity,—the principle
of absolute non-resistance seemed necessary to protect secular government from clerical interference.
In combination with other causes, this doctrine gave
birth to a theory of indefeasible hereditary right, the

---

[1] Hooker, *Supposed fragment of a sermon on civil obedience* and
Ecclesiastical Polity, Book VIII. *passim, e.g.* "God doth ratify the
works of that sovereign authority which kings have received by
men." Ch. II. § 7.

prevalence of which was largely due to the fact that both Henry IV. of France and James I. of England obtained their thrones by right of birth alone and without Papal sanction. In the seventeenth century the political side of the doctrine came out most strongly, and it is seen to be the form in which alone could become popular the theory of sovereignty. It further accomplished a work in softening or preventing political changes. Its work done, it began to become obsolete at the Revolution, and tended to pass into a mere sentiment. Meanwhile the older method of argument by means of a medley of Scripture texts had given place to the contention, that monarchy and obedience are a part of the natural order and therefore Divine. The basis of the theory was no longer Biblical and theological, but historical and utilitarian. Yet on this basis the ground could not be maintained; and the theory gave way before the doctrine of natural rights of the people propounded by Locke, which is only the Divine Right of Kings in a disguised form. There is however far more weight allowed by Locke, than by Filmer to the principle of utility. This conception may be expected to overshadow and then to supersede the artificial fiction of the original compact and the dream of natural inalienable rights. The doctrine of Divine Right not only was transformed by imperceptible degrees into the theory of natural rights, but it left behind it a legacy, in the sense that government in general is Divine, because it is natural, and that obedience to law is a religious duty.

CHAPTER VIII

PASSIVE OBEDIENCE AND THE CHURCH
OF ENGLAND

THE doctrine of the Divine Right of Kings has now been considered in respect of the process of its developement and decay. It remains to regard it *Divine* statically, so to say, to view it in relation to rival *Right to be con-* theories of government. It must be remembered *sidered in* first of all that the import of the phrase "Divine *relation to rival* Right of Kings" is mainly negative. It implies that *theories.* there is no foundation for the pretensions advanced by certain other authorities to supremacy by God's especial grant. The notion of Divine Right is in the air; all theories of government are theories of Divine Right, and most of them admit so much[1]. The Pope claims by Divine Right, so do the Presbyterians. Even the author of the *Vindiciae* contends, that since kings hold their crowns by God's grace, they may be judged by the people, as interpreters of the original Divine compact[2]. Again, most of the English writers on behalf of resistance assert for law and custom a claim to absolute authority by

[1] On this point see Leslie's able paper, *The Rehearsal*, no. 53, *Divine Right in Government acknowledged by all.*

[2] *Vindiciae contra Tyrannos*, Quaestio I. *passim.*

Divine Right. The theory of natural rights is but the theory of Divine Right under a changed guise, a fact of which the writings of Rousseau form the clearest evidence. Algernon Sidney contends that an unjust law ought not to be obeyed, since it cannot bind the conscience and lacks Divine authority[1]. This view is one which admits law to be law "simply and strictly so-called," only when it is believed to be in accordance with the Divine will. Sidney's notion, that the sovereignty of the people is inalienable, as being a grant from God, which neither human ordinance nor the people's own consent may alienate, is every whit as much a theory of Divine Right as the views of Mainwaring or Sacheverell. The doctrine under investigation does not differ from contemporary theories of politics in alone claiming Divine Right for the supreme authority, but in claiming that the King is the supreme authority. All the theories alike are at variance with modern political philosophy, for they all assert or imply a claim to Divine Right. In this respect, they differ from the thought of to-day, but agree among themselves. If the Divine Right of Kings be, as is so often asserted, the stupidest of all theories of politics, it cannot be because it seeks to find a Divine authority for government. We have no right to condemn it beyond other theories for a notion, which they all hold in common. The point to consider is, how far it was a specially stupid theory of politics, as compared with other views prevalent in the sixteenth and seventeenth centuries.

All theories of seventeenth century are theories of Divine Right.

[1] *Discourses on Government*, III. § 11.

It will be convenient first of all to examine the *Religious* theory in relation to those doctrines which most *side of the theory will* directly controvert it and assert a Divine Right for *be here* some ecclesiastical authority. In this chapter the *discussed.* religious aspect of the theory will be the main element considered. Afterwards it will be examined on its political side, and its relations to other views of politics investigated.

From the foregoing investigation it must have *Its anti-* appeared sufficiently that the theory arose out of the *papal origin.* reaction against the Papal pretensions. It was the need of a controversial method to meet the claims of the spiritual power, which produced the doctrine of the Divine Right of Kings. This has been shewn to be the case in the Empire, in France, and in England. If further evidence be required, it is only necessary to take up at random any tract or pamphlet on behalf of royal rights written during the seventeenth century. In all probability the name of either the Pope or Bellarmine will be prominent on the first page. The royalist authors have the Pope on the brain. Whoever be their immediate antagonist, the Pope is always in the background, and it is against him that the long struggle is waged. Preachers on Jan. 30th assert that the martyrdom of Charles was really the work of the Jesuits, or they open their sermons with an elaborate proof not that resistance is a sin, but that Papal interference is against the laws and liberties of this realm of England[1]. Filmer was perhaps less

[1] In a sermon preached before the King on January 30, 168¾, Dr Turner's first thought is of the Pope and of the advantage to

anti-papal in sentiment than most of the supporters
of the theory.   Yet his *Patriarcha* opens with an
attack on Bellarmine.   Hobbes was the one great
writer of the time, whose thought was not dominated by the notion of Divine Right.   Yet Hobbes
devotes a whole book of *The Leviathan* to the
consideration of *The Kingdom of Darkness*, or the
Roman Church.   Besides, the commonest term for a
Identifica- Dissenter is Jesuit.   This is used with a definite
tion of
Dissenters intention and is not merely vague vituperation.   The
with Jesuits are regarded as *par excellence* the teachers
Jesuits.
of the doctrine of resistance.   All the special tenets
of the Society go for nothing beside this one striking
fact, that its members deliberately weaken the bonds
of allegiance and argue that under certain conditions
a nation may resist and even depose its sovereign.
Now the Dissenters teach the same doctrine, and
therefore they may without injustice be dubbed
Jesuits in disguise.   It is not possible to read the
numerous pamphlets and sermons, in which this
view is set forth, without seeing that the royalist
writers were sincere and believed themselves to have
made an important discovery, as to the true nature
of Dissent.   Rome would for its own ends permit
subjects to resist.   Dissenters would for the good of
the Commonwealth permit the same.   Therefore
Dissenters are in reality Romanists, and only play at
Protestantism.   The dominant feeling is that the
supreme heresy of the Roman Church was the claim

Rome of the execution of Charles. "Is the greatest misgovern-
ment sufficient pretence for any Pope or consistory on earth to
depose a Sovereign Power?"   (23.)

put forth on behalf of the Papacy to a political supremacy over all kings and princes. The sense of this dwarfs everything else, and all the other defects of the Roman system are viewed as nothing in comparison with the cardinal iniquity of the Papal sovereignty. Every sect, which in any way approaches to the claim of Rome to limit the "true law of free monarchies," is thus regarded as consciously or unconsciously Roman in its tenets. It is impossible to deny that intense hatred of the Pope and the Jesuits, as his chief supporters, was the animating motive of the upholders of the Divine Right of Kings. Yet the hatred, be it observed, is rather political than religious. Comparatively little is said *Jesuits are* of the erroneous doctrines or corrupt practices of the *attacked on politi-* Roman communion. Here is not the place for such *cal rather* discussion. What is attacked is the Papacy as a *than religious* political authority, claiming universal Empire, and *grounds.* dissolving the bonds of national allegiance. A burning and fanatic hatred of the Society of Jesus is another note of all these writings. Yet here again it is not as the servants of a system destructive of morality or inimical to truth, that the Jesuits have won for themselves their monumental meed of execration. This is not the ground of their evil name. That comes of their ardent support of the Papal claims. It is not as believers in Roman Catholic doctrine[1],

[1] For Bellarmine's theory of the indirect political supremacy of the Pope see *De Romano Pontifice*, L. v. especially cc. 4, 6; also his contemptuous brushing aside as irrelevant of Barclay's refutation of the theory of the canonists in *De Excusatione Barclaii*, cc. 1, 2.

but as Papalists, that they are attacked. The
Jesuits, above all others, have devoted their energies
to an elaborate defence of the Pope's position.
Whether, as the canonists claim, his political power
be direct, or, as Bellarmine argues, it be merely
indirect, certain it is that far the weightiest arguments in his favour are those of Jesuit writers[1].
Others, who think themselves loyal enough to the
Pope, may reason and refine away his political power,
and argue in favour of the oath of allegiance. But
of all this the Jesuits will have nothing. They
assert on behalf of the Pope pretensions, which would
have shamed neither Boniface VIII. nor John XXII.,
and they met their reward. This is the head and
front of their offending; and it is for this cause
that they have won for themselves a name among
Englishmen, which those who hate them most nowadays would least of all be able to interpret. It may
well be that the shouts of applause, with which a
present day audience at Exeter Hall would greet
an attack on the iniquities of Ignatius Loyola, are
a tribute unconsciously, but none the less really paid
to the Divine Right of Kings. And, when the
members of the Protestant Alliance or the Church
Association devote a field-day to the exposition of
the evils and dishonesty of Jesuitry, they are,

[1] Besides Bellarmine, there stand out more particularly
Mariana, who approves of tyrannicide in general and of the
murder of Henry III. of France (*De Rege et Regis Institutione*,
I. 6) and decides against the power of the prince to legislate in
matters of religion (*Ibid.* 10); and Suarez, *De Legibus*, L. III., *De
Lege Positiva*, cc. 7, 34, and L. IV. *De Lege Canonica*, especially
cc. 9, 19.

though they think it not, uniting with Andrews and Bramhall, with Taylor and Jackson in repelling an assault, which is dangerous to the State rather than to the Church, and are exhibiting a relic of that patriotic indignation, which, in days when the political claims of Rome were real and formidable, had a meaning and a value. Anyhow, in the seventeenth century there is little evidence that the Jesuits in England are attacked, because their system is disliked or their teaching believed to be immoral. The polemic against the conquering Society is not the lofty indignation of a Pascal, denouncing a casuistry which is debasing the moral standard and destroying all principles of right action. The spirit of the English royalists is as far inferior to that which breathes through every page of the *Provinciales,* as is the form in which it is embodied. But if the irony of the believer in Divine Right be lacking in the polish of the "letters," his declamation at least surpasses them in the blind force of passion. The English hatred of the Jesuits is the narrow, but fervent enthusiasm of patriots disgusted at claims which fetter the free action of the nation, and enraged with those who presume to justify such claims with the pen or to put them into practice with the sword. The Jesuits are villains—that the royalists believe. But the cause is not that they believe or teach false dogmas in theology, not that they are paving the way for moral scepticism, nor that they (in general) urge and permit immoral actions, but merely that they are traitors guilty of high treason against the sovereignty of nations, seeking to wrest the diadem from the imperial crown of England, that they may place it on the brows of a priest: *Le clericalisme c'est l'ennemi* is the governing thought of those who cry for *Jus Divinum* and Non-resistance.

Teaching of resistance regarded as main element in Popery and Dissent.

As was said, it is this sense, that the essence of Popery is a claim to political supremacy, that is the cause of the numerous accusations for holding Jesuit or Papist views, that are levelled against the Dissenters. Filmer tells us that "the main and indeed the only point of Popery is the alienating and withdrawing of subjects from their obedience to their Prince[1]." It is not, then, surprising that Hickes is of opinion that "Popery having apparently corrupted the Gospel in the doctrines of obedience, and submission, and the divine authority of the supreme power, especially of Kings; they cannot be sound and orthodox Protestants, who hold the very same destructive principles to regal government, by which the Papists have corrupted the Gospel in these points. No they are not sound, and orthodox Protestants, but Protestants popularly affected, Papists under a Protestant dress, wolves in sheeps' clothing, rebellious and Satanical spirits transformed into angels of light[2]." To this well-known passage quotations similar in spirit might be multiplied a thousand-fold[3]. The

[1] Preface to *The Anarchy of a Mixed Monarchy*.

[2] Hickes, *Sermon on Jan.* 30, 168½. Another sermon describes Jesuits as *Rome's Fifth Monarchy Men*; Mr Gardiner's account of the Fifth Monarchy is a proof of the appositeness of this description (*History of the Commonwealth and Protectorate*, I. 32).

[3] We have one pamphlet directed against *The Six Popish Pillars, Anabaptists, Quakers, Presbyterians*, etc. (1690). Jewell writes, "Why hath he [the Pope] and his complices (like Anabaptists

reiterated charge that Dissenters are all Jesuits at heart is only to be explained upon this view of what was really the mind of the Anglican divines. The term is not employed merely as an opprobrious epithet. It is the expression of a deep sense, that since the real object of Jesuitism is to loose the bonds of civil allegiance, all who hold doctrines of resistance are believers in the only essential and distinctive doctrines of Loyola and Rome[1]. The purely theological points on which Dissenters differ even more widely than Anglicans from the Roman Church may be ignored as mere details, which do not concern the main position.

But here a distinction must be made. The theory of most English Nonconformists and of the average Whig politician, is open to the taunts of the royalist on the score of its likeness to the Jesuit doctrine of resistance. If resistance in any form for any cause be damnable, and if it be Popery to teach it, then Whigs like Locke and Sidney, and Parliamentarians like Prynne may be accused of Popery. It is true that religion is one of the main grounds for resistance in practice, but at least neither Whigs nor Independents believe that the state is to be

Some Nonconformists agree with Rome only in allowing resistance.

and Libertines, to the end they might run on the more licentiously and carelessly), shaken off the yokes, and exempted themselves from being under all civil power?" (*Apology*, 75). In *The Apostate Parliament* occurs the query, "Setting aside the Romish faith and the vow of blind obedience, tell me wherein these men differ from the disciples of Ignatius Loyola? Why only these are Popish and they Protestant Jesuits?" See Appendix C.

[1] On the political theory of the Jesuits cf. *From Gerson to Grotius*, Chap. v.

controlled in the interests of a religious body. They would not fetter its action, as the Papalist would do. Indeed, as the notion of toleration begins to develope, any general theory of clerical supremacy becomes an impossibility. That men view the mere teaching of resistance as evidence of Popery is indicative of a state of feeling, difficult for us to bring into imagination, when non-resistance is regarded as the most essential element of religion.

Presby-
terianism
advances
claims
similar to
those of
Rome.

But in regard to one ecclesiastical system other than the Roman, the taunt of Jesuitism is more truly justified. Presbyterianism, as exhibited in Geneva or Scotland, veritably claims, as did the Papacy, to control the state in the interests of an ecclesiastical corporation. The cardinal error of the royalist writers, when viewed from the modern standpoint, is that in formulating the theory of the Divine Right of Kings against that of the Pope, they were driven into the position of supporters of despotism and oppression. However much this is to be condemned, it was probably inevitable. Certainly it may seem to us a strange thing that in defending the secular power against the spiritual, men should ignore or minimize the dangers of the secular power itself becoming a tyranny. But it is not strange, that those who were inspired by a passionate indignation at the preposterous assumptions of the Papacy, should have been no less hostile to the political side of the Presbyterian system. "New presbyter is but old priest writ large" is a maxim of deeper import than is sometimes imagined. It is the felicitous expression of men's sense of the danger still to be apprehended from clericalism. *A theory* *of cleri-* The same mischievous claims to place secular *calism in* governments under the heel of an ecclesiastical *politics.* organization, as had led to so much conflict in the Middle Ages and were only finally overthrown by the Reformation, had reappeared in a yet more irritating form in the Presbyterian system. The condition of Geneva under Calvin was an object-lesson, which neither statesmen nor patriotic churchmen were likely to ignore. Affairs in Scotland would form a sufficient warning, if any should be tempted to fall out of the frying-pan into the fire, and after throwing off one ecclesiastical tyranny to rivet upon their necks another, which would differ from it mainly in being narrower, more searching, more inquisitorial, more ubiquitous, and less careful of the larger needs and hopes of humanity, less likely to force upon states and their rulers the sense that sectional and local interests are not the only rule of right. The Papacy, whatever might be said against it, was at least a standing witness to the need of international morality, and might be supposed to have the advantage of viewing political problems from a universal standpoint. Despite the evils and mischief attendant on the political claims of the Popes, it might be contended with some plausibility that these claims were the only security the mediæval world possessed for something like justice and fair-dealing between kings and princes. The fear of Papal excommunication undoubtedly tended to confine aggression within limits and to make rulers temper expediency with right

reason. No such defence could be made for the
Presbyterian system. It would have controlled the
action of the state more completely than did the
Papacy, while it would have strengthened, instead
of diminishing all the tendencies that made for a
narrow patriotism, and that would lead men to regard
local and provincial feeling as all important. The position of the Papacy could not fail to lift it in a great
degree above the limitations, that must surround
and sometimes fetter the thought and action of the
national statesman. But there was no such cause at
work in the Presbyterian system, and its rulers would,
so far as politics were concerned, have exhibited
most of the defects, without any of the merits of
clericalism. Unless it be contended that their
possession of a purer system of theology would
ensure the wisdom of their political action, it can
hardly be doubted that the Presbyterian system,
if allowed to run its course, would have made
greater havoc of politics, than did the Papacy. It
would have subordinated all state action to considerations at once narrowly local and rigidly ecclesiastical.
Thus it is not surprising that the ablest defenders
of the doctrine of Divine Right are at pains to
shew not merely that the Papal claims would dissolve
the bonds of civil society, but that they go on,
as does Nalson, to prove that the 'Presbyterian
Discipline' is equally destructive not merely of
royal power, but of Parliamentary authority and the
liberty of the subject[1]. The two systems of Papal

---

[1] "There may be many particular interests which may be
disadvantageous to the safety, security and happiness of the

supremacy and Presbyterian 'discipline' are both
clerical in essence. They both assert a claim by
Divine Right for God's minister, whether he be the
Pope or the office-bearers in the Presbyterian body;
this claim is to be superior to all civil government
whatever. Bishop Bramhall's tract *A warning to the
Church of England* is an able exposition of this
view. In this is shewn the political danger of
Presbyterianism, as an ecclesiastical system claiming
dominion by Divine Right over the secular power.
The latter part of Nalson's *Common Interest of King
and People* is a singularly lucid and well-balanced
statement of the same position.

Nor do these writers attribute to the Presbyterians any pretensions which they do not make for
themselves. Cartwright's works are almost as full
as those of Bellarmine of the claim to control the
State in the interests of the Church; in many
respects they form an exact parallel to Papalist
pretensions. The magistrate is the Lord's officer,
and must wield the sword as the Church directs,
persecute all 'idolatry' at its bidding, and grant no

*Illustra-
tions of
Presby-
terian
theory.
Cart-
wright.*

Imperial Crown of this Realm of Great Britain, and its other
dominions, as well as to the liberty and property of the People;
but there are two which are directly and fundamentally opposite
and contrary to them, both in their principles and practices, and
these are the pretensions of a universal supremacy and spirituo-
temporal monarchy of the Church of Rome or Papacy on the one
hand, and the Democratic Presbyterian on the other. That both
these are utterly inconsistent with the safety and very essence of
monarchy and particularly with that of these nations, as also with
the peace, happiness, liberty and property of the subjects is that
which I hope to prove" (Nalson, *The Common Interest of King and
People*, 173).

pardon upon the recantation of a heretic. He is
to be guided by the example of Constantine the
Great, who persecuted in favour of orthodoxy[1]. The
'discipline' is universal and immutable[2] and is to be
maintained by the magistrate[3]; the civil magistrate
is to provide some sharp punishment for all who
contemn the censure of the Church[4]. In fact the
State is to wield the temporal sword, and the Church
to dictate how it shall be wielded. The civil magistrates as they are the nurses, so they are the servants
of the Church and must throw down their crowns
before it[5]. Since the Church is prior to the State,
the constitution of the latter must be fashioned and
made suitable unto the Church[6]. Church government
is to be the model of the civil State. Cartwright
knows that the 'discipline' is regarded in the light of
a new popedom and tyranny in the Church; but so to
term it is blasphemy[7]. The author's views are as
definitely theocratic, as those of the mediæval Papacy.
He is not merely using phrases to emphasize the
spiritual subjection of the prince, as a layman, to
the officers of the Church; but he teaches that the
prince is merely the minister and executant of the
Church's decrees. Finally, his object being to move
the people to obedience, he shews no sort of inclination to popular government or liberty as such.
The only liberty he desires is the liberty of the

---

[1] Cartwright, *Second Reply*, cxv. sqq.
[2] *Declaration of Discipline*, 13. [3] *Ibid*. 187.
[4] *Second Admonition to Parliament*, 49.
[5] *Reply to Whitgift*, 144. [6] *Ibid*.
[7] *Demonstration of Discipline*, 75.

office-bearers of the Church to control the action of
the State and to use its forces at their will. The duty
of private individuals is merely that of obedience[1].

Still stronger are the views of Christopher *Goodman.*
Goodman. His book *How to obey or disobey* was
written in 1558 against the tyranny of the 'idol-
atress' Mary, and the monstrous regiment of women,
although there is flattery of Elizabeth, " that godly
lady and meek lamb void of all Spanish pride and
stranger blood." Goodman will have nothing of passive obedience[2]; idolatry must be resisted by force[3].
Like the Papalists, Goodman conceives of God as
the true recipient of civil obedience, and of all earthly
governments as subordinate to His rule, and liable to
be overturned at any moment, if they transgress it[4].
Of the nature of God's ordinances and of the question
as to whether or no they have been transgressed, he
would apparently make the rulers of the Church the
sole and irresponsible arbiters. For princes are not
to suffer their subjects to be ignorant of God's law,
but to enforce theological doctrine universally[5]. On
this condition obedience is to be paid to the magistrate and no tyranny will absolve from the duty[6].
As in the view of Cartwright or Bellarmine, the
subject's duty is mere obedience, but obedience to
an ecclesiastical corporation; only secondarily and
under qualifications, will obedience to the civil

[1] *Declaration of Discipline,* 185. The passage is quoted below,
p. 222.
[2] *How to obey,* 30, 64.   [3] *Ibid.* 77.
[4] *Ibid.* 44 sqq., 60, 110, 118, 139.
[5] *Ibid.* 105.   [6] *Ibid.* 110.

magistrate become a duty. The State exists solely
on sufferance; and the officers of the Church may
meddle with its policy and upset its organization at
their pleasure. For no heretic is truly a king; not
the clearest legal right, neither election nor succession, can give any title to a claimant unless in the
opinion of this self-constituted authority, he "be a
promoter and setter forth of God's glory[1]." The
contention that neither prince nor people are free,
but both are subject to God's law might indeed be
used to-day in an innocent sense; but, as in the
case of all teachers of the political supremacy of
ecclesiasticism, in Goodman's mouth the words imply
a claim on the part of an irresponsible person or
body of persons, not experts in politics, to control
the action of the State, in whatever direction they
please. The King is to persecute and the people
to rebel at the bidding of the Kirk[2]. There is no
appeal from their decision as to the character of the
policy that will promote God's glory or will hinder
it. How far these claims would have been carried,
if men such as Goodman had been given a free hand,
may be gathered from some hints which he lets
drop. One of the reasons for resisting Mary is her
foreign policy; since it is plainly forbidden by
God's word to make war in alliance with Spain

[1] *How to obey*, 51, 58. Goodman's contention is that an
idolatrous and persecuting king is to be regarded as a mere private
man, to whom no obedience is due (139). This is on a par with
Bellarmine's view that the Pope does not command subjects to
disobey their sovereigns, for the Papal deposition *ipso facto*
destroys the kingly character.

[2] *Ibid.* Chap. xi.

against France and "their own brethren the Scots," all Englishmen are bidden to throw off the yoke[1]. Nor does Goodman stop here, but devotes many pages to a glorification of Sir Thomas Wyatt, and the praise of his rebellion[2].

Here, then, in the writings of Cartwright and Goodman we have clear proof that the political claims of Presbyterianism were as oppressive, as tyrannical and as preposterous as those of Rome. The two systems, Papal and Presbyterian, are alike in that they both regard the State as the mere handmaid of an ecclesiastical corporation, and would, in the last resort, place the supreme direction of politics in the hands of the rulers of the Church. They differ only in the character of the theological systems, in the interests of which the policy of the secular government is to be regulated. The history of Scotland affords further evidence of the claims made and exercised under this system. And those who had most to do with the establishment of the Presbyterian Kirk in Scotland are most emphatic in their announcement of their pretensions to subject the policy of the State to their own caprice. John *Knox.* Knox declares that no idolater (by which is meant a person whose theological views differ from his own) ought to be promoted to any public office; that no oath can bind men to obey such an one; and that any prince, who after appointment becomes an idolater, may be justly opposed[3]. In the *First Book*

---

[1] *How to obey*, 173.   [2] 204 sqq.
[3] *Summary of the proposed Second Blast of the Trumpet.*
Works, IV. 539.

First Book of Discipline it is declared that rulers and ruled must
of Dis- all alike be subject to discipline[1], and that idolatry
cipline. and all monuments thereof must be suppressed[2]; that
punishment (death for choice) should be appointed
for all such as disobeyed the superintendents, and for
profaners of the Sacraments[3].   Now when these are
regarded as directions from the Kirk to the State
in order to guide its legislation, it will readily be
seen how great is the power claimed.   In subjecting
all rulers to 'discipline,' a civil supremacy is in
reality claimed for the Kirk; for excommunication
carried with it civil disabilities; it was immediately
followed by "letters of horning."

Second   The *Second Book of Discipline* claims for the
Book of
Discipline, spiritual power an indirect temporal supremacy,
1581. very similar to that claimed by Bellarmine for the
Pope.   The method of argument is not very different
in the two cases.   The magistrate commands external things for external peace and quietness among
his subjects; the minister handles external things
only for conscience' sake[4].   The magistrate is to
command the minister to observe the rule commanded in the world, and *to punish the transgressors
by civil means.*   The ministers exercise not the
civil jurisdiction, but teach the magistrate how it
should be exercised according to the word[5].   Ecclesiastical power is distinguished from civil by the fact
that it flows immediately from God[6].

[1] VII. 3.   The *First Book of Discipline* is to be found in the
Works of John Knox, II. 183 sqq.
[2] *Ibid.* III.   [3] *Ibid.* p. 253.
[4] *Second Book of Discipline*, I. 11.   Calderwood (III. 529 sqq.).
[5] *Ibid.* 14.   [6] *Ibid.* 5.

All this may seem little more than a declaration of the freedom of the Kirk, and of the divergent spheres of Church and State. It might be so in an age when all religious opinions are tolerated. But at a time when persecution was recognized as a duty, it amounts to a claim on behalf of the Kirk for complete supremacy. The civil magistrate is bound to suppress all teaching not recognized by the Kirk, to enforce its commands, to see to the execution of its views as to the administration of God's Word and Sacraments—all this, according to the theory of Knox and his successors, on pain of deposition. The Kirk is to be the nation in its spiritual capacity, yet over this vast body the State is to have no authority, but is merely in the position of an executive appointed to execute the will of the office-bearers. If the Prince will not obey the officers of the Kirk, and employ all the machinery of government to execute their decrees, he is to be deposed.

We are told that the magistrate is to assist and maintain and justify the jurisdiction of the Kirk. There is no qualification. The ministers, on the other hand, are to assist the Prince in all things agreeable to God's word[1]. Thus to the ministers is left the final interpretation of the limits of obedience, and the magistrate becomes the mere tenant-at-will of the Kirk.

Further, in the *Second Book of Discipline* the magistrate is bidden to fortify the godly proceedings of the Kirk; to see that its public estate and ministers be maintained[2], and so to secure the Church against false teachers and hirelings, dumb dogs and

---

[1] *Second Book of Discipline*, I. 15.　　[2] *Ibid.* x. 2.

idle bellies[1]; to punish civilly those that will not obey the censure of the Kirk, "without confounding always the one jurisdiction with the other[2]," i.e. maintaining his allotted position of subserviency. He is to make laws *for the advancement of the Kirk* without usurping anything that pertains not to the civil sword[3].

These constitutions in fact invest the Kirk with the absolute freedom and right of establishing its constitution and discipline in matters small and great and then of employing the secular arm to enforce them on a reluctant nation. For where the ministry of the Kirk is once lawfully constituted, all godly princes ought to obey the voice and reverence the majesty of the Son of God[4]. The *Book* proceeds to quote from the statute declaring that no other ecclesiastical jurisdiction should be acknowledged, but that which is and shall be in the Reformed Kirk and flowing therefrom[5].

The belief in persecution is the real cause of the conflict It is this that constitutes the real objection from the statesman's point of view to the Presbyterian system, and the justification of the theory of the Divine Right of Kings and of much that seems arbitrary in the treatment of religious bodies

---

[1] *Second Book of Discipline*, x. 3.   [2] *Ibid.* 4.   [3] *Ibid.* 7.

[4] A power in the Prince of reforming the Church when corrupted is indeed admitted (*Ibid.* 7), but this is merely a saving clause by which a Revolution in favour of Presbyterianism may be admitted. Knox in attacking the Roman Church where established asserts emphatically the claims of the civil magistrate (Letter to the Queen Regent, *Works*, IV. 443). Like the Pope, he will admit the power of the civil magistrate, on condition of its being exercised in subserviency to himself.

[5] *Second Book of Discipline*, XI. 16.

by the State. The acts of Henry VIII. and *between*
Elizabeth may appear harsh, and the *submissio* *Church and State.*
cleri may be regarded as depriving the Church
of its due rights. Yet no less could have been
claimed at the time by any self-respecting monarch.
For at that time toleration was not recognized
as a principle, and it was a maxim that the nation
in its spiritual capacity forms one corporation,
subject to one ecclesiastical jurisdiction and one
system of discipline. Under such conditions it can
never be other than dangerous for the State to give
the spiritual power a free hand. For it will fetter
the action of the State in a thousand ways and will
be repeatedly claiming to "handle external things
for conscience' sake." It may, as in Scotland, set
up an inquisitorial jurisdiction in every village, and
demand the assistance of the State in punishing
any and every breach of what it regards as the
moral law, from adultery to Sabbath-breaking. It
may claim, as in Scotland, that the royal pardon
shall never issue for capital crimes; it may demand,
as in 1582, that no alliances shall be made with
Roman Catholic powers[1]. The Papacy in the middle
ages claimed to regulate international differences,
and was constantly encroaching upon the sphere of
the State. But hardly at the period of its proudest
exaltation did it claim to make the civil power so

[1] Calderwood, III. 685. The General Assembly demanded that
"no society, league or friendship be made with Papists in France,
Italy, Spain, or other countries, by common or particular outset."
The whole tenor of the articles presented at this time to the King
is expressive of the determination of the Kirk to unfettered
supremacy.

completely its slave or to interfere so minutely with
the private life of individuals, as did the maintainers
of "the discipline." However, opinions may differ
as to which of the two systems was the more
meddlesome and irritating tyranny. But there can
be no doubt that, with whatever differences in
degree, both are alike in kind. Each puts forward
a claim by Divine Right to subject the secular
power to the spiritual, to make the clergy the
ultimate arbiters of political action.

The claim of clerical-ism inad-missible. And the claim cannot be admitted. The English
nation had ever been jealous of clericalism. It had
refused to surrender the right and liberty of the
English Crown to the Popes, and had upheld its
independence in matters of politics, unawed by the
majestic traditions and splendid imperiousness of
the mediæval Papacy—this at a time, when the
spiritual authority of the Pope was unquestioned.
England had in the past no quarrel with the
religious pretensions of the Papacy; but she was no
more inclined, than the French King or the Emperor,
to admit its political claims. It was not likely that
she would allow a similar claim, presented in the
less lovely form of the Presbyterian discipline.

In the Presbyterian doctrines, as developed by
Melville in Scotland and Cartwright in England, there
was however one distinction recognized, which went far
to minimize its dangers. These writers all held the
doctrine of the two kingdoms, and did not make the
mistake common to all parties in the middle ages,
and repeated by men so different as Laud and Luther.
That error lay in treating Church and State as merely

different departments of the one great society, and with this view either an ecclesiastical or a civil tyranny is almost inevitable. Knox held the older view. In the same way the doctrine of the indirect power of the Papacy, as developed by Bellarmine, leaves it possible at least in theory to admit the freedom and inherent rights of the civil State[1].

Against either claim the same controversial method was necessary. It was needful to claim on behalf of the secular power complete supremacy and the institution of God. Not until the danger was past of a relapse into Popery or Presbyterianism, can the notion of Divine Right be said to have accomplished its work. The case of France is precisely similar. On the one hand, the Papacy claimed to excommunicate and depose the King, and to keep the rightful heir out of his inheritance. On the other hand, the Huguenots made themselves the mouthpiece of a recrudescent feudalism, and strove for an *imperium in imperio* with quasi-sovereign rights in their strong places. In the result both in France and England, the central power succeeded in establishing its supremacy, even to the point of persecuting the teachers of all doctrines which it regarded as harmful.

The State can only meet its opponents by claiming entire supremacy.

The passages cited as evidence of the Presbyterian theory may seem patient of a different interpretation. They may be defended as mere humble advice to the State from persons acting with purely spiritual weapons and claiming no coercive authority. John Knox himself could not wield the sword, but

The spiritual power never has the material sword at its disposal.

[1] Cf. Appendix III.

was only able to advise subjects in certain circumstances to depose their prince. The Kirk neither
possesses nor claims the use of the material sword. It
merely demands that it shall be used in its interests.
Precisely. Yet the position of the Papacy in regard
to European nations was at no time different. Save
in the Papal states, the Pope had no direct material
power. The army under the immediate command
of the Pope or his delegates would scarcely have
been sufficient to crush the smallest of recalcitrant
sects, and could have made no head against a
hostile nation. When the mediæval Papacy is
called a tyranny, it is too often forgotten that however mischievous its effects on political action, it
was emphatically an instance of government by
consent. Whether or no the Popes from Gregory VII.
to Boniface VIII. wielded an authority that was
both despotic in its nature and oppressive in its
incidence, it is certain that their despotism did not
rest upon physical force, but upon purely spiritual
or moral sanctions. The Papacy never as a matter
of practice wielded or claimed to wield the material
sword. It merely demanded that physical force
should never be employed, save with its approval.
Presbyterianism made precisely the same demand.

The spiritual power can only grant or withhold the moral sanctions of govern-ment. All that the Pope can do by a bull of excommunication is to declare, as God's vicar, that men
are no longer bound in theory and for conscience'
sake to obey their sovereign. They may not improbably be bound to obey him in practice and by
the strength of the material sword. The English
Catholics, or those of them who favoured the

deposing power, were so bound; they were "subject for wrath." But, admitting the Pope's claims, no one will be bound for conscience' sake, so soon as he has launched a bull of excommunication. The object, therefore, of the opponents of either system must be to assert, that, despite the Papal or Presbyterian attempt to exercise the deposing power, the sanctions of conscience still remain, and that the moral claim of the State to the allegiance of its subjects may not be impaired by ecclesiastical censure. Throughout the Middle Ages, in the Wars of the League, in the plots against Elizabeth, it has been repeatedly proved that the character of men's civil obedience will be affected by other motives than the material sword or the legal sanction of government, "wrath." The success, however partial, of the Popes or of the Presbyterian leaders has proved that the moral sanction, conscience, is a real power in strengthening or loosening the bonds of allegiance. This sanction the supporters of clericalism claim to manipulate at their pleasure. The defenders of the freedom of the State are therefore perpetually driven to assert, that it is not lost or gained according to the theological opinions of the ruler, that the State has a Divine Right to exist despite the disapproval of the Church, that obedience to the secular power is due not merely for "wrath but for conscience' sake." Obedience not merely for wrath, but for conscience' sake has been asserted to be the right of the Church alone. The moral claim to obedience, as distinct from the physical power of enforcing it, does not in itself belong to the State,

And so with Presby- terianism.

Hence supporters of the State must claim that the moral sanction is on their side.

say the supporters of clericalism, save in so far as the State is the necessary instrument of the Church. The theory of the Divine Right of Kings is the contradiction of this; it asserts that the State has a claim to obedience on moral and religious grounds, that it has a right to exist as in accordance with human nature and God's will, and is based on something better than the right of the stronger. Clericalism makes capital out of its position as the guide of men's consciences, and would subject states and politics to a meddlesome control. Hence, if political security is to be obtained, conscience must be asserted to be on the side of civil obedience, and universal supremacy by God's grant asserted for the State. Otherwise ecclesiastics will at once step in and claim to decide the cases in which resistance may be lawful.

The State asserts its authority in matters of religion. Yet in doing this the State makes large claims. It first asserts its absolute competence to prescribe forms of religious belief or at least of practice, and to set up or abolish forms of ecclesiastical organization. It is only when the State consents to be guided in this matter by experts, i.e. the Church, that any religious body will allow such a claim in its fulness. Yet the omni-competence of the State had to be asserted, and asserted as of Divine Right. It would doubtless be supported in the main only by those who feel morally convinced that the State will not as a matter of fact prohibit their own religious belief.

Erastian language of certain This is in part the explanation of the Erastian language of certain Caroline divines. They exalt the supremacy of the Crown; they declare its com- *supporters* petence to prescribe forms of faith; and claim Divine *of Divine Right.* Right for these powers. By this is merely meant a claim of the secular power to be free in theory; there is not intended or implied any claim that the State in practice shall decide religious matters arbitrarily or without consulting the heads of the Church. Doubtless much of Barrow's *Treatise of the Pope's Supremacy* or Jackson's *Treatise of Christian Obedience* is Erastian in tone. Yet in reality what they were aiming at was the legal omnipotence of the sovereign power. An exponent of the same view at the present day might well take as an illustration of the theoretical powers of Parliament the undoubted fact that at any moment it might legally abolish the Christian religion and introduce Mohammedanism under the sanction of torture. Yet such a writer would not be held to mean that Parliament could effect this change, or that it would dream of attempting it. Such an act would overpass what have been called the external and the internal limits of sovereignty[1]. Similarly in the seventeenth century, against the clericalism of Rome or of Geneva the omni-competence of the State was asserted. Against the claim of Pope or Presbyter to obedience by Divine Right the Divine Right of Kings must be elaborated. Against the claims to dissolve the bonds of sentiment or conscience between governors and governed, conscience must be claimed for the secular government by the theory of non-resistance, and difficult cases solved by the doctrine of Passive Obedience.

[1] Dicey, *Law of the Constitution*, 72—78.

It may seem strange that men such as Laud, with high views of the position of the Church and the power of the priesthood, should have asserted so strongly a theory, which, as frequently expounded, involves the assertion of the authority of the Crown over the forms of Church government and doctrine. But it must be borne in mind that Laud, like Parker and Whitgift, was well aware that the political supremacy of the State over the Church was too well-established a principle to disappear, nor did he grasp the doctrine of the two societies. It could only change hands. He knew that if this supremacy were not retained by Charles, it would pass over to the Parliament, and would be wrested into the protection and establishment of Puritanism. Laud was not ignorant that the Church of England " as by law established " had its strongest supporter in Charles. Although the Roman controversy was not over, he must have felt that the danger to England from that side was daily diminishing. The supremacy of the Crown might be extolled to any extent by a Caroline divine. For it was known that, as a matter of fact, so long as it remained in the hands of the King, it would be used to promote the welfare of the Church. It was not needful to demand passionately that the King should maintain the true religion and prohibit false teaching. Nor was it necessary to fetter the royal prerogative in order that the Church might be free. Knox had been driven to both these courses. But in England the King might be trusted to maintain the *status quo* and to guard against the aggressions of Puritanism. In England the royal authority was favourable, in Scotland it was hostile to the dominant religious system. If James VI. ever felt free to throw off the yoke of the Kirk there could be little doubt that he would do so; indeed he made various attempts to strengthen his authority over it[1]. A shrewd suspicion of this disposition must tend to drive the leaders of Presbyterianism into hostility to any doctrine of the nature of the royal supremacy, even irrespective of their previous theory. James would be dangerous to the Kirk. His freedom to touch it must therefore be denied. On the other hand the greater the freedom of Charles I. the better would it be for the Church of England, or at least for the particular view of its character and ritual taken by Laud. From the time of the Elizabethan settlement onward the royal supremacy was the bulwark of the Church of England against Puritan innovations.

Thus the taunt is not justified, that the theory of the Divine Right of Kings was merely the fiction of a time-serving hierarchy, intent upon gaining court favour, whatever might happen to the Church. For the belief in this theory was the most trustworthy security for the permanence and stability of that order of things which the clergy had learnt to love. They were not serving their King instead of their God; the best defence of the Church was the support of the Crown. Nor is it a cause for blame to the clergy that the theory of Divine Right found in them its strongest and most numerous body of supporters. The theory is, as has been shewn,

Unprincipled servility cannot fairly be attributed to the Anglican clergy.

[1] Gardiner's *History of England, passim.*

essentially anti-clerical. Yet for this reason it was
necessary, if it were to be effective, that the doctrine
should be in the main formulated by a body of
clergy. The claims of a system of clericalism, such
as the Papal or Presbyterian, might indeed be
denied by laymen; but they could not be effectively
refuted save by clergy. The element of truth in
the Papal claim made it essential that it should be
met by clergy rather than laymen. For Bellarmine
and Knox were right in asserting that only the
spiritual power can give the authoritative decision
as to whether men were bound in conscience to
obey their rulers. The question as one of conscience
must be decided by the spiritual authority. It was
not in claiming for a religious body the decision of
the moral and religious question, whether or no
obedience is due to the State on religious and moral
grounds, that the Jesuits erred. Where they were
mistaken was in asserting that the secular power as
such had no moral claim to obedience apart from
the theological accuracy of the opinions which it
enforced. The assertion that obedience is a religious
duty in all states, irrespective of the opinions of the
ruler, was not merely the sole method of rendering
politics free from ecclesiasticism; it could only be
made effectively by a body of men representing the
spiritual authority. None but the clergy could
meet the Pope on his own ground. It was vain to
denounce ecclesiasticism in politics, unless the leaders
of some religious body asserted that the possession
of religious truth was not the one road to political
wisdom, and that a national Church might be truly

of God's appointment without making the civil magistrate its vassal. That the doctrine in this country was in an especial degree the product of the Church of England and her divines is undoubted. Yet it was equally the product of the Gallican Church. Indeed the Gallican liberties are one of the chief sources whence the doctrine could be drawn[1]. For the ideal of the Divine Right of Kings in matters of theology is an assertion within limits of the rights of a national Church. The Pope had claimed a superiority which rendered nugatory the name of national Church.

The Presbyterian system, while asserting national independence of Papal sovereignty, would have yet set up within the nation an organization which would have dwarfed the State and hindered the growth of the nation's life. A Geneva on a great scale would not have been a national Church. Before the Church should have established its position, the nation would have disappeared. Even Independency, which seems to leave the whole matter free, implies a denial of the right of the nation as a whole to an ecclesiastical organization. Had it ever become universal, there could not have been a single religious communion claiming to represent the nation on its spiritual side.

If by a national Church be meant a religious body which, representing the whole nation yet *The theory belongs to a national Church.*

[1] See *supra* chap. VI. The connection between the conceptions of Divine Right and a national Church appears strongly in the collection of treatises made by Pithou, *Les Libertez de l'Église Gallicane.*

leaves its political life free to develope, unaffected
by the upas-tree of clericalism, there can be no
doubt that the theory of Divine Right was in-
separably connected with the ideal of a national
Church in the seventeenth century, and that it was
necessary to secure its realization in the face of
Papal or Presbyterian or Separatist pretensions.

Signifi-
cance of
Passive
Obedience.
For the theory of Divine Right is a religious
as well as a political dogma.   The stress laid upon
the duty of Passive Obedience is a proof of this.
Non-resistance, as an element in a utilitarian
system of politics, would probably be taught
without qualification.   Little would be said of
Passive Obedience, even though it should not be
forbidden.   This is actually the case with the
Leviathan.   But, where absolutist theory is essentially religious, it is inevitable that men should
consider the cases where disobedience to law is
a religious duty.   For, when civil obedience is
inculcated as a part of God's Law, the case cannot
be ignored of the government's endeavouring to
persecute the true religion.   Under certain conditions martyrdom is a recognized duty, and this implies
the duty of disobedience to the commands of the
Sovereign.   Unless the qualification be taken into
account, no Christian could proclaim the doctrine of
indefeasible hereditary right.   Men did not desire
the exclusion of James because they expected that
he would be a tyrant, but because they knew that
he was a Papist.   Those who opposed his exclusion
were forced to lay stress upon the duty of Anglicans
in the possible case of his persecuting their religion.

The doctrine of Passive Obedience hampered, in more ways than one[1], the supporters of the Divine Right of Kings. They were taunted with shewing their want of faith in their sovereign, since they were ever considering the chance of his being a heretic and a persecutor. It was declared that no wise upholder of the doctrine of resistance would dream of inculcating the duty of disobedience as a general rule, whereas to judge by their language the supporters of Divine Right regarded the case for passive obedience as one of constant recurrence. Besides passive obedience was little better than active resistance[2]; and its supporters might be branded as advocates of rebellion. Hobbes wrote that since the Incarnation is the central doctrine

[1] Sanderson, one of the acutest minds who wrote on behalf of Divine Right, is fully aware of the danger, and endeavours to minimize to the utmost the duty of Passive Obedience. In all doubtful cases he declares the responsibility to rest with the magistrate, and active obedience to be due. He allows that, when the conscience is clear as to the iniquity of the magistrate's command, obedience must be withheld, but even here disobedience is sin; and the case is one of the choice between two evils. "In such a case certainly he may not obey the magistrate; yet let him know thus much withal, that he sinneth too in disobeying the magistrate; from which sin the following of the judgment of his own conscience cannot acquit him. And this is that fearful perplexity, whereof I spake, wherein many a man casteth himself by his own error and obstinacy, that he can neither go with his conscience nor against it, but he shall sin" (*Judgment in One View*, 156).

[2] Hobbes' *Answer to Bramhall*, 127. "Passive Obedience signifies nothing except it may be called passive obedience, when a man refraineth himself from doing what the law hath forbidden. For in his lordship's sense the thief that is hanged for stealing hath fulfilled the law, which, I think, is absurd." See also *De Corpore Politico*, chap. vi.

of the Christian faith, the prohibition of that belief
and that alone can justify men in refusing to obey
the laws[1]. No case of the persecution of one
Christian body by another can exempt men from
the normal duty of active obedience. Further,
it might be said, that even in the last resort the
case was not clear, for the Apostles, who declared
that God must be obeyed rather than man, were
eye-witnesses of the Resurrection; their case was
therefore peculiar[2]. Moreover, Elisha had bidden
Naaman go in peace, when he talked of bowing
himself in the House of Rimmon. Taunts of this
sort could easily be levelled at the believers in
Passive Obedience. That there was, indeed, some
justification for these taunts, is shewn by the sophistical quibble with which the doctrine is wrested
to cover the case of the Revolution and of the
acquiescence of the clergy in William's reign. The
doctrine of passive obedience could not have loomed
so large save to men for whom politics was a branch
of theology. The cause of its playing so great a
part in the doctrine of Divine Right is that the
latter is bound up with the defence of the Church
of England against its foes. At this time, indeed, all
theories of politics either have a religious basis or
are framed with the practical object of defending
the true faith. Politics and theology are as yet
intimately connected. And, though in the writings of Locke and Sidney we see politics seeking
to free themselves from their theological vesture, it

[1] *Leviathan*, II. 43; the passage is quoted in Appendix III.
[2] *Behemoth*, 86.

is not yet cast away. When the theory of Divine Right is thus seen to be connected with the existence of the Church of England and with its position as a Church, at once anti-papal and anti-presbyterian, we shall surely see some justification of the action of the clergy in 1688. The theory of the Divine Right *James II.* of Kings is framed for the defence of the nation *tried to use the* against Roman claims. It is a weapon forged *theory to* against the Papacy, although it may be used for *thwart the purpose* other purposes. James saw that the weapon was *for which it existed.* two-edged, and attempted to use it against the *His* Church, in whose defence it was formed, and in *failure was* favour of the very power it was fashioned to attack. *natural.* What wonder that the sword broke in his hands ! Whether or no the interpretation of the theory set upon it by James was logically justified, it ran directly counter to the intention of all who had taken part in the making of it. The Anglican clergy were moved in their action by the clear conviction that no one could have intended that the great anti-papal weapon should be used in favour of the Pope. They must have felt that James was following in the footsteps of Queen Mary, and was attempting to use the royal supremacy in order to render it a nullity for evermore. They refused him their assistance in this attempt. Who can blame them ? In neither politics nor theology are men of any age aware of the whole extent of the ground which their theories may logically be held to cover. Nor will they ever hesitate about refusing to carry a belief to its theoretical conclusion, when the conclusion conflicts with the purpose for which the doctrine was first framed. There are many nowadays who profess the doctrine *vox populi vox dei*. But it can hardly be maintained, that they are prompt to acknowledge an unfavourable verdict of the constituencies as of divine prompting. If the worshippers of democracy are at times betrayed into reading *diaboli* for *dei*, or into employing anti-democratic institutions in order to maintain their position, are we to find great fault with the supporters of non-resistance in the seventeenth century, who found that for once they had been mistaken, and that on occasion it might be well to exhibit the virtue of non-resistance, not to a Romanising king, but to a Protestant invader? The theory of Divine Right had a great work to do in assisting Englishmen to free themselves from the Papal yoke. The proof that the work was done was not reached until, in their fear of Rome, men were ready to cast aside the very weapon which had hitherto aided them in the struggle.

Work of the doctrine. So far remark has been made of the service performed by the theory of Divine Right, in asserting the profound truth that political institutions *per se* are not displeasing to God as the author of nature; that they ought to be something more than the instruments of ecclesiastical authority; that the statesman is not bound to take his policy from the priest; that the State as such is an organism with a life of its own, and is subject to laws of developement distinct from those of the Church; that the rulers of the Church will not necessarily be possessed of political wisdom above the common, and may not without danger be trusted with the tremendous power of deciding on questions of national policy with reference to the aggrandizement of that organization (which itself has an earthly side), to whose service they are devoted; or in modern phrase that the "clergy should not meddle with politics." It is thus clear, that to the derided Anglican clergy of the seventeenth century are due many of the most cherished principles of modern life. They may not justly be charged with pursuing a time-serving and servile policy. Their aims were not dictated by the interests of a class or section, but were patriotic and pre-eminently characteristic of the defenders of a national Church. They cannot truly be charged with deserting their principles the moment that they became inconvenient, for their conduct at the time of the Revolution, if inconsistent with the letter of their doctrine, only proves how deeply imbued they were with its spirit, and exhibits their thorough loyalty to the essential principle which their theory was framed to express. All this is true, and has been too often left out of account in the abuse that has been levelled at the believers in Divine Right.

Yet it must not be forgotten that much was due *The clerical theory had a value.* to that very ecclesiastical theory of politics against which men strove in the seventeenth century. That doctrine also had a practical work to perform; despite much in it that was false and exaggerated and seems to modern notions preposterous beyond measure, it has brought about the recognition of one of the most important principles that can guide the statesman. For the claims of Pope or

Presbyter to control the secular power in the interests of the spiritual enshrined in the only form possible to those times the principle of the *rights of conscience.* In ages when the enforcement of conformity by the strong hand is a recognized principle, when all nations profess the same form of religious belief, or when the maxim *cujus regio ejus religio* has become accepted, the only possible method of asserting the rights of conscience and the claims of truth is for the Church to claim superiority over the State.   It is inevitable at such times that the perennial problem of Church and State shall take the form of a struggle for supremacy; for neither can admit the entire authority of the other without the gravest danger on the one hand to truth, on the other to the free developement of national life.   If the State be admitted to be omni-competent, while the persecution of error is preached as a duty, an Emperor or King with a theological turn of mind may commit the Church to a heresy and endanger God's truth for all time[1].   For *ex hypothesi* it is recognized that the State is supreme in all departments of life; that it is the duty of the State to enforce conformity; and that resistance is unjustifiable.   The State may therefore compel the propagation of heresy, and stamp out completely the true faith, for the notion is unfounded, that persecution always fails[2].   If the rights of conscience and

It is an early form of asserting the rights of conscience.

---

[1] On the element of justice in the claims of the Church see the remarks of Dean Church in the letter to Cardinal (then Archdeacon) Manning of July 1844 (Purcell, *Life of Cardinal Manning*, I. 696).

[2] Mill, *On Liberty*, 16.

the claims of truth are to be respected at all, the Church must make herself the guardian of them and claim supremacy over the State. So long, of course, as persecution is a recognized principle, truth cannot be secure. But it is at least a step in the right direction that the power, which has physical force on its side, shall submit to take its views of truth and error from the power, whose force is moral and spiritual only. It is better that the Church should direct the State, as to what forms of faith to enforce or to persecute, than that the State should prescribe religion *proprio motu*. Even this imperfect condition of things is a tribute to the rights of conscience, to the claims of truth, and to the existence of human interests other than those which are merely material and earthly. Toleration involves the principle, that religion is a department of life which the State has no moral right to control, that opinion may not be coerced. Persecution by the State at the bidding of the Church contains the germ of this principle; for it arises from the notion that the State as such cannot meddle with opinion, but must take its views from those who know. It forms the necessary transition between the State-religion of the Roman Empire and the modern ideal of freedom of opinion. In the first stage, the State prescribes a religion of its own and compels all men to worship the Emperor. In the second, the State recognizes that it is incompetent to decide upon questions of religious belief, and must go to the spiritual authority to find truth; but it still regards the enforcement of truth as a duty, and persecution as its proper function. The third stage is that of complete toleration of all forms of belief, when the State has given up its claim to meddle with opinion, and regards religious questions as beyond its competence. Now the third stage was not reached at the period which is here being discussed. It will therefore be readily seen that in order to secure the principle which is characteristic of the second stage, and to prevent a relapse into the first, the Church must ever be proclaiming its supremacy in matters of faith and denying the right of the State to meddle therein save at its bidding. This must inevitably lead to some such claim of political authority as was put forward under the Papal or Presbyterian system. If the State admits the right of the Church to dictate to it the true faith to be enforced and to prescribe forms of ecclesiastical organization and discipline, the Church will be found continually encroaching upon the State; many matters, which are of civil import, will be treated as constructively ecclesiastical; and, in the last resort, all freedom will be denied to the State, and its unspiritual character will be made the basis of a claim for its enslavement. The State must then assert its independence; and the form of the assertion is the subject of this essay.

The conflict inevitably lasts, until toleration becomes a recognized principle.   Nor is there any means, whereby the conflict can be brought to a close, until the principle of toleration be generally accepted. Only when the State has resigned the claim to make religion co-extensive with its authority, can the Church with safety withdraw from its pretensions to make politics subservient to ecclesiasticism. When that be the case, the State, by giving up the claim to enforce truth at the point of the bayonet, will have freed the Church from the risk of destruction. The claims of the State to omnipotence may henceforward be admitted. The Church will no longer be in danger with every chance current of thought, that may sway the sovereign one or number. There is no longer any need for the Church to proclaim its supremacy over the State, for its activity is recognized as free from State interference. The State is sovereign. It may legally do what it pleases. No co-equal jurisdiction exists. No clerical organization may dictate to it. That is the principle underlying the sophistical reasoning and obsolete philosophy of the supporters of the Divine Right of Kings. Conscience must be respected. Beliefs are free. Men's forms of ecclesiastical organization must be of their own choosing. The State must not force their faith or practice. Religious toleration is to be a practical limit upon the exercise of the sovereign power. This is the principle, which out of numberless impossible claims and anarchical opinions has been won for modern citizens by those who assert the Divine Right of Pope or Presbyter. Neither side saw clearly or completely what was the essence of its claim. Neither side realized that toleration alone could set the conflicting claims at rest, and permit of both Church and State developing without injuring one another. Both sides argue with passion, with sophistry, with an uncritical assumption of God's being on their side, which must seem to us Pharisaical. Yet each side was right in its main contention. The State has a right to exist apart from the favour of the clergy; and politics should not be governed by ecclesiastical considerations. On the other hand there are departments of thought and action with which the State may not interfere without the gravest injury to the highest interests of humanity. Both sides were fighting for principles which have long been admitted to be rooted in right reason and utility. To throw ridicule upon the antiquated forms in which these principles found expression and did their work, to blame the royalist for servility or the Papalist for bigotry is to blame men for defending a just cause with the only weapons that were available. That there was too much of passion and prejudice on either side may be admitted. Even modern controversies are not quite without them. But they are frequently wanting in those solid results, which give such cause for gratitude to the controversialists of the middle ages and the Reformation. The more closely the subject is studied, the greater will be the debt of gratitude acknowledged alike to those, who by supporting the Divine Right of Kings have ministered to the stability and independence of the English State, and to their opponents, to whose labours we owe it that liberty of thought has become a recognized principle of modern life.

CHAPTER IX

NON-RESISTANCE AND THE THEORY OF SOVEREIGNTY

IT is as a phase in the conflict of Church and *Political* State that the theory of the Divine Right of Kings *aspect of the theory.* possessed its greatest significance and produced its most memorable results. Yet it has a place also in the history of the developement of the theory of government, and must be considered in relation to those political problems which occupied men's minds in the seventeenth century. It is true, that with the possible exception of Hobbes, all the political theorists up to the end of the seventeenth century either have religion for the basis of their system, or regard the defence or supremacy of some one form of faith as their main object. Hardly any political idea of the time but had its origin in theological controversy. To Roman writers in the main are due the theories of the State of nature and of the original compact[1]. Popular rights and ecclesiastical supremacy are bound up with one another.

---

[1] See especially Suarez, *De Legibus*, III. 4; Mariana, *De Rege*, I. 1, 2, 8. In the last-mentioned chapter the question discussed is "Reipublicae an Regis major potestas sit?" The course of the argument is singularly instructive, and much of it might have been written by Locke. It is notable that, although deciding

Yet since all these theological controversies have a political aspect, it is possible to isolate this aspect for the purposes of enquiry and to investigate the purely political side of the theory of Divine Right. There will be the less danger in this course, since the markedly theological character of all seventeenth century politics has already been sufficiently dwelt upon. Further, in the deluge of political literature that poured forth in the seventeenth century, it can hardly be but that views of every sort shall be found here and there in reluctant combination. An attempt to disentangle the main threads of controversy can lay no claim to comprehensive accuracy. Lines of thought apparently inconsistent will at times be united through individual idiosyncrasy. Methods of argument will change sides. Sentiments and opinions will be subject to kaleidoscopic permutations. A sketch like the present *This chapter can only describe general tendencies.* can do no more than describe general tendencies of difference or resemblance between opposing schools. It may give a rough estimate of what was the characteristic drift of thought on either side. But it cannot lay claim to finality. Nor must it be forgotten that individual writers may well be found whose personal equation obscures the main lines

in Chapter 2 that monarchy is the best form of government, Mariana would yet surround his king with all sorts of limitations, so that he really leaves the sovereignty with the people, and thus falls into the error of supporting a "mixed monarchy." "Postremo, quod caput est, Principis malo coercendi potestatem in republica residere." It is needless to say that, in Mariana's view, one of the main limits on royal authority is set by the freedom of the Church. Cf. *From Gerson to Grotius.*

of controversy, and causes them to overleap the
barriers of thought which separate opposing parties.
Still there are certain well-marked differences in
conception and standpoint between the combatants
on either side; each party appears to represent
certain distinctive tendencies. It seems reasonable
to attempt the exposition of these characteristics,
after thus premising that isolated cases may be
found in which they are not exhibited. It will then
be necessary to consider, whether or no the theory of
the Divine Right of Kings was something more
than the expression of an absurdly romantic sentiment of loyalty; how much it has in common with
other political theories of the time; whether, when
it differs from them, it differs from them for the
worse; and whether it contained within it notions
of the State, its powers and functions, which modern
thought has not discarded.

I.

There is no more universal characteristic of the *Univer-*
political thought of the seventeenth century than *sality of*
notion of
the notion of non-resistance to authority. "To *non-re-*
bring the people to obedience" is the object of *sistance.*
writers of all schools. When resistance is preached,
it is resistance to some authority regarded as
subordinate. Nor is the resistance permitted at
the pleasure or judgment of private individuals.
It is allowed only as a form of obedience, as executing the commands of some superior and ultimate

authority, God, or the Pope and the Law. It has been shewn already that the Papal theory is in truth a doctrine of obedience to a monarch. Great indeed was the indignation evoked by the airy manner in which Bellarmine or Mariana disposed of the claims to obedience of the secular prince, and fostered principles of popular sovereignty. Yet at least some Anglican writers were capable of seeing that all these notions are developed as part of a theory of obedience, and not of liberty, and that the text, "They that resist shall receive to themselves damnation," so far from being discarded or explained away, is interpreted as proving the political supremacy of the Pope. As Bishop Jackson puts it, "The principle wherein the Romish Church, the Jesuits, and we agree is this; that none may resist the higher powers; that obedience, at least passive or submissive from the outward man of our bodies, lives, and estates is due to the higher powers; the question is...which be the highest powers on earth[1]."

So with the Presbyterian view. The main object of the discipline is obedience, in Cartwright's view[2]. The strong expressions about duty to the civil magistrates which seem inconsistent, when read by the side of claims to depose them, are explained by the view, held in common with Papalists and Wycliffe, that resistance for mere oppression's sake

---

[1] Jackson, *Treatise of Christian Obedience* (*Works*, III. 971.)

[2] Cf. the following, "Under the name of the Saints are contained all the rest of the Church, which do not exercise any public office or function therein, whose duty as in all others sometimes is only this, to suffer themselves to be ruled and governed by those whom God hath set over them." *Declaration of Discipline*, 185.

is not justifiable, and that no private person may resist the Sovereign. Only the Kirk, as inspired by God, may direct the removal of an "idolater," in order to secure "freedom," i.e. supremacy for itself. Neither Papalist nor Presbyterian (except George Buchanan) contemplates the resistance of individuals[1]; nor does either make any approach to the modern notion, that obedience may be settled by utilitarian considerations.

Even with those who go further than this and look at politics from a more purely secular standpoint, God's cause is almost invariably the sole occasion of lawful resistance. Clearly, the notion of the Divine right of insurrection was not one, for which any considerable number of persons were contending in the seventeenth century. Remark has been made of the emphasis laid in the *Vindiciae contra Tyrannos* on the duty of passive obedience incumbent upon private individuals[2]. So long as a tyrant, however oppressive in his acts, is supported by the constituted authorities and estates of the realm, obedience to him is a duty. Nor was the notion confined to France. In England it found expression in the theory that resistance to the Crown is lawful, only if it be enjoined by the inferior magistrate. It was pretended that the Parliament took up arms against the person only of the King, but in support of his authority. This shews how loth men were to believe that what was legally wrong will ever

Modern utilitarian theory of obedience not held in seventeenth century.

---

[1] Mariana is apparently an exception with his theory of the duty of tyrannicide. *De Rege*, I. 7, 8.

[2] *Supra* p. 114.

be morally right. At this time some shadowy legality is always pretended for acts essentially revolutionary. Prynne's elaborate treatise is written with the object of proving that Parliament at the beginning of the Civil War had the law upon its side. The author has no notion that tyranny can justify the abrogation for the nonce of law[1]. The same notion appears more strongly in 1688, in the fiction that James, having abdicated the throne, the English legal and constitutional system is being developed with no breach of continuity. There is evidence yet more conclusive. Johnson, writing on behalf of the Exclusion Bill, declares deliberately that Christians are bound to submit to persecution in the case where the laws permit it. "When the laws of God and our own country interfere and it is made death by the law of the land to be a good Christian, then we are to lay down our lives for Christ's sake. This is the only case where the Gospel requires passive obedience, namely, when the laws are against a man[2]." So widespread was this notion, that one writer at the time of the Revolution subjects the Whig theory to the following *reductio ad absurdum.* According to the Whig view, if the King persecutes the true faith, he may be resisted. Now on this view if the law took a similar course it might be resisted. But no Whig will admit that this latter case would make resistance justifiable. Therefore it is absurd to claim the right in the former case where the King is persecutor

[1] *The Sovereign Power of Parliament and Kingdoms.*
[2] *Julian the Apostate* (Johnson's *Works*, 33).

against the law[1]. Nor, again, is the main force of
the royalist attack directed against the contention,
that resistance to the law may in certain circumstances be justified. Royalists are not concerned to
prove that the law may not be resisted on any
pretence without grievous sin. Nobody doubts
this. Their main position is quite different. They
set themselves to prove, that laws derive their
binding authority from the King alone, and therefore
that he may not be resisted when he breaks them;
for he, as the source of legislation, is himself above
positive law, and resistance to the 'sovereign' is
always sinful[2]. The real controversy between Royalists
and Whigs concerns the existence of a sovereign one
or number not subject to law[3]. The vexed question
of Julian the Apostate was a case in point. The Whig

---

[1] *Christianity a Doctrine of the Cross*, 75.

[2] See especially the above-mentioned pamphlet, and compare
the following passage: "The plea is the same on either side; the
Pope says as long as the Prince governs according to the Laws of
God and the Church (of which He is the interpreter) so long the
censures of the Church do not reach Him; and say the People,
as long as the Prince governs according to the Laws of the Land
(and of the meaning of those laws themselves are the interpreters)
so long are they bound to be obedient; but as soon as the King
doth anything that may contradict the Pope, then he is (deservedly
say the Romanists) excommunicate, deposed and murdered, and
when he usurps upon the People's liberties, then he ought to be
deposed by the people; the arguments on either side are the
same and for the most part the authorities." *History of Passive
Obedience* (1684), 84.

[3] "There is no authority upon earth above the law, much less
against it," (Johnson, 30) expresses the whole contention of the
Whigs, which is opposed to the theory of sovereignty as well as to
Divine Right.

argument is that the submission of the early Christians to persecution was owing to the fact that it was legal, while their (alleged) resistance to Julian was due to the illegality of his oppression[1]. Even Locke evades the difficulty by denying the omnipotence of "the legislative" in all states. He will not declare, that resistance to law is ever justifiable. He merely denies, that laws which transgress certain fundamental principles, are laws "properly so called[2]." So with Algernon Sidney. He declares that an unjust law is not law[3] at all, and gives as instances the persecuting statutes of the Lancastrian period[4]. No other view was possible to him; for elsewhere he is content to bow before the majesty of law. In one eloquent passage Sidney declares that "this [Law] is he to whom we all owe a simple unconditional obedience[5]." Milton in his *Tenure of Kings and Magistrates* perhaps comes nearer than most of his contemporaries to modern utilitarian views. Yet he places the sovereignty in the people by a fundamental and unalterable law[6]; and thus by a confusion between natural and positive law, similar to that

---

[1] Johnson, *Julian the Apostate*, "The first Christians suffered according to the laws of their country, whereas these under Julian were persecuted contrary to law," 28, *Answer to Jovian, Answer to Constantius the Apostate*.

[2] *Second Treatise of Civil Government*, Chaps. 11, 18.

[3] *Discourses Concerning Government*, III. § 11.

[4] *Ibid.* § 25.   [5] *Ibid.* § 42.

[6] *Tenure of Kings and Magistrates*, Prose Works, II. 11. "The power of kings and magistrates is nothing else but what is only derivative, transferred and committed them in trust from the people ...in whom the power yet remains fundamentally, and cannot be taken from them without a violation of their natural birthright."

made by Locke and Sidney, he thinks to escape the danger of asserting a doctrine which then seemed so preposterous as that resistance to law may ever be morally justifiable.

The law to which obedience is due may be Canon Law, 'Discipline,' Positive Law, Custom. But obedience to what is conceived as law of some sort, truly and not metaphorically speaking, is the universal maxim. Nearly all teach the duty of obedience to positive law, for the law of the Church is equally positive law if its claims be admitted. That some of these writers are feeling their way towards the purely utilitarian theory of obedience held in modern times is undoubtedly the case. But they had none of them reached it. One and all would have scouted the bald proposition, fundamental in utilitarian politics, that a law having all the notes of law "simply and strictly so called" may yet be disobeyed, if it be oppressive beyond measure. The practical teaching might not greatly differ from that of a modern utilitarian, for on most of these theories there would be ample grounds for pronouncing any law, to which grave objection is taken, as lacking in some essential property of law rightly so-called. Yet the theories of the seventeenth and nineteenth centuries are as wide apart as the poles. With very few exceptions, all political thinkers in the seventeenth century regard as absolute the claims of law, as they define it, to unquestioning, unvarying obedience; they teach that to the ultimate authority in the state, whatever it be, non-resistance is the last word of duty.

II.

Causes of this general belief in the duty of unvarying obedience to law.

Nor is the explanation far to seek. The history of the Middle Ages is filled with the struggle between government and anarchy. According to the Papal theory, secular governments are the anarchical powers, which would teach men to disobey their true lord in obedience to an inferior authority. From the point of view of national statesmen it is, on the one hand, the Pope claiming the deposing power, the clergy demanding immunities, on the other hand, the feudal lordships, private jurisdictions, livery and maintenance, that prevent or check the unquestioned supremacy of one all-embracing system of law. In the Wars of the Roses the evils of this latter tendency exhibit themselves for the last time. They produce the reaction in favour of despotism and peace at any price. For a long time after this, men will have ceased to regard liberty or constitutional rights as of any importance compared with strong government and the suppression of private war. Obedience is in the eyes of all men the supreme duty of the patriotic citizen; and law the one element essential to the welfare of the state.

The Common Law conceived as sovereign.

Nor is it of statute law that men are thinking; but of the Common Law, which, though containing much that may have originally been directly enacted, yet possesses that mysterious sanctity of prescription, which no legislator can bestow. The Common Law is pictured invested with a halo of dignity, peculiar to the embodiment of the deepest principles and to the highest expression of human reason and of the law of nature implanted by God in the heart of man. As yet men are not clear that an Act of Parliament can do more than declare the Common Law[1]. It is the Common Law, which men set up as the object of worship. They regard it as the symbol of ordered life and disciplined activities, which are to replace the licence and violence of the evil times now passed away. Instead of local custom or special privilege one system shall be common to all. Instead of the caprice of the moment, or the changing principles of competing dynastic policies, or the pleasure of some great noble, or the cunning of a usurper, there shall rule in England a system, older than Kings and Parliaments, of immemorial majesty and almost Divine authority. "Law is the breath of God; her voice the harmony of the world." And the Common Law is the perfect ideal of law; for it is natural reason developed and expounded by the collective wisdom of many generations. By it kings reign and princes decree judgment. By it are fixed the relations of the estates of the realm, and the fundamental laws of

[1] [Judicial Records and Acts of Parliament] "are but declarations of the Common Law and Custom of the Realm touching Royal Government," *Jenkins Redivivus*, 1; the repeated attempts beginning with 42 Ed. iii. c. 1, to declare certain Acts of Parliament unrepealable are another proof of this. Cf. also Bonham's case (Reports 118 a). "When an Act of Parliament is against common right and reason or repugnant or impossible to be performed, the *Common Law will control it and adjudge such Act to be void.*" *Majestas Intemerata* contains a long legal argument directed against the omnipotence of Parliament, and contending that "the statute is but declarative" (8). "An Act against payment of tithes is regarded as void" (16).

the constitution. Based on long usage and almost supernatural wisdom its authority is above, rather than below that of Acts of Parliament or royal ordinances, which owe their fleeting existence to the caprice of the King or to the pleasure of councillors, which have a merely material sanction and may be repealed at any moment. It is not wonderful that men should have thought of the Common Law as sovereign by Divine Right; or that they should have deemed that it owed its authority to something higher than the will of the Sovereign. In the days when English Law first took shape, men had spoken of it as superior to King and Parliament alike, and had dreamed of no sovereign's sanction as needful to make it binding. And so we find many in the seventeenth century who retain the notion, and think, that the word "Law, Law[1]" is enough. For them law is the true sovereign, and they are not under the necessity of considering whether King or Lords or Commons or all three together are the ultimate authority in the state.

III.

With the Reformation a true theory of sovereignty becomes possible in England. But this was no longer true to the facts. Legislative activity had much increased of late. In Tudor times it effected the most far-reaching series of changes known in English history. The central power had asserted its supremacy over aristocratic privilege and made good its independence against the Papacy.

[1] "Truly for these many years last past have the lawyers enslaved both the king and the people by the charm of 'Law, law'." *The Church's Eleventh Persecution*, 7.

At last there was room in English politics for a
complete theory of sovereignty. The vast increase
in the powers and activity of the legislator could not
fail to drive men to seek for the sanction of the
law in his will. They were forced to consider the
question, whether Kings are anterior to law, or law
to governments. Here there is a distinction capable
of splitting into two parties the believers in the
Divine Right of the law of the land. On the one
hand those who believe that custom is the main
element in law, and law therefore the king-maker,
naturally claimed to make the Judges, as interpreters of the law, the supreme power in the state ;
while, like Bracton, they themselves failed to see
the necessity of a sovereign one or number and
honestly believed that no power in the state is
exempt from legal limitation. On the other hand,
those who have grasped the notion, now first made
apparent by facts, that there must be a sovereign in
the state, who may give to laws their efficacy, will
claim that he is *ipso facto* above the laws, and
cannot be subject to their coercive power. The *Inevitable*
quarrel between the Crown and the Judges was not *contro-*
versy
only the forerunner of the greater quarrel between *between*
supporters
King and Parliament : it was inevitable in the *of the*
nature of things. The Judges, as professors of the *Crown*
and the
Common Law, claimed for it supreme authority, and *Common*
had their claim been admitted, would have made *Law.*
themselves the ultimate authority in the state. For
no one denied their right to interpret the law. The
King, realizing vividly that there must be a sovereign,
claimed naturally enough the position asserted for

the Judges. What the Judges really asserted was that all constitutional questions could be settled by a reference to custom, and that they alone were competent to declare it. This, as Mr Gardiner points out, would have given into their hands the decision of the great struggle of the seventeenth century[1]. Coke, like most of the opponents of the King, had not really grasped the conception of sovereignty; he maintained a position, reasonable enough in the Middle Ages, but impossible in a developed unitary state. For his claim and that of all the Common Lawyers was to personify the Common Law as sovereign, and to deny that character to any person or body in the state. Had his ideal been reached, and questions of interpretation (which made the Judges sovereign) settled once for all, England would have been in the condition of the Punjaub under Runjeet Singh, as described by Sir Henry Maine, where the person "habitually obeyed" never made a true law and was deemed incapable of making one[2]. The fact, lamented by Clarendon, that the "professors of that great and admirable mystery, the Law" were on the Puritan side, was inevitable[3]. For their view was towards a state of things that had ceased to exist, and they sought to explain the constitution of England as Bracton might have done. But the King had perceived that with the growth of legislative activity and

[1] For accounts of Coke's views and the various controversies which culminated in his suspension, see Gardiner, *History of England*, II. 35—43, 242, 279, III. 1—25.

[2] *Early History of Institutions*, 379 sqq.

[3] *History of the Rebellion*, IV. 38—41.

the victory of the central power over its enemies, sovereignty had become a fact, and past history justified him in laying claim to all that was involved in the new state of things. It is the King and his supporters, be it observed, who first saw the change. Parliament, unwilling at first to claim the sovereignty, denies that it exists. On the other hand, if the King had been permitted to retain all his traditional prerogatives, the general recognition of the idea of sovereignty would have made the government a tyranny; as Maitland said, it was only the lack of this recognition that saved England from falling into despotism in the Middle Ages. Now that the truth was soon to be recognized by the nation at large, Parliament was forced to make new claims and by degrees to grasp at supremacy, lest it should lose old rights or even forfeit equality. With many modifications, the controversies between Whigs and Royalists right up to the Revolution hinged on this question of sovereignty. One side has ever before it the vision of law conceived as a system existing by Divine Right, its origin lost in the past, independent of circumstances and men's caprice, superior to Kings, and controlling Parliament. The other side lays stress on the conception of a sovereign raised above all laws with power to abrogate them, who alone can give binding force to enactments and invest custom with legal sanctions. The supporters of the Crown are repeatedly found arguing that the King must be before and above the law, or how can it be binding? They are enraged at the stupidity of their opponents, who cannot admit so obvious a fact. The novelty of the notion of sovereignty is the explanation of the otherwise unaccountable views entertained by those judges who favoured the Crown's claims as to the King's extraordinary power[1]. They saw that law can never bind the 'sovereign' in any state, and they were therefore driven to enlarge the meaning of prerogative to an alarming extent. The very fact that the idea of sovereignty had only then disengaged itself from a belief in the supremacy of custom, would compel all those, who were imbued with the idea, to treat of the King's prerogative, as the basis and essence of the whole system of law, rather than as an aggregate of exceptional powers and discretionary authority allowed to him by well-established custom. Sovereignty presented itself to these men with all the force of a discovery, and in their enthusiasm for the abstract conception, they used language which justified their opponents in declaring that they were interpreting the law, so as to give the King a truly arbitrary, i.e. capricious authority.

This question forms the main ground of controversy up to the Revolution.

The doctrine of sovereignty was perhaps misconceived in some of its details, or not grasped with absolute precision. Yet certainly, from the point of view of political theory, the controversy between Royalists and Parliamentarians differs merely in its practical object, from the questions, which every student of Austin is driven to ask himself, "At what point does custom become law? And how is it made

[1] See especially the judgment of Chief Baron Fleming in Bates' case printed in Prothero's *Documents*, 340, and of Berkeley in Hampden's case in Gardiner's *Documents*, 46.

such ? " The point has been much debated of late years; yet it may be doubted whether there is any substantial agreement among writers on jurisprudence. If thinkers, whose only object is scientific investigation, are not yet agreed as to what is the true answer to these questions, there is no great cause to blame the disputants on either side in the seventeenth century. The problem as to the precise value of the maxim, "Whatever the sovereign permits, he commands," will not improbably continue to perplex us till the end of time. But this much is certain. The facts of English history had for the first time rendered complete sovereignty a necessity in English national life. The question, in whom the sovereignty should ultimately be vested, could only be decided by a century of struggle. The sovereignty of whatever person or body was the highest authority in the English State became a practical fact at the Reformation. Only those who were the least hampered by tradition would be gifted with the clearness of insight necessary to perceive this. All whose imaginations were dominated by the past would fail for a time to observe the change. The leaders of advance in this matter were the believers in Divine Right.

The omnipotence of Parliament is doubtless realized sufficiently at the present day by many persons, who would be at a loss to understand some of the details of the theory of sovereignty. It is not surprising that the first perception of the notion takes at first a practical, rather than a scientific form. For most men the idea will be suggested by the

observed fact of the existence of a sovereign.
They will not frame the theory, and afterwards
observe the facts. Now it is unlikely that those,
whose gaze was turned to the England of the sixteenth century, could suppose that sovereignty was
invested in any other person than the King. Here
and there, a man like Prynne or Sir Thomas Smith
may be found arguing that not the King, but
Parliament is truly sovereign[1]. Yet most men will
arrive at the idea of sovereignty because they will
seem to see it encircling the diadem of Henry VIII.
or Elizabeth. As was shewn above, the course of
circumstances would lead men to suppose that the
sovereignty was vested in the Crown and not in
Parliament. The perception of this fact inevitably
led to the exaltation of the position of the King,

[1] The very fact that Prynne knows that his treatise will seem
a dangerous paradox is proof that his views were not generally
accepted (*Sovereign Power of Parliaments*, To the Reader). Bishop
Sanderson, again, considers the mere words of the oath of supremacy as quite sufficient proof that the sovereignty is vested in the
King, and not the Parliament (Preface to Ussher's *Power of the
Prince*). The personal character of allegiance, as defined by all the
Judges in Calvin's case, was another bar to men's dreaming of
Parliament as the actual depositary of sovereign authority. The
views quoted above as to the possibility of avoiding Acts of Parliament would similarly hinder the growth of a belief in Parliamentary
sovereignty. Nor is there as yet one imperial Parliament; it is
to the King, not the Parliament that inhabitants of England,
Scotland and Ireland are united in allegiance. If the three are
to make one realm, it can only be because the King is sovereign.
The United Parliament of Cromwell made Parliamentary sovereignty a possibility. It is noteworthy that theories of popular
sovereignty in the seventeenth century are not in general theories
of technical sovereignty vested in Parliament, but doctrines of the
rights of the people in the last resort.

and to a depreciation of the rights of Parliament and the rules of Law. Only as this took place, would those, who were determined to stand by the rights of Parliament and by the ancient conventions of the constitution, gradually rise to the conception of Parliamentary sovereignty, and find in the privilege of Parliament a treasury of omnipotence not inferior in elasticity and controversial convenience to the undefined possibilities of royal prerogative[1].

IV.

The Divine Right of Kings on its political side *The Divine Right of Kings is the form taken in the seventeenth century by the theory of sovereignty.* was little more than the popular form of expression for the theory of sovereignty. As an abstract theory the idea is never likely to be widely prevalent. But sovereignty seen, as a fact, vested in a person or body of persons may lead men to frame a theory far more generally intelligible and practically effective than the academic analysis of the notion in Austin, or even in Hobbes and Bodin, can ever become. This is the case with the Divine Right of Kings. Evidence of the fact may be found in plenty. Many of the most strenuous supporters of the Divine Right of Kings declare that similar rights belong to all established governments, and that non-resistance to their authority is equally a duty. On the other hand, the opponents of the theory are frequently found attacking not so much royal authority, as the idea of sovereignty. Moreover Hobbes, who has the

---

[1] Clarendon traces the process by which the privilege of Parliament was extended by imperceptible degrees to cover an assumption of complete sovereignty. *History of the Rebellion, passim.*

reputation of being the first Englishman in the seventeenth century to formulate the complete theory of sovereignty, did not analyse it as a purely scientific notion, but had with his contemporaries the object of proclaiming the duty of invariable obedience and non-resistance to the sovereign in all states. The analysis of sovereignty is only incidental to the practical object of inculcating non-resistance. So with supporters of Divine Right.

Divine Right of Kings confused with non-resistance to all established government.

Bishop Overall's *Convocation Book* was avowedly compiled in the support of monarchy. The object of the book is to assert the Divine Right of Kings, and the duty of non-resistance. Yet it is of all established governments that this Divine authority is really asserted. True, arguments in favour of the superiority of monarchy are drawn from the patriarchal theory; yet the statement is made that after rebels have organized a government, its authority is from God. This statement is flatly subversive of the indefeasible hereditary right, and was on that ground distasteful to James I.[1] It is evident that there was confusion in the minds of the compilers, and that the element in their doctrine which was grasped with lucidity was the idea that some sovereign power existed in all states, that this sovereign power owed its authority to Divine ordinance, and that resistance to it is a sin.

Hickes, who became a non-juror, wrote his *Jovian* in the midst of the Exclusion Bill controversy. Yet he distinctly asserts that all established governments

[1] Overall's *Convocation Book*, Canon xxviii. James' Letter is printed in the preface.

are from God, and that the Biblical prohibitions of resistance are fully as applicable to the subjects of a republic as to those of a monarchy.

The work of Dudley Digges, *The Unlawfulness of Subjects taking up arms against the Sovereign*, is still stronger evidence that the most important elements in the theory of Divine Right are the conception of sovereignty and of non-resistance to the sovereign, whether King or Parliament. Except for the addition of the religious sanction to obedience, and for the use of scriptural illustrations, we might be reading a popular abridgment of the *Leviathan*. The theory of the origin of the state held by Hobbes is definitely adopted. The author does not assert that kingship as such is viewed with any special favour by God. Arguments based on the Old Testament and patriarchal society are dismissed as irrelevant[1]. All that is claimed is that England is, as a matter of fact, a monarchy, and that resistance to all established governments is a sin. Ussher, again, argues that sovereignty is a necessary natural fact[2]. Even Laud declares that he has no will to except against any form of government assumed by any state[3]. Although Filmer's sense of the need of unity in the state leads him to regard monarchy as the only true form of government[4], yet in another

---

[1] *The Unlawfulness of Subjects taking up Arms*, 16.

[2] " True it is that in several states there are admitted several forms of government." " If this be so, and that nature seeketh always to preserve itself, we may justly conclude that Magistracy is rooted in the Law of Nature and so in the Author of Nature, that is God himself." *Power of the Prince*, 12, 13.

[3] *Sermons*, III. (*Works*, I. 85).   [4] *Observations on Aristotle*.

place he speaks of the supreme power in any state, monarchy or republic, as nothing but the original power of the father[1].

Doubtless such works as the *Convocation Book* and *Jovian* exhibit less grasp of what is really involved in the theory of Divine Right than is the case with the *True Law of Free Monarchies* or the *Patriarcha*. There is confusion in the minds of the writers, yet they believe themselves, and have always been commonly regarded as, supporters of Divine Right. The essence of the theory must therefore lie in those doctrines, upon which they lay stress in common with the more accurate expounders of the notion. Those points, which are obscured or ignored by so strong a non-juror as Hickes, can at most be regarded as "organic details" of the theory, rather than as its main and vital principles[2].

The conception not grasped by the opposite party.

Still more clearly is it evident that the real question in dispute is the fact of sovereignty, and the origin of legal authority, if attention be paid to the repeated attempts made to convince Whig theorists, that no state can be without an ultimate

---

[1] *Patriarcha*, 23.

[2] The writings of the non-juror Leslie are the most vivid expression of royalist theory after the Revolution. It is plain that he is moved by no hatred of republicanism, but merely by the dread of anarchy. "There is no medium possible betwixt non-resistance upon any pretence whatsoever and a full licence to resist upon every pretence whatsoever. Because every man is left to judge of the pretence. So that *the whole dispute is Whether government or anarchy?*" (*The Best Answer.*) "For the word King, I mean no more than the supreme authority." (*Best of all.*) See Appendix.

authority, which, because it is sovereign, must be technically arbitrary. "The name of tyranny signifieth nothing more nor less than the name of sovereignty," says Hobbes[1]. "There is a necessity that somebody must be trusted, if you will not trust one, you must trust more" declares Digges[2]. "There is no such thing as a free state in the world[3]" is the thesis of another. Laud writes, "Turn the knot which way you will, all binding to obedience will be grievous to some[4]." Another asks, "What State can these rebels have that may not degenerate into a tyranny[5]?" Indeed, during the troubles of the Commonwealth the notion might easily be generated that tyranny is no less possible under a Parliament than under a King. It is a pertinent question, "The will of one man is contrary to freedom, and why not the will of five hundred[6]?" Royalists writing on this matter habitually speak with the half-amazed irritation of a teacher, trying in vain to get wilfully stupid pupils to realize how chimerical

[1] *Leviathan*, 392. Hobbes characteristically adds "saving that they that use the former word are understood to be angry with them they call tyrants." In *Behemoth*, 112, Hobbes shews that all governments are really arbitrary: and goes on, "The true meaning of Parliament was that not the King, but they themselves should have the arbitrary power not only of England, but of Ireland and (as it appeared by the event) of Scotland also."

[2] *The Unlawfulness of Subjects taking up Arms* (79); cf. also p. 43, "A necessity to grant impunity to some in all governments."

[3] *Royal Charter granted unto Kings* (Chap. XIV.).

[4] *Sermons*, VI. (*Works*, I. 180): cf. with this Mr Sidgwick's Remarks on the "coercion of well-intentioned adults," *Elements of Politics*, 623.

[5] ΕΙΚΩΝ ΑΚΛΑΣΤΟΣ, a reply to Milton's *Iconoclastes*.

[6] *Ibid.* There is much more in the same strain.

is the dream of a perfect state with no power in it exempt from legal limitation.

Locke's Treatise an attack on the idea of sovereignty.

Yet more is this apparent in the most striking exposition of the opposite theory. Locke's treatise is expressly directed against the notion that there is any sovereign power in the state. He realizes that the legislative is supreme, yet he sets himself the task of fencing it about with limitations of many kinds, such as the duty of respecting liberty and property, etc.[1] Locke does not say that the transgressing of these limits is invariably inexpedient or even universally iniquitous. This may be true; certainly it is tenable. But he tries to prove that such action would be illegal. If the 'Legislative' oversteps the bounds which Locke has laid down for it, its authority is at an end, and the state is dissolved. Perhaps it would be hard to mention a single Parliament since the Reform Act which has not overstepped the limits of its competence according to Locke, and by so doing dissolved the state, and broken the continuity of our institutions and the whole system of law and government. The more closely Locke's treatise is studied, the more clearly will it be seen that it is an attack directed far more against the idea of sovereignty, than against the claims of absolute monarchy. The notion of legal omnipotence is abhorrent to him; and he is guilty of a confusion between law natural and law positive, from which the extremest and most reactionary royalist would have been free.

---

[1] *Second Treatise*, c. 11. Johnson's writings are dominated by a disbelief in the theory of sovereignty.

Algernon Sidney's *Discourses concerning Govern-* *ment*, and even Milton's *Tenure of Kings and Magistrates*, exhibit an almost equal want of insight. The definite ground assumed is that of Rousseau, that the people is sovereign, that this sovereignty comes from God and is inalienable. All governments are in their view merely officials carrying out the will of the sovereign people, and they may therefore be removed at any time[1]. This view is apparently also that of Mariana and Suarez, and is far more consistent and logically defensible than the common Whig theory.

Yet this view is also untenable, for in no state, at that time or now, can the legal sovereignty be said to be vested in the people. It may be true that it ought to be so vested; but it certainly is not the case in any modern state. The sense in which Milton and Sidney spoke of sovereignty being vested in the people is one which proves them incapable of realizing the notion of sovereignty with accuracy. It is with them little more than the expression of the belief in a general right of insurrection against intolerable oppression. To such a belief there would be no objection, if they did not use their loose interpretation of the term sovereignty, as a ground for denying the existence of the thing. They deny the fact of sovereignty save in a perfect democracy. This may be an ideal, but it is not the expression of existing conditions. That the people ought to be sovereign is a tenable view. But to assert that they are so as a matter of fact, and that any state, in which

[1] *Discourses Concerning Government*, Chap. III. *Tenure of Kings and Magistrates*, 14.

they are not so regarded, is not truly a state, is to be
guilty of a gross confusion of ideas. Milton's view that
" to say the king is accountable to none but God is
the overturning of all law and all government[1] " would
logically lead to the denial of law and government
in the Roman Empire or the French kingdom. The
confusion of Sidney's thought is yet more startling.
After propounding the theory of popular sovereignty
he goes on to assert, quite in the Austinian manner,
that the power of the lawgiver is arbitrary. He
then proceeds to argue that this power is in England
vested in the Parliament[2]. The inconsistency is
glaring. The people is sovereign; yet a small
number of them assembled in Parliament have the
' arbitrary,' i.e. sovereign power of making laws.
Even if Parliament be held, which it cannot be save
in a loose sense, to govern in the name of the
electors, and if sovereignty be ascribed to them, yet
the electorate was very far from being identical with
the people when Sidney wrote.

Theory of compact.   Even the theory of the original compact affords
evidence that the popular party had not clearly
grasped the notion of law and sovereignty. Austin
shews how untenable is the notion, that a compact
can be binding with no sovereign to enforce it. The
widespread prevalence of the theory may therefore
be taken as evidence, that the men who held it

---

[1] *Tenure of Kings and Magistrates*, 12.
[2] *Discourses Concerning Government*, III. §§ 21, 45, 46. Sidney
regards Filmer's exposition of sovereignty as proving nothing but
" the incurable perverseness of his judgment, the nature of his heart
and the malignity of his fate always to oppose reason and truth."

believed in law as resting mainly on moral sanctions, as independent of physical force and possessed of Divine authority. The theory that government and obedience result from a binding compact could only be credited by men, who instinctively regarded law as anterior to the state.

V.

From all this it appears that all parties in the seventeenth century are at bottom united in their respect for law and in anxiety to defend government; although they differ as to the nature of both. Law must be supreme, anarchy at all costs must be prevented. This is the dominant thought of influential writers on all sides. Yet one party in their reverence for law would seek to invest it with a quasi-sovereign authority, and would deny to present and future generations the power of substantially changing it. For it is law, as a product of custom and ancient statutes hardly distinguished from custom, that is reverenced by the Whigs. The other party had deeper insight. They saw that in no civilized state can law exist without a lawgiver, and they deduced the necessity of a true sovereign. Both sides agree in inculcating non-resistance to the power which is regarded as the ultimate authority, whether law or lawgiver. Doubtless the supporters of the monarchy made mistakes. They pushed to extremes their doctrine of the theoretical omnipotence of the sovereign power, and seemed at times indisposed to recognize the importance of practical limitations on the exercise of sovereignty. Of what have been called "internal

All parties unite to respect law, but differ as to nature of law and sovereignty.

limits" on the sovereign power, restrictions imposed by temperament and environment, they admit the wisdom. But their theory of non-resistance forbids them to allow of any external limits. Yet it remains true that the royalist party had in general far clearer notions on law and government in a modern state, than had their opponents, who are often incapable of distinguishing between natural and positive law, and are ever haunted by the vain illusion of placing legal limits on the sovereign power.

Funda-mental Law.

Once the fact is grasped that the Divine Right of Kings in its philosophical aspect is merely the form given by circumstances to a doctrine of sovereignty, many of its most characteristic notions will present themselves in a fresh light. The phrase "fundamental law," of which so much is heard, signifies what a modern philosopher has classed among "the fundamental conceptions of politics[1]," and indicates merely belief that, if the state be truly such, there must be a sovereign and subjects. Hickes' division of laws into laws positive and laws imperial is another way of expressing the same notion; laws imperial merely mean those facts, which are inherent in the nature of the state, and which must exist before laws properly so called arise.

Indefeas-ible here-ditary right.

The view that hereditary right is indefeasible is another element in this conception. Or rather it is the form given to that notion of the inalienable

---

[1] Sidgwick, *Elements of Politics*, Chap. II. It need hardly be said that, in the view of all orthodox supporters of Divine Right, the statutes of the Tudor period altering the succession are one and all *ultra vires* and void.

character of sovereignty, which (however insignificant practically) is yet sure to arise with the conception of sovereignty. It is doubtless a limitation on the sovereignty to deny the power of the sovereign to alter the form of government. Yet it would be hard to find a better sanction for many branches of so-called constitutional law at the present day, than that the courts will enforce them. So with indefeasible hereditary right; so long as the view could be maintained that the courts would enforce the doctrine, it was not unnaturally regarded as a part of constitutional law.

The doctrine that the rights of Parliament are derived from the Crown only as matters of grace and favour, was characteristic of the mind of King James, and became the ground of controversy both in his own case and that of Dr Cowell. It afterwards became the accepted principle with the royalist writers. The doctrine is really an expression of the sense that sovereignty is indivisible as well as inalienable. So it is used by Bodin[1], who has an elaborate proof that the so-called power of the estates of the realm being merely grants from the sovereign does not imply any diminution or division of his power. He seeks to shew that in the case of England the assent of Parliament to new laws is not really indispensable. It is a maxim, that the donor of a right or privilege may reclaim it at any moment, because sovereignty being indivisible and inalienable, no sovereign right can be irrevocably resigned. Thus it seemed natural to assert, that

Power of Parlia-ment due to royal grant may be recalled.

[1] *De la Republique*, 139.

because King John granted Magna Charta, all the powers resigned by him still inhere in the King and may be recalled. The repeated historical proof that the Crown was at one time seised of such and such rights, and that it still possesses them in theory, is evidence of the hold upon men's minds of the notions of the indivisible and inalienable character of sovereignty. They cannot conceive that the King can really have lost any prerogative, which can be clearly shewn to have once belonged to him[1].

In the theory of the Divine authority of government all sides are agreed. In some form most men hold that non-resistance is a religious duty. It is the theory of sovereignty which differentiates the royalist writers from the popular side and unites them with Hobbes. For the *Leviathan* contains not only a theory of sovereignty, but also a demonstration that monarchy is the best form of government, that the English state is in fact a monarchy, and that resistance to the sovereign is never justifiable. Thus, then, the affinity between the theories of Divine Right and that of Hobbes' was far closer than is often supposed.

VI.

Hobbes and the clergy.

But how are we to explain the intense abhorrence with which Hobbes was regarded by the believers in Divine Right? Many causes of this dislike may be found. His philosophy, his

---

[1] *Majestas Intemerata* is a striking instance of this feeling. The author cannot conceive that the King has lost any rights which ever belonged to him.

alleged heterodoxy, his hatred of the Universities, his contempt for Aristotle (of whom Filmer has so great an admiration), his unrelieved Erastianism, his scorn of merely passive obedience, would all tend to deepen the dislike. But the head and front of his offending is different.

In the first place his system of politics is purely utilitarian. It contains far less of the religious sanction, which men of that day demanded for all governments, than do the writings of the opponents of non-resistance. His point of view is eminently modern; and his thought, therefore, for that very reason tends to be out of relation to that of the time in which he lived. It has been shewn above that in many ways his connection with his contemporary theories of politics is far closer than was once thought. Yet at bottom his system is divided from all others of his time by a far deeper gulf than that by which they were separated from one another. Alone among the men of his time Hobbes realized, that politics are not and cannot be a branch of theology. The fact that he passed to the other extreme, and committed the error of treating theology, as though it were a branch of politics, was unlikely to render him a more acceptable figure[1]

---

[1] To Hobbes religion was nothing but a "law of the kingdom," enforced for the sake not of truth but of peace, about which there must be no controversy. The duty of the clergy is solely to preach obedience. The Anglican divines could not be expected to view with favour a man who wrote in this style. "We may justly pronounce for the authors therefore of all this spiritual darkness in religion the Pope and Roman clergy, and all those besides who endeavour to settle in the minds of men *this erroneous doctrine,*

in the eyes of those, who sought their theory of
obedience in S. Paul and found the justification of
monarchy in the vision of Nebuchadnezzar.

*Theory of
original
compact
denies,
believers
in Divine
Right
assert, the
organic
character
of the
state.*

Yet there is a still greater cause of divergence
between Hobbes and the other royalist writers.
His theory of government was based upon the
original compact. This notion was, however ridiculous, the one clear conception of the opponents of
Divine Right and lay at the root of such consistency
of theory as they possessed. There is, indeed, on the
Whig side some more or less hesitating recognition
of the principle of utility, notably in the case of

---

that the Church now on earth is that kingdom of God mentioned in
the Old and New Testament" (Leviathan, 383). Now the belief of
all contemporary theorists of whatever party was the exact
converse of this ; they looked to Scripture for a complete theory
of politics. The dominant thought of Bellarmine and Suarez is
that Christ must have appointed for the Christian Church the
most perfect form of government ; and that political theory may
safely be founded thereon. The very first paragraph of the
De Romano Pontifice is to this effect ; Suarez takes the same ground
as a proof of the excellence of monarchy, (De Legibus, III. 4).
Mariana is willing to use the tenable opinion of the council being
superior to the Pope in order to prove the subjection of the King
to the community ; although he guards himself against the retort
from the opposite and more common view of Papal autocracy by
asserting that the Pope's power comes direct from God, while that
of the King comes from the people (De Rege, I. 8). Similarly it
has been shewn that for most Anglican divines politics are founded
upon theology ; e.g. Sacheverell's sermons, especially " The Political Union," which is far abler than the better known production,
are a striking instance of the belief. " It is impossible for it [govern-
ment] to subsist upon any other bottom than that of religion."
Hobbes would have transposed religion and government ; that he
arrived at the same conclusion as other royalists is as nothing to
the fundamental difference of principle.

Locke, and this connects them with the thought of the future and with the speculations of Bentham and Mill. Yet the basis on which rest all the theories of popular rights in the seventeenth century is not utility, but the original compact. It is against the original compact that the supporters of Divine Right inveigh most strongly. For it is the expression of a diametrically opposite standpoint to that of the Royalists. Amidst whatever mass of sophistry and error, the conception of the organic character of the state dominated the believers in Divine Right. The theory of compact, whether held by Whigs or Hobbists, is the denial of this. To them the state is an artificial creation. To Filmer or Hickes or Leslie it is a natural growth. In Locke or Sidney or Milton the original compact limits all forms of governments and reduces the state to a mechanical instrument, that may with ease be destroyed and manufactured afresh. In the view of Hobbes the machine of state, when created, is indeed to last for all time, but it has no quality of life, no principle of internal developement. According to the Whig view the sovereign people may repeatedly upset the constitution of the state, and might, if they were better men, do without one at all. The state in fact is a necessary evil. The popular theories of the seventeenth century are a survival of the notion proclaimed in its nakedness by Hildebrand, but hinted at by Aquinas, and more or less dominant in all the Papalist writers, that the state is a consequence of the fall existing for the hardness of men's hearts. Far different from this is the conception of the supporters of Divine Right. Political society is natural to man; government and therefore obedience are necessities of human nature. The uncritical appeals to the Scriptures, to the patriarchal theory, to past history are all governed by this one luminous thought, that the state is no mere artificial manufacture, but a natural organism, and that a wise handling of its problems can arise only from the recognition that it has distinct laws of developement, which may not be transgressed by tinkering it, as a machine. The logical issue of the popular theory is to treat the state as a lifeless creation of the popular will with no power of developement and with no source of strength in sentiment or tradition. No theory of government was ever more untrue to the facts of life than is that of Locke, and the difference between him and Filmer in this respect is all in favour of the latter. In Filmer's theory there is, indeed, a touch of unreality, which is not found in many of the less famous supporters of Divine Right. But there can be no doubt that the method of believers in Divine Right was far less unhistorical than that of their opponents. The contrast is expounded with striking force of satire and reasoning in the numerous writings of Leslie. Even Filmer's theory is based upon the notion that what has always existed must be natural to man and of Divine authority, and is therefore immutable.

Further, it is worthy of remark, that the supporters of Divine Right differed from their opponents in being the nearer to the truth. For both sides agreed in teaching invariable non-resistance to the ultimate authority, and are therefore in error according to the modern views. Neither side admitted the Divine Right of insurrection, as it is very generally held now. Both sides used uncritical methods and misinterpreted Scripture or evaded its meaning. Nor did the supporters of the Divine Right, or at least the majority of them, contend that monarchy is the only lawful form of government, and that all republican states ought to set about changing their constitution. Neither side possessed a utilitarian theory of politics. It is possible that on the popular side an individual here and there might be found, who taught a theory of utilitarian obedience; while on the side of the King some men might be found, who denied God's protection to any government save a monarchy. But in the main this was not the case. Against those who fail to perceive the true nature of law and sovereignty the royalist writers point out with truth the necessity in every state for some supreme authority above the laws. Against those who assert that the state is the artificial creation of an impossible contract they proclaim the profound truth that government is natural and necessary to mankind. The Divine Right of Kings is the expression of the supreme truth of political thought, Φύσει ἄνθρωπος ζῷον πολιτικόν. Men pride themselves on at last realizing the truth that the state is organic, or hail with enthusiasm the attempt of Austin and other modern writers on jurisprudence to clear up notions of law and government. They have then little right to charge with triviality those who announced the

Burke.

same truths in opposition to theories of law, that had ceased to represent facts, and to a system of politics only less unreal and absurd than that of Rousseau. It is true these notions found forms of expression that had relation to an order of things that has long since passed away. But if as against Rousseau prating of the rights of man, of natural equality, of popular sovereignty, men still pay reverent gratitude for the polemic, in which Burke proclaimed the historical character of constitutional life, the organic growth of the state and the value of sentiment and " prejudice," what right have they to blame Filmer or Leslie, who insist against Locke with equal truth that all men, so far from being born free and equal, are born slaves, that government has its roots deep in the past and that the state has a life which may not lightly be touched ?

Divine Right shews a belief in the moral basis of the state.

Lastly, the theory of the Divine Right of Kings was the form in which was expressed the sense of the need of some bond of moral sentiment and conscience other than the belief in its utility to attach men to any government. Burke felt the same need and expressed it in tones which yet ring in men's ears. He knew that the influences of sentiment and tradition are stronger than the calculations of interest to bind a people's allegiance to its government, and that no constitution can be stable which makes a merely utilitarian appeal on men's assistance. He was not ashamed to say that the dead weight of custom, " prejudice," was the weapon which all states should have in their hand. For he felt that an emotional tie must add strength to the civic reason in order to make it an enduring support. Now the theory of Divine Right was the expression of the same truth in forms suited to the seventeenth century. It may be that our debt of gratitude to the men of that age is no less great than that which all are willing to acknowledge to the great thinker of the last century. Nor should we be chary of giving their due to the protagonists in a struggle of which we are enjoying the fruits, merely because their fundamental principles won ultimate triumph only through the defeat of the practical maxims deduced from them, or because their methods of argument lack the persuasive charm and their style is without the majestic flow, which have given to Edmund Burke his unfading laurels.

"It is most true that all available authority is Mystic in its conditions" says Carlyle[1]. Into the true nature of the bonds, which unite men in government and subjection, Filmer and Leslie and Sacheverell perhaps had a deeper insight than the modern journalist or member of Parliament. In some form or other "loyalty to persons springs immortal in the human breast[2]," and must always survive as the basis of society, and obedience for conscience' sake remain the chief support of government[3]. The Divine Right of Kings is partly the expression of truths concerning society and the state of deeper and more universal significance than the trivialities of modern party politics.

[1] *French Revolution*, ii. 2.

[2] Cardinal Newman, *Letter to the Duke of Norfolk* (80).

[3] "There can be no firmness without law; and no laws can be binding if there be no conscience to obey them; penalty alone could, can never, do it." Laud, *Sermon* iv. (*Works*, i. 112).

CHAPTER X

CONCLUSION

*True
meaning
of Divine
Right.*
    IT will have appeared from the foregoing investigation that the theory of the Divine Right of Kings was something different in import and value from the collection of purely ridiculous propositions perversely preached by a servile church, which some have elected to represent it. It was able to gain currency by appealing to some of the deepest instincts of human nature. It gathered up into itself notions of the sanctity of the medicine man, of the priestly character of primitive royalty[1], of the divinity of the Roman Emperors and perhaps of the sacredness of the tribunician power. Yet the doctrine of Divine Right owes much to the common sentiment of Christians as to obedience; and it

[1] That this feeling had not died out in the seventeenth century is proved by the following words put into the mouth of Charles; *On their denying his majesty his chaplains:* "It may be, I am esteemed by my deniers sufficient of myself to discharge my duty to God as a priest; though not to men as a prince. Indeed I think both offices, regal and sacerdotal, might well become the same person, as anciently they were under one name, and the united rights of primogeniture." *Eikon Basilike.* This feeling was quite common at the time.

found its most effective material in the practice and teaching of the Christian Church in early ages. The sentiment of obedience to government, as of Divine authority, subsisted as a vague notion until the attempt of the Papacy to make use of the notion in its own interests, led men to examine the value of current maxims on the subject and to assert the independent authority of secular governments, in a theory which is in its essential meaning a doctrine of liberty—the freedom of political societies from subjection to an ecclesiastical organization.

It is as an anti-clerical weapon of independence *An anti-clerical* that the theory had its greatest value and fulfilled *theory.* its most noteworthy function. In opposition to the claims of the Pope to sovereignty by Divine Right, men formulated the claims of the King to sovereignty by a right that is not inferior. Thus the doctrine is anti-clerical. Yet since it was directed against a theory of clericalism, it was inevitably formed or supported in the main by divines. And the form of the theory was necessary to its success. It would have failed in its object, had it attempted to give to Parliament rather than to the King the sovereignty which it denied to the Pope. Against the traditional splendours of the tiara it would have been vain to set up any lower dignity than the Crown. Indeed no such aim could have been conceived in imagination. It would have been an anachronism. The one country, in which the resistance to the Papal yoke was of purely popular origin, threw off allegiance to the Papacy only to fall under the dominion of a power equally ecclesiastical in its aims and more galling in its incidence. In the sixteenth century it was well if a King had the strength to cast off the Papal yoke, without rivetting another clerical authority on the state. Certainly none but a King had the power.

The theory forms the necessary transition between mediæval and modern politics.

Again, we see that the theory was necessary as a transition stage between mediæval and modern politics. It is a far cry from the conception expressed in the Holy Roman Empire, that theology is the source of political theory, and that the state is an aspect of the Kingdom of Christ, to the modern view that politics and theology have little or no relation to one another. Politics are frankly secular nowadays. Even where religion is invoked as a sentiment, theology is not expected to solve the problems of statesmanship. Political theory has ceased to be anything but utilitarian, although it may be a question how far this change is an improvement and whether it is likely to be lasting. At any rate, in some form or other utilitarianism governs political thought at the present day. But for this to be the case, a long course of developement and conflict has been needful. Before political life can free itself from what may be called the theocratic stage, it must assert for itself a coequal right to exist with theology. It must claim that politics have a proper and necessary function to perform in the developement of the human race, and that therefore their independent existence must be as much a part of the Divine plan for mankind, as is the science of theology or the organization of the Church. That the state is the realization of a true idea, and has a necessary place in the world, is the claim, which was explicitly or implicitly denied by the Papalist, and only made good through the theory of Divine Right. For it is only when the claim is put forward by Divine Right, that it can have any practical efficacy against a sovereign claiming, as God's vicegerent, the overlordship of all kings and princes. That secular politics are as truly God's ordinance and that political organizations have as much claim to exist with His approval as the controversies of Churchmen and the rules of the Canon Law, is the least that can be demanded by all supporters of Divine Right.

In the Middle Ages all departments of thought *The theory* were conceived as subordinate to theology in such a *an element* way that the methods of theology fettered and *in the Re-* *formation.* strangled free developement in science or art or literature. The Reformation is the assertion of the claims of the human spirit to carry on independent work in all branches of enquiry and activity, under the consciousness that truth cannot contradict itself and that the results of every sort of labour carried on with appropriate means and for worthy objects will tend to unity at the last.

Now in politics the rise and prevalence of the theory of the Divine Right of Kings is the same phenomenon. Theology had attempted unreasonably to dominate politics, and had committed men to an unphilosophical basis and an uncritical method.

The only way to escape from the fetters imposed *Its form* by traditional methods, was to assert from the old *necessary.* standpoint of a Scriptural basis and to argue by the accustomed fashion of Biblical quotations, that politics must be freed from theology and that the Church must give up all attempts to control the State. The work of the Reformation was to set men free in all departments of thought and enquiry from subjection to a single method and a single subject. In the case of politics the achievement of this result was possible only through claiming at first theological sanction for the non-theological view of politics. Only when the result is achieved will politics be free to develope theories which shall be purely philosophical or historical. Not till then will it cease to be needful to find Scriptural authority for political theory, or Biblical counterparts to the ideals of government. Politics were able to enter upon their modern stage, only because the theory of Divine Right having done its work had emancipated them from mediæval fetters and had in so doing become obsolete itself.

Political value of the theory.
Again, it has appeared that the anarchy of the Middle Ages developed in men's minds a sense of the need of law and of the duty of obedience. Further, *Obedience to law.* the Reformation and other causes had contributed to develope so highly the legislative activity of the state, and the checks imposed upon its action by custom or the Pope or feudalism had been so generally removed, that a theory of sovereignty had become the natural expression of facts, and the sense arose, that law has its authority as being a command of the sovereign. The perception or the denial of these facts has been shewn to be the main point of political controversy between the believers in royal and in popular rights.

The other chief source of difference is that be- *The state an organism.* tween an artificial and a historical conception of the state. The believers in Divine Right taught that the state is a living organism and has a characteristic habit of growth, which must be investigated and observed. Their opponents believed the state to be a mechanical contrivance, which may be taken to pieces and manufactured afresh by every Abbé Sieyès who arises.

Moreover, it has appeared that the doctrine of *The theory fulfilled its object.* Divine Right effected its object. The political claims of the Papacy have disappeared. Whether or no Rome has technically receded from her pretensions, the temporal supremacy is not now an object for which the most ultramontane Romanist will contend. The claims still put forward by the Vatican to the temporal power in no way involve a claim to political supremacy over all princes. The doctrines of the deposing power and the *plenitudo potestatis* have vanished rather than been disproved. It would not be within the dreams of a modern Papalist to assert them, nor would there be the smallest likelihood of any Roman Catholic nation admitting them, if they were asserted. The claim to infallibility has been long since explained as in no way involving a weakening of civil allegiance[1].

---

[1] See Cardinal Newman's *Letter to the Duke of Norfolk* ; also *Life of Cardinal Manning*, I. 399.

Perhaps the Pope's complaint, that Brandenburg was erected into a kingdom without his consent is the last instance of any attempt to assert the temporal supremacy, unless the coronation of Napoleon be regarded in that light. (Lamberty, *Mémoires*, I. 383.)

Further, practical influences, among which the Union with Scotland is probably not the least important, have contributed to reduce to a minimum the claims of the other ecclesiastical body, which disputed with the Roman Church for the palm of imposing upon the state the more stifling touch. The omnipotence of civil governments all the world over is a fact no longer disputed—with one limitation. From the claim by Divine Right put forward by the Church to a freedom which meant supremacy, has grown the doctrine of toleration, by which alone, as a practical limit upon state action, religious freedom can be secured without clerical supremacy.

The theory necessary to the Reformation. That the Divine Right of Kings was not merely useful, but necessary to the political side of the Reformation, appears to be clearly proved by the evidence. Confirmation of this is afforded by the fact that the theoretical presentment of antagonism to the Papal claims had taken in earlier ages a form, which differed but little from the theories of the sixteenth and seventeenth centuries. With the Restoration the last chance of Presbyterianism becoming dominant in England disappeared. The Revolution finally removed all danger from the side of Rome. Only then did the theory of the Divine Right of Kings cease to be useful. As a matter of fact, from a doctrine with a practical aim it begins at this time to pass into a romantic belief enshrining a sentimental regret for the past, and has perhaps a value in literature which it has lost in theology and politics. Perhaps we may see in Burke the survival in substance and transformation in form of the fundamental principle, which gave to the theory of Divine Right its political value. The *raison d'être* for the rival theories was removed by the statutes of Toleration and Catholic Relief. On the other hand, as soon as the notion of the original compact had done its work in England by giving men what they regard as an intellectual justification for the Revolution, it too began to disappear and to give place to the purely utilitarian theory of politics, which became dominant through the influence of Bentham.

The theory of Divine Right did not lose its popularity because it was absurd, but because its work was done. There were just as good reasons for disbelieving in its validity in 1598 or 1660 as there were at the Revolution. Certainly some writers were well acquainted with them even at the earlier date, a fact proved by such a treatise as that of Parsons. The Divine Right of Kings ceased to have practical importance, not because its doctrines were untrue, but because its teaching had become unnecessary. The transition stage had passed. The independence of the state had been attained. Politics having made good their claim to be a part of the natural order had no longer need of a theological justification. *The belief died, when it was no longer useful.*

Again, if the theory be regarded on its purely political side, the conceptions which it enshrined are become part of our common heritage. To the sense of the organic character of the state and of the duty of obedience are due the existence of "law-abiding citizens" to-day and that dislike of all violent *Doctrine has moulded English sentiment.*

breaks with the past, which has ever been the peculiar glory of England,

> "Where freedom slowly broadens down
> From precedent to precedent."

It was due to this doctrine that the English Revolution was the most peaceful in history and that English institutions have been developed with scarcely a breach in continuity. To modern ears the 'abdication' of James II. must ever seem a fiction only the more dishonest that it was transparent. Yet the phrase was a pledge, that the old laws and customs of the realm should remain, and that no cataclysms should disturb the orderly developement of the national life. The phrase was false, but the sentiment which it expressed was profoundly true.

Its effect on politics beneficial. Nor again has the doctrine of non-resistance been anything but salutary in its results. It has, indeed, been superseded by a theory of utilitarian obedience, which, although it may be true, is likely to be fraught with greater dangers than could have attended the firmest faith in passive obedience. It is easy for modern politicians to regard the inculcation of invariable non-resistance as mere nonsense. Yet most sober thinkers would admit that only in the extremest cases can resistance be justified. It may be that obedience is owed to the law on account of its utility, but no one will make every disutility in the law a ground for disobedience. It is not doubtful that a sense of the duty of obedience must be widespread, if stability is to be secured for the state. We are willing enough to admit that "force is no remedy," and that in general a certain sentiment of loyalty is needful to the well-being and security of all governments. On what grounds then can we blame those who found expression for identically the same views in the maxim that men must obey not only for wrath, but for conscience' sake? A modern thinker has declared that laws and governments need some other sanction than that of military force. Those who endorse the aphorism "You can do anything with bayonets except sit on them" can have little reason for blaming Laud when he declares "There can be no firmness without law; and no laws can be binding if there be no conscience to obey them; penalty alone could never, can never do it[1]." That government can worthily perform its function only when obedience is enshrined in the hearts of the governed, that laws are vain without loyalty, was the truth for which the men of the seventeenth century were contending, when they asserted that all resistance was damnable. That government of any kind was better than anarchy, they were well assured. Tyranny was in their eyes a more supportable condition than disorder. But whether or no it can be maintained that no caprices of autocracy and no oppression of democracy can make resistance to a King a right or defiance of Parliament (or the County Council) a duty, all will agree that the widespread prevalence of a law-abiding sentiment is essential to the stability of the state. It is well that most men should regard resistance to laws, however unjust, as practically prohibited by the moral law. If there be "cases of resistance," they are best ignored.

[1] Laud, *Sermons* (*Works*, I. 112).

Dangers of utilitarian theory. Now it is hard to imagine a more effectual method of propagating this view than is the theory of Divine Right. Nor is it at all clear that the widespread popular acceptance of a purely utilitarian basis for obedience may not lead to great dangers in the future. Englishmen have cause for gratulation, that, in a time when the tendency is to loosen the bonds of allegiance and to proclaim (generally out of season) the morality of insurrection, there should still exist in the minds of the great majority of their countrymen a deep sense of the majesty of law and of the duty of obedience. This sense is the priceless legacy bequeathed to our own day by the believers in the Divine Right of Kings.

ERASTUS AND ERASTIANISM

WAS Erastus an Erastian? The question is not superfluous. For party names are commonly misnomers. And while there is no more frequent term of ecclesiastical vituperation than Erastianism, yet it is hardly unfair to say that many of those who make use of it appear to think that the continual employment of Erastus' name, or its derivative, is sufficient compliment to his memory to excuse ignorance of his life, his writings, and the controversy which was their occasion[1]. But we cannot understand Erastianism *in vacuo* apart from the influences which produced it, and the name alone is presumptive evidence of some relation between the doctrine and its alleged author. It may, therefore, be not superfluous to inquire a little into the influences under which the notions of Erastus were formed, and thus to gather their true import. Such an investigation may throw light on the problem of the relation between Church and State, as it presents itself to

---

[1] I find, for instance, in one of the most famous of theological encyclopaedias (Herzog) a statement to the effect that Erastus founded a sect in this country.

the minds of those who disbelieve in liberty of conscience. For, as we shall see, Erastus was concerned solely with the question as to the proper method and authority for enforcing ecclesiastical discipline in a State which was uniform in its religion[1]. He was not concerned either with the question as to the right to proclaim truth, or as to the coercive religious authority of a State which allowed more than one or persecuted the true faith. His views might have reference to modern Russia, but except constructively can have no bearing on English ecclesiastical controversies of to-day. He is concerned with moral discipline, not doctrine; with a uniform, not a tolerant polity. But it may be convenient first of all to detail the facts of his life[2]. Thomas Lüber was born at Baden, in Switzerland, on September 7, 1524. He thus came under the influence of the Zwinglian form of the Reformation, and at no time, so far as can be

[1] Canon Perry's assertion that Erastus "wrote a treatise with the object of proving that in Christian commonwealths the secular authorities are the proper TEACHERS and administrators of religious discipline," appears to me a singularly unfortunate way, to say the least, of describing the *Explicatio*. *Student's Eng. Church Hist.* II. 12.

[2] For these facts I would refer the reader especially to M. Bonnard's thesis, *Thomas Eraste et la discipline ecclésiastique*, Lausanne 1894. This is an admirable work based on manuscript as well as other sources, in which the author exhibits the whole growth of Erastianism, properly so called, and moreover gives in the footnotes frequent quotations from unpublished letters, which are most valuable. The chapter *Die Kämpfe wegen der Kirchenzucht* in Sudhoff's *C. Olevianus und Z. Ursinus' 'Leben und ausgewählte Schriften'* is also valuable in a similar way, though short and very hostile to Erastus. I shall cite these books as B. and S. respectively.

proved, inclined to any other[1], nor does there appear to be any evidence that his politico-ecclesiastical notions were directly derived from Luther, as has been suggested; the presumption, as will be seen, is the other way. In 1542 he matriculated at Basel, translating his name Lüber into Erastus, without the grammatical error which was the hard fate of the great scholar of whom he was so nearly a namesake[2]. He attached himself to the philosophical faculty and studied classics, mathematics, and theology. After two years a visitation of the plague led to his quitting Basel. Thence he went to Italy, where he appears to have been supported by a rich patron, spending three years at Bologna and six at Padua, and greatly distinguishing himself by his studies in medicine. In Italy he married a lady of noble birth, who, when a widow, was to marry the man, also an Italian, through whose action alone the fame of Erastus has survived. After this he spent some years as court physician at Henneberg. He rapidly attained distinction as an exponent of the most enlightened medical science of the time, and wrote works on this subject, larger and more numerous than the little volume by which we remember him. He opposed the views of Paracelsus, and was a great assailant of impostures, such as alchemy and astrology, though he was a believer in witchcraft, and did

[1] I say this, assuming that the question as to his alleged Arianism is decided in his favour. The very interesting letter of Silvanus reproaching Erastus with having been the cause of his apostasy, does not really contain any evidence as to the unorthodoxy of Erastus. S. App. B. p. 507.

[2] Cf. Jebb, Rede Lecture, 'Desiderius Erasmus.'

not in that matter rise above his age[1].   But his
ability, at once general and special, was recognized
by contemporary opinion, whether that opinion were
friendly or hostile—and it was both.   Beza at Geneva
was a friend, and apparently remained so, in spite of
the controversy.   Bullinger and Gwalther at Zurich
were not merely supporters, but intimates, into whose
ears the troubles of the libertarians at Heidelberg
were continually poured.   And Erastus, universally
recognised as the chief of his party, appears to have
had one great quality of a leader, the power of at-
tracting loyalty.   Yet on the other hand he would
appear to have been a mark for virulent hostility,
and to have been treated with as much contumely
by his opponents as Erastianism has been since his
time by many who have hardly heard his name[2].

But, at any rate, he was an outstanding man as
a scientific physician.   And whether or no we agree
with his views on ecclesiastical politics, there can be

---

[1] This may be the cause why a modern writer tells us that he
was not an enlightened man in the modern sense of the term.
Personally I should say that in the only sense of the term which
we have a right to apply to the sixteenth century Erastus was
eminently an *Aufgeklärter*.

[2] Cf. Bullinger's remarks to Dathenus, "Modestiam ergo in te,
mi frater Dathene, requiro, ne forte non sine causa eam nobis
iniicias cogitationem si quando potestatem consequamini in Ecclesia excommunicandi, *fore ut omnes, quotquot per omnia vestra
non approbarint, atheismi sitis condemnaturi ac expulsuri ad ipsos
usque religionis nostrae hostes truculentissimos.*"   *Explicatio*, 358;
and Gwalther to Beza, "Quid vero de iis, qui Heydelbergae hanc
causam agunt, sperare possimus, satis nos una haec audacia
admonet, qua suae sententiae subscribere nolentes atheismi ac-
cusant, et eos quidem viros in quorum fide, doctrina, moribus
nemo bonus aliquid unquam desideravit."   *Ibid.* 379, 80.

no doubt of the skill and lucidity with which they were propounded.

In 1557 he received the appointment which was to fling him into such bitter controversy, and to carry his name down the centuries. His presence being sought at the courts of Dresden and Heidelberg alike, Erastus preferred the offer of the Elector Otto Henry, who was founding a chair of therapeutics, and remained at Heidelberg until, three years before his death, he was driven out by an 'Erastian' religious revolution. His energies found scope in the work, so necessary, so arduous, and so frequent in universities, of drawing up new statutes and a fresh programme of studies. He was elected Rector of the University in 1558, and became also a member of the church council of Heidelberg, a post which he voluntarily resigned in 1564. This is some evidence of the weight he was already acquiring as a theologian. But we have more. The situation of religious parties at Heidelberg, when Erastus arrived there, was briefly this: The Elector was a tolerant Lutheran, and Heidelberg appears to have been a refuge for theological eccentrics of all nations, just as in our century London has been for political exiles[1]. In the city there were two parties, Lutheran and Swiss, in

---

[1] Bullinger argues that Erastus' services to the exiles should be a good reason for treating him with consideration. "Si fideles labores eius non praecessissent, tibi aliisque exulibus vix tale patuisset hospitium, quali nunc frueris una cum aliis multis. Beneficia eius tum in peregrinos tum domesticos collocata, eruditio item eius eximia et singularis, denique vera eius et sincera pietas, ob quae a bonis laudatur omnibus, aliud sane ei destinarat praemium, quam nunc ipsi rependitur a nonnullis." *Explicatio*, 366.

sympathy. These again were divided into groups, the former into the strict party, and those who followed Melanchthon, the latter into Calvinists and Zwinglians, of which last Erastus was the most distinguished lay representative. Each party in turn, we may say, gained the upper hand, tolerant Lutheran, Zwinglian, Calvinist, strict Lutheran. The Erastian controversy was the result of the conflict, closed as it was by a Lutheran revolution and the retirement of Erastus. The latter had early won the hatred of the Lutherans by his successful support of the claims of a certain Etienne Sylvius, who, presumably a Zwinglian himself, refused to do the bidding of the theological professor Hesshus and attack the sacramental doctrines of Catholics and Zwinglians alike.

In 1559 Otto Henry died, and was succeeded by Frederic III., a man of austere piety and strongly anti-Lutheran in sympathy. Colloquies took place in 1560 between the parties, and Erastus secured the enthusiastic praise of the great Calvinist Olevianus, who declared that few theologians were his equals in learning and wisdom, and looked to gaining much advantage from his support[1]. He was so successful that in August the Elector definitely introduced the 'reformed' faith, and proscribed

[1] "Utinam vir ille totum se abderet sacris literis ad quas propendet eius zelus, sed nescio quo pacto vix medendi vocationem audet relinquere, neque reliqui senatores ecclesiastici tam sunt cordati ut eum extrudant in messem, licet maxima et pene incredibili ministrorum penuria laboremus, ipse vero incredibili dexteritate polleat. Ausim dicere Germaniam paucissimos habere tantae doctrinae et prudentiae viros theologos." Olevianus to Calvin, B. App. II. p. 203.

alike Catholicism and Lutheranism[1]. In 1563 the
'reformed' catechism of Heidelberg, composed by
Olevianus and Ursinus, was introduced, being supported by Erastus, who is the probable author of the
Büchlein vom Brotbrechen. Erastus also took part
in the colloquy of Maulbronn (1564), and published
two other books on the Ubiquitarian controversy.

As has been seen, the anti-Lutheran Protestant
party had triumphed in Heidelberg, and won the
Elector to their exclusive support. It was natural
that, so much being accomplished, those who looked
to Geneva for guidance should desire the introduction of that famous 'discipline,' which was for them
almost the *raison d'être* of religious organization.
By discipline is meant an organized Presbyterian
police des mœurs, beginning with the parish or
church as its unit, with a hierarchy of consistory,
classis, provincial and national synods, all ecclesiastical, all claiming to be *jure divino*, independent of
the civil power, occupied in pronouncing sentence of
excommunication upon all those persons whose lives,
in some small[2] or large particular, had failed to meet
with the approval of ruling elders, or did not submit
to a friendly admonition or repent in time. This

[1] The author of the historical introduction to the tercentenary
edition of the Catechism is of opinion (pp. 43—5) that the Elector
did not intend to break with the followers of Melanchthon or the
confession of Augsburg, even by the introduction of the Catechism,
but that intolerant Lutheranism refused to regard him any longer
as anything but an enemy.

[2] It is fair to say 'small,' for one of Beza's arguments for the
necessity of the discipline is that the magistrate, if left to himself,
might leave unpunished some *offendiculum*. *Tractatus*, 120.

was claimed to be of Christ's institution; if not a necessary note of a true church, at least its most desirable accompaniment. It flourished in Geneva, its birthplace, in the Netherlands, in France, and was for centuries the most overwhelming ecclesiastical force in Scotland[1]. The divine right of the discipline was the occasion first under Queen Elizabeth, and then under the Westminster Assembly, of furious controversy in this country. Now the life of Erastus might be described as a polemic against ruling elders. It was only in subservience to his design of protesting against what seemed to him a monstrous usurpation of arbitrary power that he developed—so far as he developed at all—his theory as to the functions of the civil magistrate.

It appears that so early as 1556 a suggestion was made for the introduction of excommunicating elders into Heidelberg. This, however, came to nothing. But Heidelberg being a camp of refuge, there came exiles from France and the Netherlands anxious, regardless of the carnal appetites of the population, to see this holy inquisitorial system at its work of saving souls and protecting the sacrament[2]. Erastus declares that, irrespective of right, it seemed to him highly inexpedient to set about excommunicating a population who in reality needed conversion, for not one-thirtieth of the people were

---

[1] Buckle considered the effects of the system worse than those of the Spanish Inquisition.

[2] Cf. Bullinger to Beza, *Explicatio*, 371, "Non sine causa murmurant quod omnia fere administrat Princeps per Niderlandos sive Belgas, homines peregrinos, suis illis penitus praeteritis."

in sympathy with the new order of things[1]; and it was scarcely politic to employ spiritual censures for not being good Calvinists against persons who had not yet become Calvinists at all—for the jurisdiction claimed was to be unaccompanied by civil penalties. Probably, however, Erastus did not believe in this limitation, for he declared in a letter that the discipline would be no whit better than the Spanish Inquisition, except that its supporters would hardly dare to quaff the cup of human blood for which they seemed to be thirsting[2].

At first, Erastus tells us, he had accepted the prevailing views as to excommunication, as a divinely appointed prerogative of the Church, but when he came to study the authorities, ancient, mediæval, and modern, he saw that the reasons given were flimsy; then betaking himself to Scripture he found no sanction at all for it there, and the texts alleged in its support patient of, and indeed needing, a different interpretation[3].

Having thus convinced himself that the belief in ruling elders was a 'fond thing vainly invented,'

[1] *Explicatio*, preface.   Even Sudhoff (369) in this respect appears to side with Erastus, much as he dislikes his principles: "Die Ungunst der Verhältnisse, namentlich die aus Unverstand und Lauheit hervorgehende Opposition in den Heidelberger Kreisen des Hofes, der Universität und der Bürgerschaft, die Haltung der Züricher, trugen dabei weitaus die grösste Schuld, *wenn auch zugegeben werden muss, dass eine Kirche welche, wie die pfälzische, zumeist durch den staatlichen Impuls entstand und gehalten wurde, in der ersten Zeit kein günstiger Boden für ein schnelles Gedeihen der Disciplin sein konnte.*"

[2] B. p. 73, n. 1; cf. also p. 65, n. 2.

[3] Preface to *Explicatio*.

Erastus was ready to do battle for the liberty of the
subject and of the prince, in a word for the laity,
against a clericalist party. "New presbyter is but
old priest writ large" is the import of Erastianism as
expounded by its author, save that he would class
with the clergy those ecclesiastically-minded laymen
who were likely to be eager elders. He complained
that all the changes at Heidelberg were really the
work of a camarilla of five men, foreigners, who had
the ear of the prince and turned him to their own
ends[1]. Of these the most important were Dathenus,
a Netherlander, and Olevianus, a refugee from Trier,
who arrived in 1560, and at once raised the question
and wrote to the Genevan authorities to ask advice.
By 1562 he was able to report that the Elector recognised the necessity of introducing the discipline.
Apparently, however, the matter was not easy, for
he speaks of the opposition of those who cared for
human wisdom, by which is probably meant Erastus,
and of lawyers, who at Heidelberg, as later in England,
opposed the introduction of a power which seemed to
trench upon their own prerogatives[2].

[1] "Consiliarii omnes, nobiles, ignobiles, populus, aula, adver-
santur, illi tamen fortiores sunt omnibus." B. 76, n. 3.

"Clandestina ineunt iam etiam cum principe concilia, qui in
hoc totus est, ut contra voluntatem filiorum, conciliariorum,
ministrorum, subditorum omnium, exceptis belgis et gallis, nescio
quam disciplinam instituat." S. 341, note.

"Princeps pergit cudere excommunicationis formulam resistente
toto consilio magno. Sed plus potest quinqueviratus." S. 342.

All these passages are from letters of Erastus.

[2] Calvin's remarks are notable: "Si tibi cum iureconsultis
certandum est, scias hoc hominum genus ubique fere esse Christi
servis adversum, quia non existimant se gradum suum posse tueri,

The steps of the introduction of the discipline were as follows: The Catechism (1563) laid down the principle of excommunication for the impenitent and hypocrites, and declares the excommunicate to be excluded by God from the kingdom of Christ[1]. An ordinance expressing the same principles was issued in 1563, and another in 1564 went a little further towards organizing the discipline, but by its provisional character and through the final authority reserved for the central civil power came very far from meeting the views of Olevianus. Then in 1568 there came to Heidelberg an English refugee, George Wither, who had left this country owing to the Vestiarian controversy. Desirous of a doctorate he offered a thesis on the subject of the ceremonies, which was then agitating England. The theological faculty had no mind to quarrel with Parker and the Anglican Church, and so they forbad Wither to dispute on this subject, but suggested instead that of excommunication. Erastus bitterly complains that in their care for English susceptibilities the authorities recked little of setting their own city by the ears[2]. On June 10 Wither offered his theses

si qua vigeat ecclesia autoritas." Calvin to Olevianus; *Opera*, xix. Ep. 3869.

[1] "Nach dem Befehl Christi diejenigen, so unter dem christlichen Namen unchristliche Lehre oder Wandel führen, nachdem sie etlichemal brüderlich vermahnet sind und von ihren Irrthümern oder Lastern nicht abstehen, der Kirche oder denen so von der Kirche dazu verordnet sind, angezeiget, und so sie sich an derselben Vermahnung auch nicht kehren, von ihnen durch Verbietung der heiligen Sacramente aus der christlichen Gemeine *und von Gott selbst aus dem Reich Christi werden ausgeschlossen.*" Fr. 85.

[2] Preface to *Explicatio*.

in support of the discipline of excommunication as existing *jure divino* apart from the magistrate, and as including the power to excommunicate the prince. Erastus was not present, but one of his friends opposed the theses, declaring the authority claimed to be utterly contrary to Scripture. The debate was adjourned, and on the second day Erastus was present. What the grounds of opposition were, is indicated in the notes, taken at the time, of Ursinus' replies to them[1]. We gather that the arguments used were much the same as those of Erastus' theses, and that like them the main object was not to magnify the civil power, but to oppose the discipline. The discussion did not stop here. Erastus started working up commentaries on the subject. These he reduced later to the form of 100 theses. His opponents were infuriated, assailed him with a torrent of abuse, and attempted to prevent a man who was not a divinity professor from discussing theological topics[2]. Eventually he reduced the theses to seventy-five, and circulated them in manuscript, sending a copy to Beza at Geneva. The latter naturally disagreed with Erastus, and wrote the *Tractatus pius et moderatus de Excommunicatione*, the longest and most important contemporary reply to Erastus. Though it does not belie its title, and is moderate and respectful in tone, it is uncompromising for 'the

---

[1] *Opera*, i. 301—6.

[2] Cf. Rutherford's description of him: "One physician who in a cursory way diverted off his road of medicine, of which he wrote learnedly, and broke in on the by upon the deepest polemics of Divinity, and reached a rider's blow unawares to his friends." *Jus Divinum*, Epistle to the Reader.

prerogative of Christ,' as later Presbyterians called
it, and against laxity towards those accused of *lèse-
majesté* to the kingdom of heaven. Erastus on the
other hand received letters of sympathy from the
Zwinglian divines at Zurich, more especially Bullinger
and Gwalther, who quarrelled with neither side, but
declared distinctly their general approval of Erastus'
views. They added that, while not desirous of con-
demning other churches, they would never be *tam
dementes* as to introduce the discipline into their own
city[1].

The poor Elector was overwhelmed with the
controversy, and tried, like Laud and Charles in a
later controversy between Calvinists and Arminians,
to prevent either side discussing the matter further[2].
He was not obeyed. Soon after, in 1569, he took
a step which greatly pleased the disciplinarians. He
married the widow of Bredenrode, the Belgian noble,

---

[1] See the letters published at the end of the *Explicatio*. Bullinger did not go far enough, perhaps, for Erastus, who urged the
necessity of repressing the tyranny of these men, and bade him
beware lest by his desire to be charitable to two Churches he should
bring ruin upon many. Bullinger, it was said, had admitted that
this power of excommunication did more than anything else to
ruin Churches. What Bullinger and Gwalther both disliked
was the confusing of ecclesiastical discipline with the Christian
mysteries.

[2] "Cives murmurant, Princeps affligitur, consiliarii importunis
supplicationibus, et tantum non enecantur. Si hactenus omnino
fuissem cum Belgis, iam cessarem, quia impie tyrannice impuden-
tissime rem agunt." Jezler to Ulmer. B. 78, n. 1. (It is curious
to note that the Arminian controversy in Holland was apparently
one of the first cases in which the writings of Erastus were largely
used.)

familiar to all readers of Motley. This event led
naturally to the increased influence of Dathenus and
his party. A further check to Erastus was the
accusation of heresy levelled at Simonius, who was
driven away. Various attempts, described as in-
credibly base, were made to intimidate other supporters with exile, and not all were unsuccessful.
The Elector now demanded from Ursinus and Zanchi
their written opinions on the subject. Both supported
the discipline, although Ursinus, who was very reluctant to be drawn into the discussion, made so
many qualifications in favour of the civil power,
the consent of which was always to be necessary to
excommunications, that had the real object of Erastus
been to support the prince rather than to attack
excommunication, he might have agreed with his
adversary quickly, and indeed is said to have regarded
this opinion with some sympathy[1]. Zanchi's views

[1] Ursinus, on the one hand, has no wish to give power to an
oligarchy apart from the Christian community or the prince. But
he will not, with Erastus, accept the individual's desire to receive
the sacrament as sufficient evidence of repentance. *Explicatio
Catechesis, Opera*, I. 296 sqq., and *Judicium*, III. 802 sqq. He
avers further that any discipline of the kind desired cannot be
effective without the magistrates' assistance (as in 1646, powers
to compel attendance, &c., would be needed).

(a) "Si item sic intelligi vellent, quod non debeat esse aliquis
peculiaris senatus in Ecclesia, qui vel excommunicare etiam
blasphemos, vel constituere quidquam possit, invito magistro et
populo Christiano, ego cum ipsis non contendero." Ursinus to
Bullinger. B. 159, n. 1.

(b) "Nam ut novus senatus constituatur, qui invitis etiam
praecipuis Ecclesiae membris excommunicare possit aut alia
gerere in Ecclesia, in ea sententia nunquam fui." *Ibid.*

(c) "Nihil in hac re tentetur nisi tali consensu magistratuum

and arguments are much the same as those of Beza[1].
But the disciplinarian party was determined, and
Erastus speaks with disgust of their clandestine
intrigues with the Elector to induce him, against
the wishes of his children, his counsellors, and all
his subjects save French and Belgian refugees[2], to
lay upon their necks a burden which their fathers
were not able to bear, in the support of a view
held merely by men fired with the lust of power[3].
A catastrophe clinched the matter. In a negotiation
between the Prince of Transylvania and the Empire
for aid against the Turks, it had come out that Neuser

ministrorum et populi vel totius vel potioris partis ut nullae neque
politicae neque ecclesiasticae turbae inde oriri possint." *Ibid.*

(*d*) " Claves non sunt ministrorum tantum, sed totius ecclesiae."
Exp. Cat., Opera, I. 298. Further, the whole tone of Ursinus'
' opinion,' insisting so strongly on the need of the consent of the
whole Church as a preservative against tyranny, is on a par with
the attitude of certain believers in majority rule, who ignore the
fact that a majority may exercise a tyranny just as much as an
oligarchy.

[1] *Opera*, VIII. App. 139. Zanchi gives the magistrate the
custody of both tables, the duty of reforming the Church, punishing idolatry, securing suitable ministers, but condemns of course
those "qui mutant pro suo placito religionem, non ut servi Dei
sed ut Domini ecclesiae sese gerunt." *De Ecclesiae Militantis
Gubernatione*, VIII. 555. This shews how much power all in those
days granted the prince. Knox would have said the same.

[2] " Non filios non conciliarios, qui ei, uno excepto Ehemio, con-
stantes advertantur omnes, non nobiles, non doctos, non plebeios,
audit. Episcopus est aulae Dathenus." S. 344. " Summa est,
Genevenses et Belgos oportet esse, seu velimus seu nolimus."
Ibid. 341.

[3] "Vestra igitur excommunicatio nil aliud est quam inane
figmentum hominum imperare aliis cupientium." Erastus, *Confirmatio*, III. 3, p. 196.

and Sylvanus had written letters expressive of anti-Trinitarian and even Mahomedan sympathies. The scandal brought discredit upon Erastus, and the need of repression was felt to be so great, that in 1570 the discipline was definitely established by Electoral ordinance, though even this ordinance left the ultimate power to the Elector. Erastus himself described it as tolerable[1]. Neuser, it should be said, escaped, and became first a Mahomedan, then an atheist. Sylvanus was tried. There were different views as to executing him. Beza wrote strongly in favour of severity. He argued that repentance was all but impossible, and even if it were not, death would be the only sure way of saving him from like blasphemy in the future. The case dragged on. Eventually the Elector decided for execution, in virtue, as he said, of a special gift of the Holy Ghost, the guide into all truth[2]. But there is no evidence to connect Erastus with these heresies.

The discipline was not popular. Some refused to act as elders. Those who did act quarrelled. The masses hated the system and rendered it ineffective, as was the case throughout the greater part of England when it was established in the next century. The discipline was in fact Erastian in the worst sense of the word. It was imposed by the civil power at the bidding of foreign influence within and without the State, against the wishes of the great majority of the people.

[1] B. 96, n. 2.

[2] "Er habe auch den H. Geist, welcher in dieser Sache ein Lehrer und Minister der Wahrheit sei." B. 92, n. 1.

In 1572 Erastus was again Rector. It may be that, like Gibbon's hostility to the Revolution, of which Mr Bagehot says, " the truth is, he had arrived at the conclusion he was the sort of person revolutionists are likely to kill," that of Erastus to the discipline was inspired by a feeling that it would not leave him long unscathed. For he too was excommunicated for a couple of years, 1574–6. In 1575 he was accused of anti-Trinitarian tendencies, but was acquitted. In 1576 the death of the Elector wrought another change. A Lutheran reaction under his successor followed, the hostile parties were once more united, and Erastus resigned his professorship and left Heidelberg. Had he been an Erastian in the ordinary sense, he would not have done this. He went to Basel, where he was treated with distinction. Having lectured on ethics, he died in 1583.

Let us now follow the fortune of his works, since it throws light upon their meaning. In the interests of peace his own contribution to the controversy and that of Beza had been kept in manuscript. Before Erastus died, however, he appears to have changed his mind. But this is not certain. In 1589 both Theses and *Confirmatio* (the reply to Beza) were published under the title *Explicatio gravissimae quaestionis, utrum Excommunicatio, quatenus Religionem intelligentes et amplexantes, a Sacramentorum usu propter admissum facinus arcet ; mandato nitatur Divino, an excogitata sit ab hominibus.* The publisher called himself Baiocius Sultaceterus, and described his action as due to a death-bed wish of

Erastus and to the love of truth; more probably it
was to the love of money. The place of publication
was given on the title-page as ' Pesclavii.' Beza was
annoyed, and declared that Erastus would never have
sanctioned such proceedings. It appeared that Pes-
clavium was really London, that the real editor was
Castelfeltro, the husband of Erastus' widow, and that
John Wolf was the real publisher. Now the disciplinarian controversy had been raised some years
back in England by Cartwright and Travers. Beza
hinted at Whitgift's being at the bottom of a publication which was so opportune[1]. He said he was
not. But he certainly knew about it. And from a
statement of Selden in his *De Synedriis*, there would
appear to be evidence that Wolf was rewarded by
the privy council[2]. There can be little doubt that
the treatise was published with the object of finally
settling the disciplinarian controversy in England.
Hooker shews himself well acquainted with Erastus,
and goes into some of the questions he raises. In
his main principles about Church and State he held
Erastus', *not* Erastian, views; though he did not
share his disbelief in the power of the keys. But

[1] It was opportune, for Baillie speaks of Beza as afraid to
answer Erastus' book (II. 227). This must, of course, refer to
the *Confirmatio*. Cf. also pp. 265, 311. And the whole controversy of the Westminster Assembly is a proof of the ingenuity of
the arguments of Erastus. Selden's *De Synedriis* is only a developement of one part. Cf. *Jus Divinum*, or Collinges' *Responsio
Bipartita*, in both of which Erastus is regarded as the most
formidable opponent.

[2] Selden gives a long account of the whole matter (*De Syn.*
I. 1016—21). Cf. what Beza says in his preface, and also the
letters in Strype's *Whitgift*, I. 168, and App. III, 302.

he is strongly imbued with a sense of the iniquity of excommunicating the prince.

In the Arminian troubles in Holland the name of Erastus was invoked[1]. We have a treatise of Grotius *De Imperio Summarum Potestatum circa Sacra*, 1614, said to be entirely Erastian. Grotius, however, like Erastus, is guarded. He will grant to the magistrate no power to contradict the word of God, to promulgate new articles of faith, or to prohibit preaching or the sacraments[2]. This would assuredly have seemed a poor and ecclesiastical view to writers like Hobbes and, perhaps, Selden. Further, Grotius, though he cites many supporters, among them Wolfgang Musculus, does not cite Erastus, nor do the views of the two about excommunication agree. The debates of the Westminster Assembly naturalised the term Erastianism in this country. In the attempt of the divines to draw up a scheme of uniform Presbyterian Church government, the greatest difficulty of all was raised by the claim to the power of the keys. The English Puritans were strongly Calvinist in the modern sense of the term. But they were loth to exert a power which they deemed arbitrary and unlimited, and to put it in the hands of an ecclesiastical body. The Independents objected, not to suspension of individuals in each congregation, but to any attempt to make parishes

[1] Arminius and his friends leant on the civil power, and were much attacked for having appealed to the superior magistrate against the ecclesiastical authority; see *Articles of Synod of Dort*, translated by Dr Scott, and *History of Preceding Events*, 137 and *passim*.

[2] *Opera*, III. 214.

unite in a larger organization for the review of decisions[1]. They appear to have been willing to admit a final right of appeal to the civil magistrate. This brought them very near to the Erastians[2]. Many are the groans of Dr Baillie over the influence of these latter. He describes them as follows:

"In the Assembly we are fallen on a fashious proposition, that has keeped us divers dayes, and will do so divers more, coming upon the article of the church and the church-notes to oppose the Erastian heresy, which in this land is very strong, especially among the lawyers, unhappy members of this Parliament. We find it necessary to say that 'Christ in the New Testament had institute a Church government distinct from the Civil, to be exercised by the officers of the church, without commission from the magistrate.' None in the Assembly has any doubt of this truth but one Mr. Coleman, a professed Erastian, a man reasonably learned but stupid and inconsiderate, half a pleasant, and of small estimation. But the lawyers in the Parliament making it their work to spoil our Presbyterie, not so much upon conscience as upon fears that the Parliament spoil their mercat and take up most of their country pleas without law, did blow up the

---

[1] "The proposition we stick on is that no particular congregations may be under the government of one Classical Presbytery." Baillie, ii. 139 (1644).

[2] Neal's remarks are notable. Except that he calls Erastus a divine, he gives a very fair description of his teaching. The pastoral office, he says, was according to Erastus only persuasive, like that of a professor of the sciences over his students, without any power of the keys annexed.

poor man with much vanity; so he is become their
champion, to bring out in the best way he can
Erastus's arguments against the proposition, for the
contentment of the Parliament. We give him a free
and fair hearing; albeit, we fear, when we have
answered all he can bring and have improved with
undeniable proofs our position, the Houses when it
comes to them shall scrape it out of the Confession;
for this point is their idol. The most of them are
incrediblie zealous for it; the Pope and the King
were never more earnest for the headship of the
Church than the plurality of this Parliament. However they are like for a time by violence to carry it,
yet almost all the ministry are zealous for the Prerogative of Christ against them. We are at this
instant yoked in a great and dangerous combat for
this very thing. Often we have been on the brink
to set up our Government, but Satan to this day
hath hindered us. The ministers and elders are not
willing to set up and begin any action till they may
have a law for *some power to purpose; all former
ordinances have been so intolerably defective that they
could not be accepted.* The Erastian and Independent
party joining together in the Houses to keep off the
Government so long as they were able, and when it
was extorted, to make it so lame and corrupt as they
were able; yet at last yesterday an Ordinance came
forth to supply the defects of all the former, that so
without much further delay we might go to work.
We laboured so much as we were able before it came
out to have it *so free from exceptions as might be*,
but notwithstanding of all we could do, it is by the

malignity of the forementioned brethren in evil so filled with grievances, that yet it cannot be put in practice. We for our part mind to give in a remonstrance against it; the Assembly will do the like; the City Ministers will give the third; but that which by God's help may prove most effectual is the zeal of the City itself. Before the ordinance came out, they petitioned against some materials of it. This both the Houses voted to be a breach of their privilege, to offer a petition against anything that is in debate before them till once it be concluded and come abroad. This vote the City takes very evil. It's likely to go high betwixt them. Our prayers and endeavours are for wisdom and courage to the City. I know to whom this matter has cost much labour. *The Independents have the least zeal to the truth of God of any men we know.* Blasphemous heresies are now spread here more than ever in any part of the world. Yet they are not only silent, but are patrons and pleaders for liberty almost to them all. We and they have spent many sheets of paper upon the toleration of their separate churches. At the last meeting we concluded to stop our paper-debates, and on Thursday next to begin our verbal disputation against the lawfulness of their desired separation. When we have ended, the Houses will begin to consider this matter. The most there and in the army will be for too great a liberty; but the Assembly, the City, and the body of all the ministry in the Kingdom are passionately opposite to such an evident breach of the Covenant[1]."

[1] Baillie, *Journal*, II. 360, 1 (1646).

Mr Gillespie in his *Aaron's Rod Blossoming* (table of Contents) describes the genesis of the party thus:

"The Erastian error not *honestis parentibus nati*. Erastus the midwife, how engaged in the business. The breasts that gave it suck profaneness and self-interest. Its strong food arbitrary government. Its tutor Arminianism. Its deadly decay and consumption, whence it was? How ill it hath been harboured in all the reformed churches? How stifled by Erastus himself? Erastianism refuted out of Erastus. The divers who have appeared against this error. How the controversy was lately revived."

Rutherford occupies the greater part of *Jus Divinum* with an able answer to Erastus, and thinks that in answering him he has fully answered Prynne's objections[1]. He describes the attempts of the Erastian party thus: "It is not an enriching spoil to pluck a rose or flower from the crown of the Prince of the Kings of the earth. Diamonds and rubies picked out of the Royal Diadem of Jesus Christ addeth but a poor and sorry lustre to earthly supremacy; it is *baldness instead of beauty*." He makes use of the argument to be made famous by Pascal, "In things doubtful conscience hath refuge to the surest side. And Christian rulers would not do well to venture upon Eternity, Wrath, the Judgement to come, confiding on the poor plea of an Erastian distinction, to encroach upon the Prerogative Royal of Jesus Christ."

The arguments are much the same as in the case

[1] Epistle to the Reader.

of Heidelberg, though there was a great deal more here about the civil magistrate; but Collinges in his *Responsio Bipartita* declares his opponents' arguments to be all derived from Erastus, "the first worker in that sort of brass[1]." The extension of the term Erastian to mean not opponents of excommunication, but upholders of the view that the magistrate could order religion as he liked and command obedience, was due to this controversy[2]. Now of course its original significance has been largely forgotten.

The *Explicatio* was reprinted in 1649 at Amsterdam. The theses (not the *Confirmatio*) were translated into English in 1659 under the title of *The Nullity of Church Censures*. Another translation appeared in 1682.

In our own day the disruption of the Church of Scotland caused Dr Lee to republish in 1844 the old translation, with an elaborate preface of his own, vindicating Erastus from the charge of Erastianism as commonly understood, and the Church of

---

[1] p. 20.

[2] It is fair to say that Rutherford regards Erastus as more, not less Erastian than his followers, but I think he does not reflect (1) that Erastus' remarks as to the civil magistrate were *obiter dicta*; (2) that the power he gives him, as to *sacra*, would go to any Christian under a doctrine of the priesthood of the laity, held as strongly as Erastus undoubtedly held it; (3) Erastus always contemplates the magistrate not as changing religion at his will, but as the orthodox head of an orthodox church; (4) Erastus does *not*, as Rutherford thinks (513), ever say that it is the magistrate's business to excommunicate apostates or any one else. He merely says that his objections to the discipline do not apply to them.

Scotland from being either Erastian or a supporter
of Erastus.

Having thus detailed the relevant facts, I proceed
to a few points which may serve towards the elucida-
tion of the problem with which I started, How far
was Erastus an Erastian? But a definition of
Erastianism is necessary. Perhaps the theory is
expressed in the barest and therefore most complete
form by Selden in the words "Whether is the Church
or the Scripture the judge of religion? *In truth
neither, but the State*[1]." Such a view is clear enough.
It places all truth at the mercy of the civil power
and utterly denies any rights of conscience to either
individual or church. It places the claims of expediency above those of reason. It makes political
convenience the sole test of belief. And it is such
a view as this that gives its *locus standi* to the
hierarchical theory of the State; although, indeed,
it might perhaps more fairly be said that it was the
hierarchical theory and its consequences which produced Erastianism by way of repulsion. Still, the
great argument in favour of theories of ecclesiastical
supremacy, whether propounded by Jesuits or Presbyterians or Fifth Monarchy Men, is always the same.
In an age in which uniformity in religion is the
political ideal, the spiritual organization must claim
a deciding view in matters of faith, or religious belief
will become merely a question of political convenience.
The only safeguard for truth is a claim, which seems
preposterous to those living in a world where toleration

[1] *Table Talk*, Op. III. 2067; cf. also 2016.

has solved the problem. Theories of ecclesiastical supremacy may be bad, but they are better than the view which makes religion or atheism a mere political instrument, the shuttlecock of State or private interests. They are, in fact, the form which a regard for the rights of conscience takes in an age in which persecution is regarded as a duty. The Roman Empire had made of religion a mere political engine. In the inevitable reaction the Christian Church was led to put forth a claim nearly equally indefensible to dominate the civil authority. Then the Reformation witnessed the uprising of the laity against this view. And nearly all supporters of change were willing to allow to the civil ruler more power in the direction of taking the initiative[1] in reformation than our own age would be disposed to do. Some went further. The *Leviathan* exhibits true Erastianism in its most full-blown form. Hobbes regards religion as under the absolute control of the State, which for its own ends may establish and prohibit what forms it pleases, and demand not only on loyal, but on moral grounds the obedience of every member. The conscience is in fact bound to any religion the State

---

[1] Cf. even Knox' Letter to Queen Regent Mary, *Works*, iv. 433; and also *Second Book of Discipline*, x. 7, in Calderwood, iii. 545. Knox, like the Pope, was willing to exalt the civil power, so long as it could be used as an instrument. A great deal of so-called Erastianism is little more than the extravagant support of the one power that could carry through or maintain the particular religious views of the writer; as a later writer says, "Only this honour the Presbyterians give to their magistrates, they must be the executioners of their judgements to hang whom they condemn," and cf. the Confession of Puritan exiles in Holland.

imposes. It is true Hobbes makes one reservation, in which a merely passive obedience is permitted, but it concerns only the case where the State denies the Incarnation, and is besides so contemptuous, that he leaves little doubt that he himself would regard conformity to any and every conceivable State-imposed religion or negation as a moral duty. The king is at once priest and bishop. Bishops have no right to call themselves so by *divine permission,* and the clergy ought to preach of nothing but the duty of civil obedience.

But perhaps the simpler definition of Erastianism as the theory that religion is the creature of the State may serve; and I suppose that no one will deny that the word as commonly employed means at least this much. Now did Erastus teach this or not? If not, was his doctrine at all an approximation to it? And how, then, did the theory become attached to his name? To the first of these questions, I believe that the answer is in the negative; to the second an affirmative, although opinions will probably differ as to how far such approximation extends. And the third can be answered from the history of the controversies mentioned above.

(1) We must always remember that Erastus did not write directly in support of the State, but had the object of crying down excommunication. Any views he expresses as to the functions of the magistrate are mere *obiter dicta* introduced in support of the main position. He is bound in fact to shew that morality will not suffer, if his views be adopted. And so he goes on to say that excommunication is

not only unscriptural and a usurpation, but that the magistrate can effect all that it aims at; not that he himself can excommunicate. His argument runs on these lines: (*a*) Excommunication was not practised among the Jews; (*b*) it has no authority in the New Testament; (*c*) in a state where every one is of the same opinion, (*not* excommunication, but) all coercive jurisdiction belongs to the magistrate alone. The argument is of the character of the times, and there is no need to go into it at length. The alleged instances among the Jews are disposed of. The Sanhedrin[1] is shewn to be a political not merely a religious body, and to have had coercive power. This point was elaborated by Selden in the *De Synedriis*[2]. The passages from the New Testament cited as favouring the discipline are then examined and explained. The most important of these is Matthew xviii. 17. Erastus argues that Christ's

---

[1] The Disciplinarians based their argument partly on the assumed fact that the powers of the Sanhedrin were continued in the Church, and that they were essentially ecclesiastical. Both Bancroft in his *Survey of the Pretended Holy Discipline* and Bilson in *The Perpetual Government of Christ's Church* appear to have held the same views as Erastus on the matter.

[2] Baillie was very anxious to have him answered, e.g. "The Erastian party in the Parliament is stronger than the Independent, and is like to work us much woe. Selden is their head. If L'Empereur would beat down this man's arrogancy, as he very well can, to show out of the Rabbins, that the Jewish State was diverse from their Church, and that they had the censure of excommunication among them, and a double Sanhedrin, one civil, another ecclesiastical; if he would confound him with Hebrew testimonies it would lay Selden's vanity, who is very insolent for his Oriental literature" (II. 277). Gillespie was also very strong on this point.

command has nothing to do with excommunication. It refers to private wrongs. The aggrieved party is to go either to the Sanhedrin or to a similar body acting in a non-Christian State as a court of arbitration. If that fails, the erring brother is to be treated as a heathen and a publican. This means not that he is excommunicate, but that an action in the State courts may be brought against him. He will not act as a Christian, let him therefore be treated merely as a citizen[1]. St Paul's delivering over to Satan of the erring Corinthian is also discussed. This is interpreted as a prayer for his removal from this world, not as excommunication[2]. Lastly, Erastus declares that in a Christian State the magistrate is the proper person to punish all offences. He is not to excommunicate. That would be to give him a purely religious function[3]. He is merely to act on a law inspired by religious principles. Erastus does not touch doctrine, and therefore gives the magistrate

[1] This argument appears in Musculus, *Loci Communes*, *De Magistratibus*, p. 631, Ed. 1611.

[2] Lightfoot, *Horae Hebraicae*, shares Erastus' views on many of these points.

[3] Cranmer indeed does this in his *Questiones*, *N. O.* 116, *Remains and Letters*, 117. "A bishop or a priest by the Scripture is neither commanded nor forbidden to excommunicate, but where the laws of any region giveth him authority to excommunicate, there they ought to use the same in such crimes as the laws have such authority in; and where the laws of the region forbiddeth them, there they have none authority at all; and they that be no priests may also excommunicate, if the law allow them thereunto." But to the whole of this is added: "This is mine opinion and sentence at the present, which I do not temerariously define, and do remit the judgement thereof wholly unto your majesty."

no power over truth. For he says that he is only
considering the case where prince and people are all
of the same religion, and that the true one. All this
appears to me to shew that the views of Erastus are
not relevant to modern Church controversies, which
take place in a State which recognizes every religion,
and which presuppose a 'magistrate' (Parliament)
composed of persons of a thousand conflicting views.
It is only through the ignoring the two provisoes:
(1) that the true religion is supposed to be established
and none other allowed in the State; (2) that the
magistrate has no power to transgress the Word of
God: that it is possible to identify the views of
Erastus with those of Hobbes or Selden. His
objection is clearly to two governing coercive
authorities in one State.

"Ut in rebus profanis curandis ei non licet ter-
minos et fines aequitatis, iusticiae, ac honestatis, hoc
est praescriptionem legum et statutorum Reipublicae, transcendere; sic in disponendis et ordinandis
rebus sacris vel ad cultum Divinum pertinentibus
longe minus ei licet ulla in parte a praescripto verbi
Dei discedere: quod tanquam regulam in omnibus
debet sequi, ab eoque nusquam vel latum pilum
deflectere. Summa est, Magistratum in Christiana
Republica unicum esse cui a Deo commissa sit *gubernatio externa rerum omnium quae vel ad civilem vel
ad piam et Christianam vitam pertinent; ius et au-
toritatem imperandi ac ius dicendi neque ministris
neque aliis ullis concessum esse. Intelligi hoc debet
de ea Republica dictum, in qua Magistratus et subditi eandem profitentur religionem, eamque veram.*

In hac dico duas distinctas iurisdictiones minime
debere esse. In alia, in qua videlicet Magistratus
falsam tuetur sententiam, certo quodam modo tole-
rabilis videri fortasse possit divisio rationum[1]."

"Oppugno tantum iudicium de moribus, quod
hodie Ecclesiasticum nominant, distinctum a iudicio
politici magistratus. Nempe duas iurisdictiones sive
duo discriminata de moribus iudicia *publica et externa* nego in una Republica esse oportere, cui pius
Magistratus a Deo praepositus est[2]."

Is this substantially different from Elizabeth's
claim for herself in *The Admonition to simple men
deceived by the malicious*? Erastus' magistrate is in
fact merely a sovereign, "over all persons and in all
causes within his dominions supreme," no more[3].
Further he says that in matters of faith the magistrate will of course consult the leaders of theological
opinion, who will teach him what is or is not the
Word of God. And he admits it may be well that
for moral offences he may delegate power to bodies
composed at least partly of ecclesiastics or of persons
elected by churches[4], who shall inquire into such
offences and bring the offenders to justice. But he
objects to the assumption of jurisdiction by the
spiritual authority, which he deems essentially non-

[1] *Confirmatio*, III. 1, pp. 161–2. In another place he says
"Verbum Dei et Sacramenta nulli potestati subiiciuntur."

[2] *Ibid*. IV. 1.

[3] "Non hoc dico, Deum voluisse magistratum sacrificare atque
alia huiusmodi, quae sacerdotibus imperata solis fuerant, facere,
sed illud assero Deum soli magistratui concredidisse curam et
gubernationem tam sacrarum quam profanarum rerum." *Ibid*.
III. 1, p. 163.   [4] *Ibid*. 172.

political[1]. His opponents claimed without justice
that their discipline in no way usurped the power
of the State. He retorted by asking them why, if
this was so, they required an act of State to introduce their discipline. He also objects to any attempt
to introduce it among an unwilling population as too
'Erastian' in our sense, and as depriving the Christian
community of its rights[2]. They made the cardinal
error of all clericalist parties in arguing that their
decisions, being concerned with religious matters,
were of a radically different order from those of other
men. They claimed infallibility. "An apud solos Allo-
broges *homines non falluntur in iudicando?*" asks
Erastus pertinently[3]. Beza's argument was that the
sentence of the Church was merely declaratory,
announcing upon earth a sentence of exclusion from
Paradise previously passed in an invisible court
above[4]. This in his view differentiated the decisions
of ruling elders from those of earthly courts. Erastus
saw through this (unconscious) sophistry. He saw

---

[1] Cf. the description of Baxter's views in Calamy's *Life of
Baxter*, and his reasons for disliking the Presbyterians, *Reliquiae
Baxterianae*, 142, 3.

[2] "Si verum est Christum nomine Ecclesiae intellexisse totam
multitudinem, falsum est magistratui hoc permitti, ut nolente
Ecclesia hos ei Presbyteros imponat. Quanquam enim *Magistratus praecipuum est Ecclesiae membrum*, tamen ipsismet inter-
pretibus non iussit Christus membro primario et principi judicare,
sed Ecclesiae toti: in qua non facit alios aliis potentiores quod ad
hanc rem attinet." *Confirmatio*, vi. 1, p. 329.

[3] *Confirmatio*, iii. 4, p. 223.

[4] In excommunicating "Deum ipsum constituimus et presbyterii et huius iudicii auctorem, cuius dumtaxat minister et interpres
fit presbyterium." Excommunication is really the supplement to
an act previously done in heaven: "ut videlicet nihil aliud si

that the attempt to judge whether a man desirous of communicating was sincere or no in repentance involved an impossible claim to a knowledge of motive, and was therefore in this respect an encroachment on the divine justice, no less than it was in another a usurpation of human. It judged motives, i.e. it claimed infallibility; it affected reputation, i.e. it had a civil aspect[1]. The fact is that the conception of the Church entertained at that time by Presbyterians and Papalists alike is largely political, just as rigid predestinarianism is the theory of legal sovereignty applied to the actions of God. The Deity of Calvinism is Hobbes' *Leviathan*, with power unchecked by law, justice or conscience. To both Papalists and Presbyterians the Church is a State, *the* State indeed—though not all would have admitted so much[2]. But Erastus saw the dangers of the system

excommunicatio in terris quam declaratio alterius occultioris factae in coelis, ex qua nimirum merito colligatur eum qui in coelis eo quidem tempore non approbatur, indignum esse qui inter fideles in terris censeatur: quae *posterior* etiam declaratio in terris facta, rata est in coelis." Beza, *Tractatus Moderatus*, 4. "Nos autem ...tam credimus rata esse in coelis, quam Christum scimus regnare in eorum ministerio quos ecclesiae suae hic regendae praefecit; neque haec legitima vero presbyterii iudicia secus arbitramur reformidanda, quam si filius ipse Dei aeternus illa ore suo pronuntiaret." *Ibid.* 8.

[1] "Nos enim de solis illis loquimur, ut saepe monui, qui cupiunt cum Deo reconciliari; at hoc unum contendimus, non esse a Deo institutum Presbyterium, quod de cordibus hominum dicentium se poenitere iudicet, verene an false dicant; atque sic vel ad sacramenta admittant, vel ab eisdem removeant." *Confirmatio*, ii. 1, p. 152. Cf. also i. 4.

[2] The developed doctrine of Presbyterianism does admit the theory of the two kingdoms; but this was hardly the position of either Calvin or Knox. Cf. the lecture on *Ius Divinum in 1646*.

it was proposed to introduce[1]. He saw the power which the right of excommunication would give to ecclesiastical oligarchies in a community all of one faith. Excommunication in our heterogeneous modern world would have far less effect, although even here it might affect a man's business prospects and be therefore a proper subject for the courts[2] to investigate. But in a society of uniform religious belief, if practised as had been desired, it would have been defamation of character raised to the level of a divine ordinance and relieved of every civil penalty. To claim such a power was certainly to claim what lay within the magistrate's functions, unless there was appeal to him, and that was the thing most disliked. There can be no reason why a preacher who spoke of certain individuals in his sermons should not suffer the pains and penalties of slander, if his allegations were unjustifiable. Excommunication was the same sort of thing on a grander scale. It is not calculated to advance a man's prospects in this life to tell his neighbours that his prospects are

[1] He regards it as on a level with Papal oppression. "Haec enim vere fortis Deus fuit, qui omnes Reges et principes, omne robur, omnes conscientias, ipsam etiam sacrosanctam scripturam, Pontificis Romani pedibus subiecit. At nos, inquies, aliter instituimus, Pontificum factum non probamus. Audio quidem hoc dici, *sed contrarium video et experior*. Permulta alia in Pontificibus recte reprehendimus; at eadem deinde fecimus et facimus, postquam nobis paulum confirmati videmur. Nolo exempla dissipatarum Ecclesiarum, iniquorum iudiciorum, et aliarum confusionum atque malorum, quae aetate nostra ex hac vel sola vel praecipue orta sunt, commemorare; quia sunt odiosa." *Confirmatio*, v. 1, p. 298.

[2] *Ius Divinum*, 632.

unpleasant for the next, *if they believe you.* And it is noteworthy that this, though under different names, and not always explicitly stated, was the main ground of dispute at the Westminster Assembly. It was argued by the supporters of the discipline that the jurisdiction was in no sense coercive, but purely spiritual. Erastus is not much blamed in his own day for ascribing too much power to the magistrate. Beza says little on the subject, nor do any anti-Erastians deny in set terms that all coercive authority belongs to the State[1]. They are rather concerned to shew that theirs does not conflict with it. Here indeed Ursinus breaks away from his party and asserts that the magistrate must be consulted and give his assent to excommunication. Prynne, a great disciplinarian and anti-Erastian, was attacked for supporting the discipline on what we should call Erastian grounds—on the ground, that is, that the government was supporting or was about to support the system, and every one must therefore obey it. He is asked, why he did not act upon that view in the days of prelatical tyranny[2]. Moreover the thing most hateful to the Presbyterians in England was the insistence by Parliament on a right of final appeal

[1] Beza indeed declares the magistrate to have the custody of the two tables. *Tractatus*, 99. The real point between the two was not as to the power of the magistrate, but as to the divine origin of excommunication. We may compare, as showing the Erastianism of the anti-Erastians, the appeal of Ursinus at the end of his *Judicium*, begging the Elector to cause questions of new doctrine to be brought before him.

[2] Cf. *Certain Brief Observations on Mr Prynne's Twelve Questions.*

to the civil power[1].   They object to all limiting of
excommunication and want to free it alike from
exceptions and all other jurisdiction[2].   There is
indeed no doubt that in England the main force of
the hostility was fear of clerical tyranny[3].   Selden

[1] "But we deny that (in a well constituted Church) it is agreeable to the will of Christ for the Magistrate either to receive appeals
(properly so-called) from the sentence of an Ecclesiastical Court,
or to receive complaints exhibited against that sentence by the
party censured, so as by his authority upon such complaint to
nullify or make void the censure." Gillespie, 253.

"Great wrestling have we for the erecting of our Presbyterie;
it must be a divine thing to which so much resistance is made by
men of all sorts; yet by God's help we will very speedily see it
set up in spight of the devil....

"Our greatest trouble for the time is from the Erastians in
the House of Commons.   They are at last content to erect Pres-
byteries and Synods in all the land, and have given out their orders
to that end; yet they give to the ecclesiastic courts so little power
that the Assemblie, finding their petitions not granted, were in
great doubt whether to set up any thing till, by some powerful
petition of many thousand hands, they obtain more of their first
desires.   The only means to obtain this and all else we desire is
our recruited army about Newark." Baillie, II. 317, 18 (1645).

[2] "To limit the censure of excommunication in matter of
opinion to the common and uncontroverted principles, and in the
matter of manners to the common and universal practices of
Christianity, and in both to the parties' known light, is the dangerous doctrine of the Arminians and Socinians, openeth a wide
door and proclaimeth liberty to all other practices and errors
which are not fundamental and universally abhorred by all
Christians, and tendeth to the overthrow of the Reformed religion." The Reformation cleared, 21.

[3] "The Clergy, who, what Church forms soever they set up,
will be ever imposing their private opinions in matters of religion
for infallible truths, and incensing prince against people and people
against prince, and one sort of men against another, making their
followers to espouse and maintain their unjust quarrels, till they

declares that "Presbyters have the greatest power of any clergy in the world and gull the laity the most[1]."

become insensibly slaves to their ambition and boundless power, instead of attaining to any solid real or truly Christian reformation.

"Whether that wisdom and power of the Clergy which hath taken upon it in all ages to suppress heresy and schism by human laws and penalties, have not been a perverting and interrupting of that law of love amongst the members of Christ's body which he commands? And whether they, under the pretence of composing differences and settling a government over the body of Christ, by endeavouring to reduce all the members of the body to unity of judgement and uniformity of practice in matters of religion upon grounds of outward compulsion have not discovered in themselves that true spirit of schism described 1 Cor. 12 (which they would seem to extirpate), which despises all below it and envies all above it as unnecessary members, and fit to be cut off from the body, so defacing and dividing the body of Christ by labouring to make the whole body but one member, and where then is the body?" *Twelve Weighty Queries*, p. 8.

"Lay no more burden of government upon the shoulders of ministers than Christ hath plainly laid upon them; have no more hand therein than the Holy Ghost clearly gives them....I fear an ambitious ensnarement, and I have cause. I see what raised Prelacie and Papacy to such a height. When once they had a hand in the work they soon engrossed it, and then made it the main, the sole point of religion. 'Christian perfection,' saith one of them, 'doth not consist in almsdeeds and devotion, but in exalting the ecclesiastical jurisdiction, the true cement of that perfection.'" Coleman, *Hopes Deferred and Dashed*, p. 25.

"O ye honourable worthies, open your eyes and see whither you are going or whither some are leading you. Once the Pope had your predecessors at his beck, and you may again, for you will lose your freedom under a Presbyterian domination. The Lord of heaven grant that England never see that day wherein Parliament must not meddle with Church government because a spiritual thing." Coleman, *A Brotherly Admonition*, p. 6.

[1] *Table Talk*, Op. III. 2064. One of Baillie's complaints was

That the discipline really aimed at a function
not of persuasion, but of government is proved (1) by
the argument of one supporter that its object was
the external peace of the Church, not the mind of
the member[1]; (2) by another's argument that the
proper persons to maintain order in the churches
and prevent brawling are the ecclesiastical authorities[2]; (3) by a case of which both Erastus and
Bullinger speak, where the presbytery, in their
anxiety to secure jurisdiction, were actually driven
into a course which led to the impunity of a man
accused of unnatural vice[3].

that in a form of discipline at one time proposed it would have
been possible for the ministers to be controlled by laymen in the
kirk-session (III. 452). A good account of the clericalist character
of Calvin's *régime* is given by Bancroft, *Survey*, chaps. II. and III.

[1] "Neither is it the internal or nearest aim of Discipline in
Church government to work upon or rule the mind, which is not
known to the Church or Church governors, *but to procure the
external peace of the Church, which may be obtained, the mind
remaining still unconvinced.*" *Answer to a Libel*, 55.

[2] "Suppose there should be any disturbance in the church
assembled for the public worship of God by some drunkard or
madman or any heretic, either by sporting or by railing or seducing
or any abominable action, where lies the power to suppress it?
Is it in the magistrates or in the church officers? I answer it is
in the hand or power of the church officers first, because they were
charged to keep the door, that there be no such occasion for disturbance in the midst of divine worship." *An Answer to those
questions*, 15.

[3] Cf. Gwalther's letter, who states the case. "In palatinatu
nulla prius scandala tam atrocia incidisse quam ea sint, quae
seniorum illic constitutorum culpa acciderint....Quod si ergo
novam in Ecclesia tyrannidem his principiis stabilire posse
metuemus, quis nos absque causa id timere dicet?" *Explicatio*,
379.

It is the competing jurisdiction and its clericalist character that frighten Erastus. Yet it must be allowed that he writes largely of the civil power. He quotes Musculus to the effect that the worst of heresies is to regard a Christian magistrate as on the same level with a heathen[1]. Nor can there be any doubt that like all the reformers he would have been ready (and indeed probably helped) to impose his faith by the help of the civil power upon an unwilling people. There is no hint of toleration in his writings, yet his crusade was one in favour of popular liberty as well as the civil power, against those who were duping the latter into assisting an attempt to crush both. If the thing is to be introduced, in Erastus' view the people as well as the prince should be consulted. Further there are one or two passages in which he says that the magistrate

[1] Musculus, though in many ways more Erastian than Erastus, yet saves himself from the charge of enslaving religion to the State policy. "Horum consideratione manifestum redditur etiam si ad magistratus Christianos cura religionis pertineat, haud tamen illis competere, ut citra verbum Dei quicquam in religione constituant. Nequit enim fieri ut arbitrarii cultus Deo placeant, quia non sunt voluntati ipsius conformes : nec possunt conscientias hominum de eo certas reddere, quod Deo vere serviant, hoc est, rem gratam faciant." He goes on to show that Moses in the Old Testament, and the Apostles in the New, were given explicit directions, nothing being left to their arbitrary will. "*Haec praecedentibus adiicere voluimus, ne damnabilem eorum magistratuum temeritatem approbare videamur, qui absque Verbo Dei quamcunque volunt religionis formam subditis suis proponunt, et pro potestate sua a Deo accepta authenticam esse servarique volunt: et si quis illam sequi recusaverit, mox contumaciae ac rebellionis damnant, quasi Christiana religio a potestate magistratuum et non magis ab infallibili divinorum eloquiorum certitudine et auctoritate pendeat.*" *Loci Communes*, 646.

might teach, if he had time, which he had not, and might even act as a minister[1]; yet Erastus was very anti-sacerdotal and bases these views on general principles about the priesthood of the laity[2]. And even then we must remember the true religion is supposed to be established; there is no notion of a right in the prince to change religion at will. Nor is there any evidence that he would have put truth under the heel of policy, and like Hobbes have dragged religion under the Juggernaut car of reason of State. He regarded the function of the Church as purely persuasive[3]. It is a pity that, seeing this, he did not go further and deny the right of the State to persecute, whether or no at the bidding of the Church[4]. But at least it was liberty, not tyranny for which he contended. He could not be deceived by the specious pretence of spiritual illumination into regarding as harmless upon earth a jurisdiction, whose only virtue in the eyes of its supporters lay in the fact that it rested upon fear, that is compulsion, and therefore needed the sanction of the State[5]. Indeed his views may be summed up in

[1] *Confirmatio*, IV. 2, p. 265.   [2] *Ibid.* III. 1, p. 175.

[3] He did not, for instance, object to the rebuking of the magistrates in sermons. What he could not endure was the claim to examine them judicially. This, in his view, meant an assumption of governmental authority. v. 1.

[4] If the truth that "my kingdom is not of this world" be a valid reason for giving no coercive jurisdiction over morals to the Church, it is equally valid against any coercion in matters of belief by the State, irrespective of the question as to whether or no the State is advised by the Church. Cf. *Confirmatio*, p. 173.

[5] Cf. *Reformation cleared* 23 : "*There cannot be so much as trial and examination of the offence without authority unless the*

the following passage from the life of Baxter, hardly an Erastian in our sense. "The Erastians, I thought, were thus far in the right in asserting more fully than others the magistrate's power in matters of religion, that all coercive power is only in their hands, which is the full sense of the Oath of Supremacy, and that no such power belongeth to the pastors or people of the Church." " He could not but approve their holding the pastoral power to be only persuasive, though authoritative and by divine appointment; and that pastors were officers of God's institution, who were not only to persuade by sermons general and special, but by particular oversight of their particular flocks; and could as the ground of their persuasion produce God's commission or command for what they said or did. But that as pastors they had no secular or forcing power; and that unless the magistrate authorised them as his officers they could not touch men's bodies or estates, but had to do with conscience only[1]." This is also the exact line taken by Coleman.

It is the impossibility of two co-equal jurisdictions in a State which strikes Erastus. And this is obvious. One of them must be final, so far as the State be

party be willing to appear; that persuasion and jurisdiction, that the delivering over to Satan and thereby striking the conscience with the terror of God by the authority of Jesus Christ, which hath the promise of a special and strong ratification in heaven, and any other ecclesiastical way whatever, which must be inferior to this, and depend only upon persuasion on the one part, and free will on the other, can be supposed to be alike efficacious." Here the appeal to force is evident.

[1] *Reliquiae Baxterianae*, 139; Calamy, p. 113.

united[1]. In a State where the magistrate is non-Christian, and therefore *ex hypothesi* persecutes the Church, he would allow jurisdiction to the Church. But where this is not the case, he saw, like the Papalist, the need of unity. He, indeed, points out that the Popes had based their claim to a universal monarchy on the fact that since there was only one supreme authority, the inferior, i.e. the secular, must yield to the superior, the ecclesiastical power. Erastus held the modern view that the office of the Church as such is purely persuasive[2]. But since he identified Church and Nation, he naturally added that the public policy must be inspired by Christian maxims, and would punish all sins as well as crimes, so far as needful. In a State where men are all of one faith, crime and sin become interchangeable externally, and many things forbidden by religious sentiments may be punished by civil means without injustice. Where this is not so, the attempt to enforce morality as such on the community is a form of persecution; but of course in such a case the jurisdiction of various religious bodies may appear in some form, for they may regard as wrong acts of their members which the State, looking to the whole variegated mass of the people and their opinions, must treat as indifferent. It may be added that what we know of the actual

---

[1] Cf. Coleman. "I could never yet see how two co-ordinate governments, exempt from superiority or inferiority, can be in one State, and in Scripture no such thing is found that I know of." He explains, "Government I take strictly for the corrective." *Hopes Deferred*, 25.

[2] He asks why the duty of ministers to teach is to be expanded into a right to judge (IV. 3).

working of the discipline lends confirmation to the views of Erastus, and proves it to have acted as a restraint upon individual liberty[1].

The main object then of Erastus was not to magnify the State, nor to enslave the Church, but to secure the liberty of the subject. He regarded the discipline as a narrow and illiberal form of persecution, which if not entirely clerical was ecclesiastical to the core, and if allowed to work unchecked was

[1] The following passage from the ordinance imposing the discipline in England (1648) gives some notion of the liberality of the system. The undermentioned classes of persons are to be excommunicated : " All worshippers of images, crosses, crucifixes, or relics ; all that shall make any images or pictures of the Trinity or of any person thereof [this would condemn all religious art]; all religious worshippers of saints, angels, or any meer creatures ; any person that shall profess himself not to be in charity with his neighbours ; all persons in whom malice appears, and they refuse to be reunited...any person that shall upon the Lord's day use any dancing, playing dice, or cards, or any other game, masquing, wakes, shooting, bowling, playing at football, stool-ball, wrestling, or that shall make or resort unto any plays, interludes, fencing, bull-baiting, bear-baiting, or that shall use hawking, hunting, or coursing, fishing or fowling, or that shall publicly expose any wares to sale, otherwise than is provided by an ordinance of Parliament of the sixth of April, 1644; any person that shall travel on the Lord's Day without reasonable cause ; any person, father or mother, that shall assent to the marriage of their child to a Papist, or any person that shall marry a Papist; any person that shall repair for any advice to any witch, wizard, or fortune teller." And see the whole story of the attempt to introduce the discipline into England in Neal, who was by no means unfavourable to the Puritans. Cf. also a letter of Gwalther's complaining that, whereas the episcopal excommunication was always accompanied by reasons, in Heidelberg persons had been excluded from the sacrament and no reason given. *Explicatio*, p. 387.

liable to ruin the State[1]. He asks pertinently enough, Who will be best obeyed, the magistrate or those who have power to excommunicate him? For though his throne be intact, and civil obedience be still preached as a duty, are men in a State, where all are earnestly convinced of their religion and all united, likely to pay much respect to one who has been, although desirous of taking part in the sacrament and declaring himself repentant, excluded from it because the presbytery disbelieves his sincerity[2]? What Erastus disliked was not only the attempt to steal from the prince his power, but also the arrogant assumption of ability to do God's office and read the thoughts of the heart. If a man desired the sacrament, was orthodox in his belief, and declared himself penitent, that was for men sufficient proof of repentance. For we can only judge externally, and cannot put our own authoritative interpretation upon the sincerity of the act without claiming

[1] Bancroft, *Survey*, 208: "There is but only this difference between them and the rankest Jesuits in Europe, that what the one sort do ascribe unto the Pope and his shavelings, the other do challenge unto themselves and their aldermen."

[2] "Dicitis quidem Magistratui excluso nihilominus obedientiam deberi. Sed quis credat me illi parere velle, cui ego vitae totius modum cum potestate et coactione praescribere me posse arbitror? Facile est obedientiam praestare ei, qui contra voluntatem tuam facere nihil ausit. Sane Magistratus quem sibi subiecit Presbyterium, nihil aliud est, quam servus Presbyterii: dum pro eius arbitratu cogitur in quoslibet molliter, duriter, cruciatu corporis, exilio, vinculis, morte, etc. animadvertere." *Confirmatio*, v. 1, p. 301. Bancroft deliberately connects Buchanan's doctrine of deposition with the alleged right to excommunicate princes (*Survey of the Pretended Holy Discipline*, 204); cf. Knox, *Exhortation to England*, Works, v. 516.

infallibility. Thus excommunication usurps not only man's authority by its claim to jurisdiction, but God's by its assurance of certainty. The Popes had seen this, and argued logically enough that an excommunicate King could not rule a Catholic people, and so they proceeded to claim a deposing power. Erastus feared lest the Presbyterate should do the same, and a glance at the writings of Knox will convince us that his fears were not unreasonable.

It is then, I think, not so easy to answer the question, Was Erastus an Erastian ? as many people imagine; or if we answer in the affirmative, we shall have to surrender a favourite nickname for our opponents. He was, I believe, less Erastian than Whitgift[1], perhaps less so than Cranmer[2], far less so than Selden or Hobbes[3]. Strangely enough, even Pareus[4] uses phrases about the power of the magistrate in religion, which many would call Erastian. As Dr William Cunningham says, " Erastus is less Erastian than some who in modern times have been ranked under that designation, not perhaps without

---

[1] See *Defence of the Answer to the Admonition*, Tractate xx., Works, iii. (295–325), especially p. 306, where he quotes with approval "*princes deciding in matters of religion, even in the chief and principal points.*"

[2] See his works *passim*, more especially the Corrections of the Institution, *Questions concerning the Sacraments*, ii. p. 117.

[3] Cf. Lee, preface to the Theses, who says that Erastianism is not to be identified with the tenet of Hobbes that the civil power may establish whatever religion it pleases, and exact obedience to it, which the subject is bound to render for conscience' sake, or even set up any form of Church government it pleases, and change it as often as it likes (xlv. vi.).

[4] *Aphorisms*, § xi.

some injustice to him, but most certainly with no
injustice to them[1]."

But though this may be the case, it is not therefore true either that Erastus was right or that his
views have no relation to Erastianism or Byzantinism.
He saw one side in a debate which had lasted for
centuries, and even yet is hardly concluded. Taught
by experience Erastus desired to prevent the establishment of what seemed to him an ecclesiastical
tyranny. In the course of his argument he asserted
that in a State of one religion all that was needed
for the enforcement of piety and morality could and
ought to be done by the magistrate; and that for
any other persons to assume a coercive control without appeal was a usurpation on the one sovereign
authority. Yet the powers which he admitted to be
the magistrate's were sufficiently large even within
the limits laid down. And these limits could not
endure. Erastianism is not rightly named, if we
mean by it the explicit tenets of Erastus. Yet the
attribution is not altogether wrong. For the word
describes the actual and inevitable, if not the logical,
development of his teachings when torn from their
context and shorn of the careful qualifications with
which he surrounded them. Erastus did not mean
to do more than assert that all coercive authority
is vested in the State. But he added to this the
prevailing notion that the State must support one
religion and tolerate no other. It was then not
many steps to the theory of Hobbes that the State
could support any religion it pleased out of motives

[1] *Hist. Theol.* II. 572.

of State policy and with no regard to truth. In fact the power which Erastus claimed for the Christian might soon be asserted to belong to the non-Christian magistrate, although such a claim was far enough from the thought of Erastus and from that of many Erastians. Erastus paved the way for a theory more imposing, more systematic, more antagonistic to reason than his own. For assuredly there is no less reasonable view than that which permits a magistrate to set up a Church on purely political grounds and to prohibit all others. This position, if ever thoroughly carried out, might be more destructive to free inquiry than any ecclesiastical tyranny. It did not indeed, I think, directly follow from the doctrine of Erastus or the Erastian reformers. But they might easily be misunderstood or misrepresented as if it did.

The opposite (or ecclesiastical) view had held the field, though not unassailed, for centuries. The Reformation was in one respect the uprising of the laity against the clergy; in another an assertion of State rights against a federal imperialism in Church matters. It was in fact individualist and particularist, as opposed to a system which was socialistic and centralised. And the circumstances under which it took place made men rely very largely on the prince's authority as their most effective support. It made some reformers, such as Erastus abroad and Anglicans and many Independents at home, dread the Presbyterian discipline as being the counterpart of that bureaucratic clericalism from which they believed themselves to have escaped. The Erastians' aim, or that of most of them, whether at Heidelberg or Dort or Westminster, was rather to protect the individual than the State, though the latter object was a good deal more prominent at Westminster. This indeed was the main cause of the later use of the word Erastianism as a term having no reference to excommunication and a large general reference to State authority. The conflict was inevitable between Church and State, so long as persecution was to be enforced. For such enforcement required the aid of the State, which could not be expected to give it without being consulted. The remedy lay beyond the vision of Erastus and the men of his day, though not far beyond that of some of his opponents in the synod of Westminster. With liberty of conscience proclaimed as the State policy, the conflict of the two jurisdictions is at an end for all practical purposes. When the State leaves off the hopeless task of imposing one faith and worship by force, and the Church leaves off preaching persecution as a duty, there would be no cause for a serious struggle, and on the principles of Erastus no ground for interfering with the jurisdiction of religious bodies over their members: while the existence of other religious bodies would prevent such jurisdiction doing serious civil damage to a man in cases where the whole community irrespective of creed was not on his side[1]. Excommunication to be seriously effective needs the

---

[1] For instance, supposing for the sake of argument it were right to excommunicate a man or woman who had married a divorced person. Such an act might have effect on devout Churchmen,

absence of competing Churches or systems. But
this way out of the difficulty was not clear to
Erastus. He, it may be thought, would unduly exalt
the State. Certainly Erastians did, just as Olevianus,
Knox, and the disciplinarians would use the State as
the handmaid of the Church, with more outward
deference, but with no more real respect, than Gregory VII. or Boniface VIII. Neither party could be
at peace so long as Catholics and Protestants alike
were agreed as to the import and efficacy of an *auto-
da-fé* as the means of promoting the 'one faith.' For
this view made the forces of Church and State necessary to one another, and yet brought them into
incessant conflict. The problem was not solved, it
was transcended. The battle was over only when
men saw that peace being the end of the State,
social well-being would be attained by leaving all
religious bodies the fullest liberty to organise, to develop, and to preach. To employ a familiar method,
toleration was the higher unity in which were resolved
the contrary, but complementary ideals of secular
authority and spiritual independence. The victory
was won by both sides and by neither. On the one
hand, ecclesiastical pretensions, however preposterous,
burnt into men's minds (and indeed their bodies) the
sense that society needs some basis other than force.
We owe to them the belief that a duty is laid upon
men to secure freedom for the expression of spiritual
aspirations, a freedom which might otherwise have

but unless the general sentiment of the community, Churchmen,
Dissenters, and Agnostics, was in favour of it, it would be unlikely
to injure such persons seriously in their business or profession.

been sacrificed to the shock of national ambitions or the jealousies of competing dynasties. On the other hand, but for Erastus and his followers, even Hobbes and the supporters of the Divine Right of Kings, who insisted so strongly on the right of the State to be, on the essential need of political society to human well-being, and on the duty of preserving men against the evils of a domination, which on its own showing was human in administration and divine in its sanctions and claims, and therefore likely to be the more unrestrained in its tyranny, there might have been—there nearly was—an agelong enslavement of human thought and action to a system in some respects more narrow because more complete, less broadly human, less careful of culture and intellectual enlightenment, than was the system of the mediæval world taken at its worst.

APPENDIX A

EXTRACTS FROM STATUTES RELATING TO
THE SUCCESSION

THE progress of the idea of inherent right and the complete decay of the doctrine of election may be illustrated from the statutes passed between 1483 and 1603, which attempt to settle or declare the succession.

(1) In the *titulus regius*, which gave the Crown to Richard III., we see the two notions of elective kingship and title by inheritance blended together. It is noteworthy that the statute seems to regard Parliament in the light of a supreme court competent to declare the law without appeal, rather than as a legislative body creating new law. Parliament claims no right to alter the succession, but merely to declare it, so as to remove perplexity.

" We consider that ye be the undoubted son and heir of Richard, late Duke of York, very inheritor of the said crown and dignity royal, and as in right King of England by way of inheritance;...and by this our writing choose you High and Mighty Prince, our King and Sovereign Lord. *To whom we know it appertaineth of inheritance so to be chosen*.......We pray and require your most noble grace that according to this

election of us the three estates of this land ; as by your
true inheritance you will accept and take upon you the
said Crown and royal dignity with all things thereunto
annexed and appertaining as to you of right belonging as well by inheritance, as by lawful election.......
Albeit that the right title and estate which our
Sovereign Lord the King Richard the Third hath to
and in the Crown...of England...been just and lawful
as grounded upon the laws of God and of nature ; and
also upon the ancient laws and customs of this said
realm and so taken and reputed by all such persons as
been learned in the above said laws and customs ; yet
nevertheless for as much as it is considered, that the
most part of the people is not sufficiently learned in the
above said laws and customs, whereby the truth and
right in this behalf, of likelihood may be hid and not
clearly known to all the people, and thereupon put in
doubt and question. And over this, how that the court
of Parliament is of such authority and the people of
this land of such a nature and disposition, as experience
teacheth, that manifestation and declaration of any truth
or right made by the three estates of the realm assembled
in Parliament, and by the authority of the same maketh
before all other things most faith and certain, and
quieting of men's minds removeth the occasion of all
doubts and seditious language, therefore &c."—Speed's
History, 724.

(2) The statute granting the Crown to Henry VII.
is far different in its businesslike brevity of tone. In
this the authority of Parliament to do what it wills
with the succession is unmistakeably implied.

"Be it ordained established and enacted by authority
of this present Parliament that the inheritance of the
Crowns of the Realms of England and France with

all the preeminence and dignity royal to the same appertaining...be, rest, remain, and abide in the most royal person of our now Sovereign Lord, King Henry the Seventh and the heirs of his body...and in none other."—*Statutes of the Realm*, ii. 499.

(3) The statute declaring Elizabeth queen, although it admits her title by descent, and is fulsome in tone, yet has no scruple about regarding an Act of Parliament as the true title to the Crown. The second clause ratifies Henry's testamentary disposition and thus traverses the doctrine of hereditary succession.

"Your highness is rightly, lineally and lawfully descended and come out of the blood royal of this Realm of England in and to......whose princely person ......the imperial and royal estate, place, crown, and dignity are and shall be most fully...invested and incorporated,......as the same were since the Act of Parliament made in the thirty-fifth year of King Henry the Eighth. ......For which causes......we beseech that it may be enacted, That as well this our declaration...as also the limitation and declaration of the succession contained in the said Act (35 Hen. VIII. c. 1) shall stand the law of this realm for ever."—*Statutes of the Realm*, iv. 358 ; Prothero's *Statutes*, 21.

(4) Lastly, the statute recognizing the title of James I. is saturated with the notion of inherent birthright, and knows of no other title. The act carefully guards against granting the succession, but claims merely to declare it.

"A most joyful and just recognition of the immediate, lawful, and undoubted succession of Descent and Right of the Crown.

"We (being bounden thereunto both by the laws of God and man) do recognize and acknowledge (and thereby express our unspeakable joys), that immediately upon the dissolution and decease of Elizabeth...the imperial crown of the realm of England...did, by inherent birthright and lawful and undoubted succession descend and come to your most excellent majesty, as being lineally, justly, and lawfully next and sole heir of the blood royal of this realm as is aforesaid."— *Statutes of the Realm,* IV. 107; Prothero's *Statutes,* 251.

APPENDIX B

EXTRACTS ILLUSTRATIVE OF POINTS DISCUSSED IN CHAPTERS VIII. AND IX.

1. *Popery, as involving a belief in the deposing power, a disloyal doctrine.*

"I will not say (though it has been said) the Romanists' faith is faction and their religion rebellion; but this I must say, that they teach and broach such doctrines as are very scandalous to Christian religion, and very dangerous and destructive to Kingdoms and States; as having a direct and natural tendency to sedition, rebellion, and treason."—Duport, *Sermon on the Fifth of November*, 64.

"I do not, I will not, say All our Romanists are enclined to rebellion; I doubt not but there are many faithful and loyal subjects among 'em; but this I must say, As long as they own a foreign jurisdiction, either spiritual or temporal, which they must do if they are thorough-paced; and as long as the Pope usurps the power to depose and dispose, to depose Kings, and dispose of their Kingdoms, and to absolve subjects from their oaths of supremacy and allegiance; so long the Romish religion must needs have a natural tendency to disloyalty; and therefore, if Papists be good subjects,

no thanks to their Popery; and I fear, 'twill be hard
for 'em to be good Catholics at Rome, and good subjects
at home; for if they be so, it must be only *durante bene
placito,* so long as the Pope is well-pleas'd, but if once
he be angry with Kings and call 'em heretics, then have
at 'em fowlers, let 'em look to themselves."—*Ibid.* 68.

"The Reformation of our Church was laid upon the
subversion of one of the most fatal and pernicious
principles to government, that any religion can maintain, namely the precarious conditions of allegiance to
the true and lawful sovereign, upon the falsehood and
ruin whereof our constitution both civil and ecclesiastical was founded and established."—Sacheverell,
The Political Union, 54.

The following passage shews how the whole controversy between the temporal and spiritual authority
must be viewed from the standpoint of an age, when
the enforcement of uniformity in religious practice was
regarded by all parties as the duty of the State.

"No king or prince by their [the Romanists']
doctrine can truly be accounted a freeman or denizen in the State
wherein he lives, seeing no king can have so much as a
voice or suffrage in making those ecclesiastical canons,
unto which he, his people, all his laws temporal and
spiritual are subordinate and subject. For no man
could think him to be a freeman in any corporation,
that has no voice in making the temporal laws by which
he is to be governed or at least in choosing such of
them as have interest in the making of Public Laws."—
Jackson, *Treatise of Christian Obedience* (*Works,* III. 909).

"The Jesuits the principal authors of resistance to
all higher powers."—*Ibid.* 971.

"The deposing doctrine and placing the power in
the people is but the spittle of the Jesuits which our

Whigs and Dissenters have picked up."—Leslie, *The Wolf stripped of his Shepherd's Clothing*, 4.

"Your mobs are all papists, they are for the deposing power, which is perfect popery."—Leslie, *A Battle Royal*, 174.

Papal supremacy divests the prince of his absolute sovereignty, of his legislative power and renders monarchy insecure of possession or succession, by bereaving it of the guard of the laws, of the strength of alliances, of the fidelity of their people. Papal supremacy destructive of the people's liberty and property.—The Common Interest of King and People, Chap. VII.

"These men cry out against Popery, and yet profess, what all good Protestants esteem the most malignant part of Jesuitism."—Dudley Digges, *The Unlawfulness of Subjects Taking up Arms*, 64.

2. *Identification of Papists and Dissenters.*

"It is most manifest, that all our late horrid civil wars, rapines, bloodshed and the execrable and solemn murder of His Late Majesty, and the banishment of our present sovereign were effected according to the fore-contrivance of the Papists, by the assistance which the Dissenters gave them and the opportunities they had to preach them into rebellion under the pretence of a thorough Reformation, that all late commotions and rebellions in Scotland sprung from the same counsel and conduct."—*Foxes and Firebrands*, 32.

"Let us now come to take a view of the younger antagonists of monarchy, the popular supremacy of Presbytery, that Lerna Malorum, that revived hydra of the Lake of Geneva, with its many-headed progeny, Anabaptists, Quakers, Levellers &c., all which unnatural offspring are as kind to their dam as vipers, and as inconsistent with monarchy, as they pretend to be with the Papacy (with which Presbytery jostles for universal supremacy) or any of them with Loyalty, Royalty or true religion."—Nalson, *Common Interest of King and People*, 201.

" The Puritans were mere tools to the Jesuits (as they are to this day), from them they learned the deposing doctrine, and to set up the private spirit against the Holy Scriptures, and all the authority of the Church."— Leslie, *The Rehearsal*, No. 84.

"Sure the hand of Joab, the Jesuit with his King-killing doctrine, was in all this, and every one of the regicides had a Pope in his belly, to give him a dispensation, and absolve him from his oath of allegiance."—Duport, *Sermon on Thirtieth of January*, 11.

" Those *fratres in malo*, those red-hot fiery zealots o' both sides ; your furious hair-brained fanatic, and your perfidious disloyal Loiolite : I join 'em together, *Bithus cum Bachio*, for I know not which is the worse o' the two ; and I think they plough with one another's heifer."—*Ibid.* 22.

" Do you think our Roman Catholics, at least the Jesuits, were idle spectators all the while and had not a hand in the 30th of January, as well as in the fifth of November ? Is it not well known that the train to entangle us in that horrible snare, and intrigue of the late confusions, was laid by a great Cardinal minister of State, and perhaps the whole conclave ?......Is it not yet apparent, that the Popish emissaries and incendiaries were sent hither on purpose under the name of Anabaptists, Seekers, and Quakers, and I know not what to blow the coals and foment the flames of our late dissensions ?"—Duport, *Sermon on Fifth of November*, 72.

"Our factious, fanatic, turbulent, and schismatical spirits are but the Jesuits' journeymen."—*Ibid.* 76.

3. *Clericalism of the Presbyterian System.*

"Their [the Presbyterians'] Church government is pernicious to Civil Power, grievous to such as must live under it, and apt to distort the Common Peace." —Leslie, *The Trojan Horse of the Presbyterian Government Unbowelled*, 3.

"They claim power to abrogate the laws of the land touching ecclesiastical matters, if they judge them hurtful or unprofitable.......They require the civil magistrate to be subject to their power."—*Ibid.* 5.

"It may be that the general disaffection to regal power, in these distractions, may render some men less apprehensive of the dangerous consequences of this doctrine, and the former claims; as supposing them to have no other drift than to clip the wings of royal prerogative. But this is a gross and dangerous mistake and whosoever shall be invested with that Civil Power, which shall be taken from the King, be it the Parliament or whosoever else, must look to succeed him in the heavy enmity which this Presbyterian power will exercise against the Civil Power (when it doth not comply with them), in what hands soever it be placed. For these encroachments of theirs are not upon the King as distinguished from other magistrates, but upon the civil magistrate in common whosoever he be."—*Ibid.* 8.

"The King and Parliament must be subject not only to their general assembly, but (in subordination to that) to the dictates of every petty parochial session, where their personal residence and abode shall be. Lastly if the King and Parliament will govern contrary to their will and pleasure, their principles will allow them to incite the people to resist them."—*Ibid.* 8.

"They determine that the temporal magistrate is bound to punish adultery with death by God's own law.......They hold it unlawful for the civil magistrate to pardon capital offenders."—*Ibid.* 9.

" By their platform they may deal with all civil causes for a spiritual end, which the Pope usually expresses with this clause *In ordine ad bonum Spirituale,* and these men by the same effect *in ordine ad bonum ecclesiae.* But both he and they do by this distinction usurp upon the Civil magistrate."—*Ibid.* 10.

"This discipline which they do so much adore is the very quintessence of refined Popery, or a greater Tyranny than ever Rome brought forth, inconsistent with all forms of civil government, destructive to all sorts of policy, a rack to the conscience, the heaviest pressure that can fall upon a people, and so much more dangerous because by the specious pretence of Divine institution, it takes away the right, but not the burden of slavery."—Bramhall, *A Warning to the Church of England,* 2.

That it [the Discipline] exempts the ministers from due punishment.—Ibid. Chap. IV.

The Disciplinarians cheat the magistrate of his civil power, in order to religion.—Ibid. Chap. VII.

"They ascribe unto their ministers a liberty and power to direct the magistrate even in the managery of civil affairs."—*Ibid.* 25.

"They assume a power in worldly affairs indirectly and in order to the advancement of the Kingdom of Christ."—*Ibid.* 26.

"The Parliament will restore to the King his negative voice ; a mere civil thing. The commissioners of the Church oppose it, because of the great dangers that may thereby come to religion. The Parliament name officers and commanders for the army; a mere civil thing. The Church will not allow them because they want such qualifications, as God's word requires, that is to say in plain terms because they were not their confidents. Was there ever Church challenged such an omnipotence as this? Nothing in this world is so civil or political, wherein they do not interest themselves in order to the advancement of the Kingdom of Christ."— *Ibid.* 27.

"This is the Presbyterian want, to subject all causes and persons to their consistories, to ratify and abolish civil laws, to confirm and pull down Parliaments, to levy forces, to invade other Kingdoms, to do anything respectively to the advancement of the good cause and in order to religion."—*Ibid.* 31.

Chapter VIII. *That the Disciplinarians challenge this exorbitant power by Divine Right.*

Chapter IX. *That this discipline makes a monster of the Commonwealth.*

"We have seen how pernicious this discipline (as it is maintained in Scotland and endeavoured to be introduced into England by the Covenant) is to the Supreme Magistrate, how it robs him of his supremacy in ecclesiastical affairs, and of the last appeals of his own subjects, that it exempts the presbyters from the power of the magistrate, and subjects the magistrate to the presbyters, that it restrains his dispensative power of pardoning, deprives him of the dependence of his subjects, that it doth challenge and usurp a power paramount both of the word and of the sword, both of peace and war, over all courts and estates, over all laws civil and ecclesiastical, in order to the

advancement of the Kingdom of Christ, whereof the
Presbyters alone are constituted rulers by God, and all
this by a pretended Divine Right, which takes away
all hope of remedy, until it be hissed out of the world;
in a word that it is the top-branch of Popery, a greater
tyranny, than ever Rome was guilty of. It remains
to shew how disadvantageous it is also to the subject.

"First, to the Commonwealth in general which it
makes a monster, like an amphiscian or a serpent with
two heads, one at either end. It makes a coordination
of sovereignty in the same society, two supremes in
the same Kingdom or State, the one civil, the other
ecclesiastical, than which nothing can be more pernicious
either to the consciences, or the estates of subjects, when
it falls out (as it often doth) that from these two heads
issue contrary commands."—*Ibid.* 35.

The striking similarity of this passage to the argument
of Ockham against the Papacy is plain.

Chapter X. *That this discipline is most prejudicial
to the Parliament.*

Chapter XI. *That this discipline is oppressive to
particular persons.*

Nalson, *Common Interest of King and People*, Chap. ix.

*Presbytery in reality as great an enemy to Democracy
and Parliaments as to monarchy. A short view of their
tyrannic consistorian government over the magistracy,
clergy and laity. Of the latitude and power of scandal
to draw all affairs into the consistory.......The small
difference betwixt a Jesuit and Geneva Presbyter. Both
aim at supremacy.*

"We shall find that it is absolutely inconsistent
with all government (except its own oligarchic spiritual
tyranny) and even that adored Democracy, which it
pretends to hug and embrace with so much tenderness

and affection.......The real design is to dash a Parliament against a King, to break them both in pieces ; and like the ape in the story to make a cat's foot of the House of Commons, to pull the nut out of the hot ashes of rebellion, into which they shall have reduced the monarchy ; for when once by that assistance they shall have procured their own establishment, they will render it as absolute a slave, as they would do monarchy."—*Ibid.* 241.

" It is not the persons or names, but the superiority of the authority, against which this faction of Geneva levels all its aims."—*Ibid.*

" These saints who pretend to a power of binding Kings in chains will without scruple so claim the honour of shackling the nobles in fetters of iron."—*Ibid.* 242.

" It is the desire of sovereignty under the colour of religion at which they aim ; and to which whatsoever is an obstacle, whether King, Parliament, Prelates, Lords, or Commons, shall all be declared anti-Christian and unlawful powers."—*Ibid.* 244.

" The great assembly and the moderator for the time being is the absolute and supreme sovereign power of the nation, where Presbytery bears the sway."—*Ibid.* 247.

"They [Presbytery and Jesuitry] are both inconsistent with monarchy and indeed with all government ; over which they pretend a power and jurisdiction by Christ, the one for the Pope, the other for the Presbytery ; from which there lies no appeal."—*Ibid.* 257.

Chapter X. *Presbytery as destructive of the People's liberty and property as it is dangerous to monarchy and all government.*

" No person whatsoever, let him pretend never so much religion, sanctity, or innocence, can possibly be a good subject, so long as he continues a true Presbyterian

or of their offspring; in regard they always carry about
with them as the main of their religion such principles,
as are directly contrary to monarchy and destructive
of loyalty; to which he can never be a firm, true and
assured friend, who owns a power superior to that of
his prince within his dominions; and that such a power
may of right depose him, and take away his crown and
life, which has been proved to be the avowed doctrine
of the consistorians of Geneva, Scotland, and England,
both in point and practice."—270.

"That Presbyterian popular consistorian supremacy,
is, and ever will be, the unchangeable, irreconcilable
enemy of monarchy, law, liberty, peace, property, and
the true Protestant Catholic religion."—279.

"Having thus taken the whole civil government
into their own hands as the Pope has done, and by
virtue of the same distinction in *ordine ad spiritualia*
they followed him likewise in that which is a natural
consequence of the other, to exempt themselves from
being accountable to the civil power even for civil
crimes."—Leslie, *The New Association*, Part II. 33.

4. *The Divine Right of Kings in reality a defence
of all secular governments against ecclesiastical aggression.*

"It shall suffice to note that the Romanist makes
an unequal comparison and sets the terms of his
proposition awry, when he compares spiritual power
indefinitely taken with power royal or monarchical,
which is but a branch though the highest branch of
power civil or temporal. The question should be
betwixt authority spiritual or ecclesiastic indefinitely
taken; and between power civil or temporal alike
indefinitely taken. Power temporal or civil thus taken

is immediately from God, and government temporal
itself in some one kind or other (that is Monarchical,
Aristocratical or mixed or &c.) is *de Jure Divino,* as
well as power spiritual or ecclesiastic is."—Jackson,
Treatise of Christian Obedience (Works, III. 903).

" That this nation should be governed by a King,
another by peers and nobles, another by the people, or
by magistrates of the people's choosing, either annual
or for term of life, this is not determined *Jure Divino*
by any express or positive law of God, but is reserved
unto the guidance of his ordinary Providence, who
sometimes directs one people or nation to make choice
of this form, another to make choice of that.   But the
choice of government being made by the people or
imposed upon them by right of war, to yield obedience
to the form of government or power established, this is
de Jure Divino positively and peremptorily determined
and enjoined by the law of God.   And whosoever
doth resist the form of government established in the
commonweal, whereof he is a member, be it of this
form or that, he doth resist the higher powers ; and
by resisting them *resisteth the ordinance of God.*"—
Ibid. 963.

5.   *Inevitable conflict between temporal and spiritual powers, so long as the principle of toleration is
unrecognized.*

" It is indeed impossible that a coordination of these
powers should subsist; for each will be continually
encroaching on the other, each for its own defence and
support will continually be struggling and clambering
to get above the other ; there never will be any quiet
till one come to subside and truckle under the other ;
whereby the sovereignty of the one or the other will be

destroyed; each of them soon will come to claim a supremacy in all causes and the power of both swords; and one side will carry it...."—Barrow, *Treatise of the Pope's Supremacy*, 144.

The divergence of this view from that of Barclay, the representative of strict Gallicanism, is noteworthy. Barclay strongly emphasizes, that need of two coordinate authorities, which Barrow denies to be possible. "A free Church in a free State" was the ideal of the Gallican writer; the Anglican is aware, that the dream is incapable of realization.

6. *Connection of English politics with French controversies.*

"This pretence of the King's authority against his person was hatched under the Romish territories and made use of in the Holy League of France."—Falkner, *Christian Loyalty*, 356.

7. *The theory of Hobbes regarded as dangerous, notwithstanding his practical conclusions, owing to his basing it upon the original compact.*

"Though Mr Hobbs sometimes hath over-large expressions concerning the power of governors; yet he having before laid the same formation for the original of political government, doth also undermine the safety and stability of governors and government....... But as these positions are framed upon such suppositions, as look upon man in his beginning, to stand without due respect to God, and the rules and notions of good and evil; so the dangerous aspect they have on peace and government doth speak the folly of them, and they will be sufficiently in this particular confuted by asserting the divine original of sovereignty."—Falkner, *Christian Loyalty*, 409.

"I consent with him about the rights of exercising government, but I cannot agree to his means of acquiring it. It may seem strange I should praise his building, and yet mislike his foundation, but so it is, his *Jus naturae* and his *regnum institutivum* will not down with me; they appear full of contradiction and impossibilities."—Filmer, *Observations touching the original of government*, Preface.

8. *The patriarchal theory of kingship based on a belief in the state of nature and in Scripture as the only authentic testimony for it. Natural rights are Divine rights.*

The original state of nature shewed to be a state of government and subjection not of independency.—Leslie, *The Rehearsal*, No. 55.

"The first state of nature to which all our whigs do refer, makes clearly against them, and is wholly on your side, who plead for government and the divine institution of it; against that original independent state of nature, which the whigs do suppose, but can never prove, unless they can find some other original of mankind than the holy Scriptures have told us."—*Ibid.* No. 56.

"If being born under Laws and a government whose legislative has an absolute despotic and unaccountable power over our very lives as well as our estates without staying to ask our consent, if this is to be free born, then all the world are so and ever have been so since Adam : otherwise not one, unless a King be born after his father is dead."—Leslie, *The New Association*, Part I. 15.

" 'Supposing therefore that Adam was universal monarch or civil governor over the whole race of mankind, during his long life this will not prove he had a Divine right to be so?' Will it not? Then I am very sure no after-King can claim it. If Adam had no Divine Right, what right had he?"—Leslie, *The Finishing Stroke*, 18.

"I go upon fact plainly recorded in Scripture."—*Ibid.* 38.

"The Rehearsal had blamed those who went to heathen authors for the original of government, because none of their histories reached so high, and they knew not how the world or mankind begun.......The only and the certain account of it,......is to be found in the Holy Scriptures."—*Ibid.* 89.

"The Rehearsal places the original of government in the positive institution of God, though at the same time he shews it to be consequential, and most agreeable to the frame of our nature, as being all deduced from one common father. Which patriarchal or fatherly authority is not only founded in Nature, but most expressly and originally in the first institution of government placed by God in Adam."—Leslie, *A Battle Royal*, 128.

"A family is a little kingdom, but a kingdom is nothing but a great family. Therefore such a state of mankind, where all are upon the level and the consent of every individual made necessary to the erection of government, as Locke and others suppose it, because that every man is freeborn and that no man's life and liberty or property can be disposed of but by his own consent, I say such a state cannot be called the state of nature because nature implies fathers and mothers; it may be called a state of mankind, but not of such men as we are, but of a shower of men rained down from the clouds or new created in multitudes, like the beasts, fish, and fowl at the beginning and no one dependent upon the other. So that even the Hottentot cannot represent this state, which yet is necessary to make the people the original of government."—*Ibid.* 128.

" But to them that believe the truth revealed in Holy Scripture, 'tis strange they should make question about it, seeing the world began in one man, that lived nigh one thousand years, at puberty the first hour ; so that he could not have a less monarchy than any now extant in the world considering the vast increase there may be from man and woman in a perfect state of health examined by the surest rules of progression. Against him should anyone in the world rise up, it had been rebellion and parricide. Nothing but the authority of God would justify the suspension of obedience to him the natural father of the world."—Leslie, *Obedience to Civil Government clearly stated,* 14.

The divergence between Leslie and the French School is shewn in the different views taken of Nimrod. To the French school he is the founder of monarchy, to Leslie he is the first instance of a successful usurper.

" If it [Self preservation] were a natural law, it would be a sin to resign it over to any.......Self Preservation is only an instinct."—*Ibid.* 72.

9. *Gulf between Adamic society and modern times bridged by theory of prescriptive right.*

"Possession gives right, tho' wrongfully come by,...... [if] there is none who claims a better right than the possessor."—Leslie, *The Sham Sermon Dissected,* 2.

10. *Question of source of Law.   There must be a*

supreme lawgiver. A sovereign needful to invest laws with binding authority.

"Laws must be made by Kings. Therefore Kings must be before Laws."—Leslie, *Cassandra,* 22.

" Kings were kings before there were Laws.......The King's Power is antecedent to Law which hath its force from him."—*The Apostate Protestant,* 41.

"He gives the prince no right but what is vested in him by law. Tho' his right is prior to the law, for he gives sanction to the law, and who gave him the right to do that? And here we are enjoined to give the prince no more than what is vested in him by law. Then he can no more give sanction to any law; unless we can find a law before there was any King, to make that King, and give him a right to give sanction to laws for the future."—Leslie, *The Sham Sermon Dissected,* 5.

"This manifests the fundamental error in politics, of those persons who make laws to have a priority, before Kings and governors; as if the laws made Kings and magistrates, when in truth God and nature vested primogeniture with the right of Kings and magistrates; and they made the first laws."—Nalson, *Common Interest of King and People,* 13.

"There can be no laws, till there be some frame of government, to establish and enact such laws; nor can anything have the force or power of a law, or oblige men to obedience, unless it does proceed from a person or persons, as have a right to command it, and authority to punish the disobedience or neglect of those who ought to be subject to it."—*Ibid.* 14.

"[The common law] follows in time after government, but cannot go before it, and be the rule to government by any original or radical constitution."—Filmer, *Anarchy of a Limited and Mixed Monarchy,* 267.

11. *There must be in every state a sovereign, not bound by positive law.*

" There must be a *dernier ressort* or there can be no government. And where there is in an assembly that assembly is one body, as one person."—Leslie, *Cassandra,* 23.

" *Hoadly.* We are free because the government cannot hang us on what they please but they are bounded by law, and we must have a fair trial, and by our peers too.

Hottentot. So you are free, because you are hanged by a jury! But what think you of an Act of Attainder, which can hang without any trial or giving you any reason for it?

Hoad. This is part of our constitution, that the Parliament should have such a power in extraordinary case.

Hott. Yet you are free! And these cases happen, as oft as the Parliament pleases. They are not tied to any rule, but may make use of this power, whenever it comes into their heads.

Hoad. Well, but the King cannot hang us at his pleasure.

Hott. That is, you are not at the mercy of one man, but of five hundred. O delicate freedom."—Leslie, *A Battle Royal,* 142.

"After laws and society come in, all under it are born slaves, that is under the absolute dominion of what you call the legislature in every society. And whether that be in the hands of one or more it is all the same as to the destruction of liberty. For what is it to me, whether I am hanged by the command of one or of five hundred?"—*Ibid.* 159.

" Every government has absolute power over the

lives, as well as estates of all their subjects without asking their leave or making any contract with them. They are born in subjection, without conditions."—Leslie, *The Best Answer that ever was made*, 8.

"Without a last resort there can be no government. And if this be in the people, still there is no government. And if you stop short of all the people, then wherever it rests, there is 'absolute unaccountable' &c."—*Ibid.* 15.

"These men have strange notions of monarchy, and of absolute government, which, as I have often said, is the same in all sorts of governments whatsoever. All the difference is in whom this absolute power shall be placed, whether in one, in a few, or in many?"— Leslie, *The Rehearsal*, No. 59.

"All governments in the world must be arbitrary, in some hands or other; for there must be a last resort in every government, and that must be arbitrary and unaccountable, as having no superior upon earth."— *Ibid.* No. 36.

"If any man can find us out such a kind of government, wherein the supreme power can be, without being freed from human laws, they should first teach us that......a legislative power cannot be without being absolved from human laws."—Filmer, *Observations upon Mr Milton against Salmasius.*

"*A necessity to grant impunity to some in all governments to avoid confusion.*"—Dudley Digges, *Unlawfulness of Subjects*, 43.

"If, as Mr Locke says, and says he has proved it, *No man can subject himself to the arbitrary power of another*, no man can subject himself to any government of what sort or size soever. Nor can there be such a thing as government kept up in the world."—Leslie, *The Rehearsal*, No. 38.

"In all kingdoms or commonwealths in the world, whether the prince be the supreme father of the people or but the true heir of such a father, or whether he come to the crown by usurpation, or by election of the nobles or of the people, or by any other way whatsoever; or whether some few or a multitude govern the Commonwealth; yet still the authority that is in any one or in many or in all these is the only right and natural authority of a supreme father."—Filmer, *Patriarcha*, I. § 10.

"The true debate amongst men is not whether they shall admit of bonds......but who shall impose them; the question is not *an servirent, sed an uni vel pluribus*; it is commonly called liberty, to serve more masters."—Dudley Digges, *Unlawfulness of Subjects taking up Arms*, 29.

12. *Sovereignty indivisible.   Anarchy of a mixed monarchy.*

"They know very well that there can be no sharing of power, it must be one and entire; and the contest for it is anarchy and confusion."—Leslie, *The New Association*, Part II. 11.

"All power is one indivisible whether in the hands of one or many."—Leslie, *Cassandra*, 23.

"He lays his stress upon a constitution like ours. And as he has dressed our constitution, we may well say there is not a constitution like ours upon the face of the earth.   He has made it up of coordinate powers, all opposition, nonsense, and contradiction."—Leslie, *The Sham Sermon Dissected*, 5.

"It doth not follow, that the form of government is, or can be in its own nature ill, because the governor is so; it is anarchy, or want of government that can totally destroy a nation."—Filmer, *Observations upon Mr Milton against Salmasius*, 494.

"This mixed monarchy, just like the limited, ends in confusion and destruction of all government."—Filmer, *Anarchy of a Mixed and Limited Monarchy*, 272.

"There cannot be such a thing as *mixtum imperium* ......because if there are divers supreme powers it is no longer one state. If the supreme power be but one,......this must be placed either in one man,...... or in some nobles......or if the civil constitution of a state directs us to appeal to the people, this is an absolute and true democracy."—Dudley Digges, *Unlawfulness*, 77.

"I have shewn before that a mixed monarchy is a contradiction."—*Ibid.* 168.

13. *Theory of Divine Right a defence of government against anarchy, far more than an apology for monarchy.*

"The endeavouring to settle sure and lasting foundations of government in opposition to these popular no principles, of sedition and eternal confusion, is all the reason I know that has stirred up the wrath of these orators of the populace."—Leslie, *Cassandra*, I. 41.

"[Government] in the largest sense is a communion of superiors and inferiors united for the safety of the whole; to disunite them is overturning it."—Leslie, *Obedience to Civil Government clearly stated*, 8.

"The reasons against Kings are as strong against all powers, for men of any titles are subject to err, and numbers more than fewer."—*Ibid.* 63.

"This doctrine may disturb the present, and threaten all future governors and governments whatsoever."— *Ibid.* 64.

"All the arguments used to justify self preservation, are grounded only on supposition that men may be wronged or oppressed by God's magistrates or rulers ; and therefore conclude as well against all civil government, as against the magistrate in being."—*Ibid.* 90.

"If the last resort be in the people, there is no end of controversy at all, but endless and unremediable confusion."—Leslie, *The Best Answer*, 14.

"It is unlawful to resist him or them in whom the supreme authority (that is all the legal power of the kingdom) is placed, and no dispensation......can excuse such resistance from the sin of rebellion. Upon this pillar not only monarchy stands firm, but all other governments are equally supported."—Dudley Digges, *Unlawfulness of Subjects*, 10.

"*Liberty to resist those in whom the law places* jus gladii, *the right of the sword, destructive to the very nature of government.*"—*Ibid.* 8.

"This argument [of equality] doth not conclude for one form above another but equally destroys all."— *Ibid.* 29.

"*Hoadly.* He is ever representing me as maintaining such principles as are inconsistent with the safety of all government."—Leslie, *Best of All*, 8.

"Obedience is due to commonwealths by their subjects, even for conscience' sake, where the princes from whom they have revolted have given up their claim."—*Ibid.* 27.

"The power of the people which you set up is equally destructive of commonwealths as of monarchies. ......And with that it is impossible for any government to subsist."—*Ibid.* 30.

"I was the more willing to make this observation, that when I speak of sovereign princes I may not be

maliciously traduced as if I spoke of them exclusively
and not of other sovereigns, as if monarchy were of sole
Divine right. For want of this distinction other writers
have had this invidious imputation laid upon them; but
this reason of not resisting the sovereign, because he is
God's vicegerent and only subject to Him, is a common
reason of passive obedience to all sovereigns, as well as
unto Kings, and unto Kings, as well as unto any other
sovereigns."—Hickes, *Jovian*, 240.

14.   *Necessity of Divine institution for government.*

"Now I say that none has or can have any power
or authority, but what is given him by some other,
except God alone, who is the sole fountain of all power
and authority on earth as well as in heaven. And
therefore that God not having given man power over
his own life, nor in his natural state over the life of any
other man; consequently the power of life and death
(which is necessary in all government) could never have
come from the gift or grant of the people in their
natural state. But that the positive institution of God
is necessary to found government, and invest magistrates
with the power of life and death. And that without
this, no obligation of conscience can be laid upon any
man to submit to any government whatsoever."—Leslie,
The Best Answer, 9.

"I have you consider that there is no authority
but what is derived from God. It would be to set
up another God to suppose any other or independent
authority."—*Ibid.* 18.

"What man is he who can by his own natural
authority bind the conscience of another? That would
be far more than the power of life, liberty, or property.

Therefore they saw the necessity of a divine original of government."—Leslie, *The Rehearsal*, No. 37.

"*R.* Whatever founds government must be superior to it, and above it. Government must derive its original and whole authority from it, and must be accountable to it, and dissolvable by it, at its pleasure whenever it thinks fit.

"Now human cannot be superior to human, therefore government among men cannot be derived from mere human authority. This is so very obvious that all governments whatever and of whatever sort, and among all nations and religions, do pretend to a divine right.......On all hands it is confessed that no government can stand without a divine original right, and authority; for what else can give one man power over another, over his life, liberty, and property?"— *Ibid.* No. 53.

15. *The views of Hobbes on Passive Obedience.*

"Having thus shewn what is necessary to salvation, it is not hard to reconcile our obedience to God, with our obedience to the civil sovereign; who is either Christian or infidel. If he be a Christian, he alloweth the belief of this article, that Jesus is the Christ; and of all the articles that are contained in or are by evident consequence deduced from it : which is all the faith necessary to salvation. And because he is a sovereign, he requireth obedience to all his own, that is to all the civil, laws; in which also are contained all the laws of nature, that is all the laws of God ; for besides the laws of nature and the laws of the Church, which are part of the civil law (for the Church that can make laws is the Commonwealth), there can be no other laws Divine. Whosoever therefore obeyeth his Christian sovereign, is not thereby hindered, neither from believing nor from obeying God. But suppose that a Christian King should from this foundation *Jesus is the Christ* draw some false consequences, that is to say make some superstructions of hay, or stubble, and command the teaching of the same; yet seeing S. Paul says, he shall be saved; much more shall he be saved, that teacheth them by his command and much more yet, he that teaches not, but only believes his lawful teacher. And in case a subject be forbidden by the civil sovereign to profess some of those his opinions, upon what just ground can he disobey? Christian Kings may err in deducing a consequence, but who shall judge? Shall a private man judge, when the question is of his own obedience? Or shall any man judge, but he that is appointed thereto by the Church, that is by the civil sovereign that representeth it? Or if the Pope or an Apostle judge, may he not err in deducing of a consequence? Did not one of the two, S. Peter or S. Paul, err in superstructure, when S. Paul withstood S. Peter to his face? There can therefore be no contradiction between the laws of God, and the laws of a Christian commonwealth.

"And when the civil sovereign is an infidel, every one of his own subjects that resisteth him sinneth against the laws of God (for such are the laws of nature), and rejecteth the counsel of the Apostles, that admonisheth all Christians to obey their princes, and all children and servants to obey their parents, and masters, in all things. And for their faith it is internal, and invisible; *they have the licence that Naaman had, and need not put themselves into danger for it.* But if they do, they ought to expect their reward in heaven, and not complain of their lawful sovereign, much less make war upon him.   For he that is not glad of any just occasion of martyrdom, has not the faith he professeth, but pretends it only to set some colour upon his own contumacy."—*Leviathan*, III. 43.

"Whatsoever a subject, as Naaman was, is compelled to do in obedience to his sovereign, and doth it not in order to his own mind, but in order to the laws of his country, that action is not his but his sovereign's, nor is it he that in this case denieth Christ before men, but his governor and the law of his country."—*Ibid.* 42.

16.   *The views of Dudley Digges on the Patriarchal Theory.*

"Though it be most true that paternal authority was regal, and therefore this of God's immediate constitution, and founded in nature, yet it is not much pertinent to the present decision, nor can it necessarily concern modern controversies between Rulers and people.   Because it is most evident, no king at this day, (and much less other governors) holds his crown by that title, since several paternal powers in every State are given up, and united in one common father who cannot pretend a more immediate kindred to Adam, than all the rest of mankind."—*The Unlawfulness of Subjects*, 16.

INDEX